DANCING THE FAIRY TALE

DANCING THE FAIRY TALE

Producing and Performing
The Sleeping Beauty

Laura Katz Rizzo

TEMPLE UNIVERSITY PRESS
Philadelphia • *Rome* • *Tokyo*

TEMPLE UNIVERSITY PRESS
Philadelphia, Pennsylvania 19122
www.temple.edu/tempress

Library of Congress Cataloging-in-Publication Data

Katz Rizzo, Laura.
  Dancing the fairy tale : producing and performing *The Sleeping Beauty* / Laura Katz
Rizzo.
     pages cm
  Includes bibliographical references and index.
  ISBN 978-1-4399-1121-1 (hardback : alk. paper) — ISBN 978-1-4399-1122-8
(paperback : alk. paper) — ISBN 978-1-4399-1123-5 (e-book)
  1. Sleeping beauty (Choreographic work) I. Title.
  GV1790.S55K37 2015
  792.8'2—dc23

                                                              2014017519

♾ The paper used in this publication meets the requirements of the American
National Standard for Information Sciences—Permanence of Paper for Printed
Library Materials, ANSI Z39.48-1992

Printed in the United States of America

9 8 7 6 5 4 3 2

To the community of embodied thinkers and movers who work to carry on the beautiful and meaningful traditions of dance and ballet in their performance, choreography, writing, and advocacy for the arts

To the women who, by the very nature of our patriarchal, capital-driven, competitive society, work against all odds to contribute their voices and artistic visions to the world while also supporting the growth and success of younger artists—in particular, the following artists, scholars, and teachers: Dr. Kariamu Welsh, Dr. Judith Bennahum, Dr. Laura Levitt, Tensia Fonseca, Maria Tallchief, Christopher Boatwright, Sonia Arova, Raymond Lukens, and John White, who inspired me not only to pursue my love of the many divergent histories of dance and allow this research to inform my own dancing, choreography, teaching, writing, and living but also to follow my passions without knowing where the path would lead

To pioneers Catherine Littlefield and Barbara Weisberger and the hundreds of professional ballet dancers and pedagogues who take their art and its evolution seriously and make fundamental sacrifices in how they live their personal and professional lives; who contribute locally and globally by giving young artists, especially young girls, the technical, artistic, and emotional skills to succeed in the difficult dance profession; and who "walk the walk" by supporting, encouraging, and mentoring young women through the formidable world of life as an artist

To my husband, Richard Rizzo, and our three children, Isabella, Talia, and Orion, who inspire me to be the best I can be every day and to model for them that good choices are often difficult choices, as so many wonderful teachers, family members, and friends have modeled for me

To my parents, who not only looked after my children so that I could pursue my writing and dancing but also respected the choices I made in my life and allowed me to pursue the passions evident in the text of this book

Contents

Acknowledgments   *ix*

Introduction/Prologue   *1*

1 • Women Creating Ballet: The Case of *The Sleeping Beauty*   *9*

2 • From Saint Petersburg to Philadelphia: Reviving and Reanimating Classicism in America   *28*

3 • Catherine Littlefield and *The Sleeping Beauty*'s American Premiere (1937)   *45*

4 • Aurora Streamlined and Accelerated: Barbara Weisberger and the Second U.S. Production (1965)   *69*

5 • Aurora Speaks: What Ballerinas Have to Say about *The Sleeping Beauty*   *99*

6 • The Power of Dance Technique and the Agency of the Ballerina   *141*

Conclusion/Curtain Call   *163*

Appendix: Plot and Stage Action   *167*

Notes   *169*

Index   *191*

Acknowledgments

I am deeply indebted to the wide community of dancers, scholars, editors, librarians, archivists, academic advisers, anonymous and known readers, friends, and family who supported me as I worked through this book. This book began as a research question in the doctoral course "Dance and the Gendered Body," taught by Joellen Meglin. As I worked through the assignments for the class, guided by the intelligent and astute Dr. Meglin, I realized that I had stumbled upon a subject that resonated deeply with me as a performer and as a historian of ballet. Without the support of Meglin and my fellow students in the course, including Andrea Di Donato, Tresa Randall, and Lester Tome, as well as my participation in feminist theory seminars run by Rebecca Alpert and Laura Levitt, I would not have been able to connect the disparate ideas I had into a coherent research plan. The paper I wrote for "Dance and the Gendered Body" evolved into my dissertation, which was guided by Kariamu Welsh, Laura Levitt, Joellen Meglin, and Linda Caruso Haviland. The input of these readers helped me to think through what I wanted the project to do; it also encouraged me to trust not only my own instincts but also that the women I knew, who influenced my practice and understanding of ballet, were indeed authorities, regardless of how they had been overlooked in dance studies texts I had read over the course of my graduate career. I am also deeply indebted to Luke Kahlich, who urged me to finish the project. His insistence on meeting deadlines, along with my husband's belief in my abilities, pushed me to complete the dissertation and receive my doctorate in dance and women's studies.

After a brief hiatus in which my three children were born, I returned to this project, as well as to teaching in the studio and the classroom. I will always appreciate my family's patience and support while I spent long mornings and afternoons at the computer, away at interviews, or in archives. I am also deeply grateful to them for making real to me the idea of women's agency and the creative power of women's work by transforming my identity into that of not only dancer and scholar but also mother and caretaker.

Sherril Dodds, my current department chair, was inordinately helpful in encouraging me to develop this project into a book, and her deep understanding of dance scholarship inspired me to see the work as a cluster of ideas that could be theorized and presented to a reading public. Her editorial comments and organized and professional approach to dance research taught me much about the realities of publishing. Miriam Peskowitz, the founder and chief executive of WriterVision Strategy, was truly influential in turning this manuscript into a book. When I saw her Facebook post late one summer night offering to help twenty female writers of nonfiction, I immediately reached out to her. Her editing drew out the narrative threads of the story of women working in Philadelphia in new and more organized ways.

This book would not have been possible without the generosity of artists such as Dede Barfield, Martha Chamberlain, Roy Kaiser, Arantxa Ochoa, Janek Schergen, and, above all, Barbara Weisberger, as well as Phil Juska, Barbara Vogdes, and others in the administration of the Pennsylvania Ballet who facilitated my access to company records and gave me time to speak about these ideas with company staff in personal interviews and phone conversations. These dancers, choreographers, and directors opened up to me in ways that allowed me to tell this story in their words, and their candor about their experiences staging, casting, rehearsing, and performing *The Sleeping Beauty* truly contributes a new perspective to this old ballet.

I thank Dean and Vice-Provost for the Arts Robert Stroker at Temple University for his constant belief in me and support of my creative and scholarly efforts; the librarians at the Special Collections Research Center at Temple University; Executive Editor Micah Kleit, Anne-Marie Anderson, Sara Cohen, Gary Kramer, and Joan Vidal of Temple University Press; and freelance copyeditor Susan Deeks. I am grateful for all of the feedback I have received about this manuscript over the years, and I will always appreciate the time that others in the dance research community took to speak to me about this work—I could not have done this alone.

DANCING THE FAIRY TALE

Introduction/Prologue

The Sleeping Beauty as Ballet:
Aurora's Reanimation across Time and Space

The Sleeping Beauty is perhaps the most magnificent of the classical ballets that emerged from the extensive canon of work produced during the late nineteenth century by Marius Petipa, in collaboration with Pyotr Ilyich Tchaikovsky, in Saint Petersburg, Russia. Hailed as the jewel of the canon, *The Sleeping Beauty* is a ballet to which writers, dancers, and choreographers often refer as a stunning example of both the grand style and the academic form of ballet during that period.[1] The choreographic vocabulary of *The Sleeping Beauty*—the academic danse d'école—was expanded and perfected during the Petipa–Tchaikovsky collaboration in Russia, and the training methods and aesthetic qualities crystallized in this ballet have made their way into ballet schools and companies the world over. In *Dancing the Fairy Tale*, I argue from a dance studies perspective—a perspective focused on the work dancers do in the studio that is embedded in the physical practice of dance itself, which incorporates poststructuralist research methods drawn from American feminist theory—that *The Sleeping Beauty* is both a metaphor for ballet itself and a powerful case study for examining ballet and its performance in the twenty-first century.[2]

This book focuses on the important role of women in reanimating *The Sleeping Beauty*. It looks especially to the surprising stories of female directors and choreographers who staged and starred in the work in the United States at significant intervals during the twentieth century. Although significant contributions have been made by women such as Bronislava Nijinska (Diaghilev's choreographer and the sister of Vaslav Nijinsky), Dame Marie Rambert (founding director of the Ballet Rambert), Dame Ninette de Valois (founding director and choreographer of the Royal Ballet), Lucia Chase (director, principal dancer, and financier of American Ballet Theatre), Ruth Page (founding director and choreographer of the Ruth Page International Ballet and the Chicago Ballet), Celia Franca (founding director of the National Ballet of Canada), and Dame Peggy van Praagh (founding director of the Australian Ballet), I have chosen to focus on the significant and primarily unacknowledged contributions of Catherine Littlefield and Barbara Weisberger, two women who carried out the bulk of their careers in Philadelphia. In addition, I focus on the labor of more recent interpreters of the ballet who also worked in the city of Philadelphia.

The book revolves around the choreographic content of the ballet and the details of its embodied performance in the studio and on the stage. Seeking to remedy the situation for ballet dancers and ballet studies that Linda Nochlin chronicled so well for art history in her classic article "Why Are There No Great Women Artists?" *Dancing the Fairy Tale* demonstrates how women shaped the trajectory of ballet and its establishment in the United States, doing so in their roles as producers and as performers of this particular ballet.[3] The field of ballet studies is several decades behind the breakthrough gender studies of art history and other disciplines. Despite recent contributions to this area of research, the efforts still are primarily theoretical and ignore the actualities of specific women doing practical work that has remained unknown and unexamined. *Dancing the Fairy Tale* intervenes in the usual practices of ballet history and places women at the center of a historical narrative. I chose to focus on women who are not necessarily internationally known ballerinas and who have either produced or danced in successful stagings of *The Sleeping Beauty*. This is a choice made to delimit the work to a specific geographic context that is often overlooked because of the shadow New York casts over achievements in a city so close by yet smaller in size.

The feminist poet Adrienne Rich challenged scholars to engage in "re-vision: the act of looking back, of seeing with fresh eyes, of entering an old text from a new critical direction." She claimed that "for women this is more than a chapter in cultural history; it is an act of survival."[4] In keeping with this feminist charge to reformulate the methods with which we create academic knowledge, *Dancing the Fairy Tale* attempts to dismantle the entrenched hierarchy of mythologized male choreographers who are cited as singularly responsible for the canon of work that ballet companies and training academies across the United States and all over the world study and perform. My book therefore complicates the well-established ballet meta-narrative that traces influence directly from King Louis XIV to Jules Perrot and Jean Coralli, to Enrico Cecchetti, to Marius Petipa and Lev Ivanov, to Michel Fokine and George Balanchine, and to contemporary choreographers such as William Forsythe and Alexei Ratmansky. Instead, by researching female producers and performers of *The Sleeping Beauty*, and by looking at regional performances outside the U.S. dance and cultural center of New York, *Dancing the Fairy Tale* widens our understanding of the web of ballet influence. The book rejects a conceptualization of dance history as a river in which one influence flows directly into the other. Instead, it visualizes dance history as more weblike and as created by many mutually significant strands. This is a significant shift and new trend within dance studies, in which anything that ballets have produced outside New York (and the stark abstract ballets of Balanchine) is currently seen as a regional anomaly and therefore as having less historical importance.

Dancing the Fairy Tale also challenges the usual idea that female dancers are the tools of male choreographers. This is the standard view of ballerinas: that they are mere clay asking to be molded into objects meant for display. Drawing on both archival sources and the lived experience of coaches, performers, and teachers of classical ballet, *Dancing the Fairy Tale* underscores the ways in which women have been important as articulate producers, stagers, and interpreters of classical ballet and the reality that they are not just muses for men.

Heeding the feminist theorist Linda Alcoff's classic advice that "anyone who speaks for others should do so out of a concrete analysis of the particular power relations and discursive practices involved,"[5] I am transparent in placing my subjectivity at the center of this research and book, acknowledging that its field-shifting perspective emerges from my own experience and passion as both an academic and a classically trained dancer. Thus, this work is in a prime position to speak to both dance studies scholars and performers, a vast bridge that is rarely traversed. Alcoff urges writers to "interrogate the bearing of our location on what we are saying,"[6] and this is the very heart of this project. I write as not only a dancer with a career in professional ballet learning and performing canonical works but also as a scholar with academic training in the creative process and dance making, as well as world history, historiography, dance history, feminist theory, anthropology, and cultural studies.

From these combined vantage points, I create an argument drawn from a bricolage of sources, including my experiences performing, setting, and coaching *The Sleeping Beauty*; participant observations of rehearsals and performances; the archival evidence of clippings and playbills; and transcripts of interviews that I conducted with dancers and producers. This wider-than-usual array of sources for a book in ballet studies works to highlight the agency of female ballet artists and the contributions they have made to the perpetuation and evolution of the balletic genre in the United States and across the globe.

Overview

After this introductory section poses the question of why the study of ballet has not yet been reimagined using the critical feminist theoretical lens that has been applied to other disciplines, including arts-related disciplines, Chapter 1 expands on ballet and ballet history from the perspective of women on and behind the stage, shifting the critical discourse from the audience, where the critic sits, to the stage, where women dance, and from male to female bodies. These discursive shifts create the ground for associated others. Once women are brought more actively into the way that ballet history and ballet studies are executed, the usual ballet history meta-narrative about men's creativity using women's bodies as their muses or vessels falters—in ways that are exciting for the discipline of dance studies. The fact that much of this history of female choreographers and producers of ballet took place not in New York but one hundred miles south, in Philadelphia, highlights not only the importance of regionalism in ballet but also the concept of the history of ballet as more than the transfer of the Western European tradition to New York.

I do not consult much of the literature published outside the United States. I also do not reference the developments of British ballet during the mid- to late twentieth century and make no claim to deal with ballet outside the United States during that time frame. I have chosen to focus on Philadelphia to highlight the multifaceted nature of dance history. Although scholars often envision history as a linear progression with important developments taking place in one single cultural center at a time, and they see these places as the most important sites of cultural development, there are in actuality many equally important and significant places in which important developments and strands of cultural work have occurred but been overlooked. Far from "provincial," the women working in Philadelphia in the 1930s and 1960s trained with internationally renowned pedagogues and choreographers. Their work has simply been ignored because they saw Pennsylvania as a legitimate site from which to share their vision and artistry. In fact, Weisberger and the dancers of the Pennsylvania Ballet were not Philadelphians. They came to Philadelphia as part of a national movement generating the decentralization and professionalization of American ballet in the 1960s. When considering the importance of what these women achieved as artists, entrepreneurs, and cultural leaders, however, I argue that Philadelphia can be viewed as one of many significant sites of American dance history.

A second critical issue that emerges is explored in Chapter 2, which sets the stage for thinking about issues of classicism and tradition and how these issues shift when we investigate the stories of the two female producers, Catherine Littlefield and Barbara Weisberger. When we consider the role of the dancers themselves—and not the choreographers—in transmitting dance traditions, the grounds for considering reanimation and restagings shift. These are key issues in the ballet tradition that especially emerge in productions of *The Sleeping Beauty*. This book, however, is not a philosophical exploration of the meaning or definition of ballet as an art form; although it does touch on those subject areas by virtue of its content, it is truly a story about the work of women in Philadelphia establishing the legacy of classical ballet in the United States, not about the nature of dance itself. Such a book would certainly be interesting but not what I have undertaken for this project. The focus of this project has been on bridging the world of professional ballet and academe, as well as that of popular readership with a scholarly audience, and I am dedicated to producing a readable story about the work of real women in real the world of ballet.

Together, Chapters 3 and 4 present a new history of productions of *Sleeping Beauty* in America, with the intriguing stories of *Beauty*'s premiere and second production in Philadelphia, both organized by female producers. These productions were key to bringing the internationally known *Sleeping Beauty* to American audiences who would come to love the evening-length production so well. Chapter 3 investigates the American premiere of *Beauty* in 1937 under the direction of Catherine Littlefield, a ballerina and a choreographer coached by dancers from the Maryinsky Theater and the Ballets Russes, as well as an alumna of the Ziegfeld Follies. Chapter 4 discusses a second full-length American production of *The Sleeping Beauty*, in 1965, which was also staged in Philadelphia, this time under the direction of Barbara Weisberger. In addition, the chapter engages a set of questions about what constitutes authenticity, classicism, and tradition in ballet. This is especially germane because Weisberger envisioned classicism as a fluid concept.

Having considered the roles of these two female producers, the focus shifts in Chapter 5 to the dancers who perform the role of Aurora and to reflection on how their dancerly perspectives shift our understanding of the ballet and the concepts of "the real." As Katerina Kolozova has addressed in *Cut of the Real: Subjectivity in Poststructuralist Philosophy*, the idea of a "real" or "authentic" version of *Beauty* is based on a falsehood. In her words, "Poststructuralist (feminist) theory sees the subject as a purely linguistic category, as *always already* multiple, as *always already* nonfixed and fluctuating, as limitless discursivity, and as constitutively detached from the instance of the real. This reconceptualization is based on the exclusion of and dichotomous opposition to notions of the real, the one (unity and continuity), and the stable. It also liberates theory from ideological paralysis, recasting the real as an immediately experienced human condition determined by gender, race, and social and economic circumstance."[7]

Therefore, Chapter 5 points to the problematic ideological issues tied up with much of the discourse around Weisberger's production and its adherence to concepts of what a "real" *Beauty* should do. By the time *The Sleeping Beauty* reappeared in Philadelphia in 1997, under the direction of Roy Kaiser, followed by a second performance in 2002, its performance was neither rare in the United States nor, in its conservative and conventional presentation, unusual. Thus, it is not the performance itself—its choreography or subject matter—that is intriguing in this chapter. What is interesting, however, are the circumstances that led a female producer to gain control of, build, and then lose control of a major ballet troupe in a large American city. This version of *Beauty* was directed by a man after Weisberger was ousted from the Pennsylvania Ballet by a board of directors. The stars of the chapter are the dancers themselves and the manner in which a scholarly consideration of their reflections shifts the terms of analysis of ballet. For the 1997/2002 production, I was able to interview the ballerinas and hear their views on the process of learning and performing *Beauty*. This completes the shift from analyzing ballet from the audience to analyzing it from the rehearsal studio and stage. The ballerinas' perspectives add an embodied understanding of ballet and *The Sleeping Beauty* and shift the terms of what it means to interrogate authenticity and tradition in ballet, as I show.

Chapter 6 collects and expands these arguments, first by looking back and returning to reconsider the original creation of *Beauty* in the collaborations of Petipa and Tchaikovsky, and by placing the dance choreography of *Beauty* into the context of a larger story about how the sleeping beauty theme was also treated in literature and painting, to show the difference that embodied animation makes. Further, the chapter builds an argument for how the dancers operate in a creative space in which they are not just muses to the great choreographer but actively create their ideas through embodied performance.

A brief Conclusion discusses the implications of *Dancing the Fairy Tale*'s exploration of the creative agency of women creating ballet in the United States throughout the twentieth century, and the dynamic physical power of female performers of classic ballet, guiding readers to think about the ways we understand dance studies and ballet history.

1.

WOMEN CREATING BALLET

The Case of The Sleeping Beauty

The Ballerina as Agent and the Ballet Stage as a Space of Women's Creativity

Waiting in the wings, in costume and full makeup, a dancer prepares herself for performance. Focusing her breathing and thinking, she shakes out her tight muscles, rolls her head from side to side to relax the tension in her shoulders, and prances from foot to foot to keep the blood circulating in her feet and legs. She concentrates her energy and clears her mind so she can enter the stage with poise and confidence, allowing the hours of coaching and rehearsal in the studio, as well as her years of training, to flow from her body freely. The female principal ballet dancer is an articulate artist who brings inanimate choreography to life through her embodied representation of ideas. So often looked to as a vehicle or instrument of a choreographer, the dancer is more than a medium; she is a creator.

Until a dancer embodies the work, choreography is trapped in the abstract realm of ideas. Classical ballet is a specific language built on the court dances of the Baroque period from which it evolved. This syntax reflects its Enlightenment origins in its absolute reliance on structure, progression, and categorization of the body and its movements. In the development of technique—historically within a technique class and on an individual level for dancers—the progressive and developmental character of ballet technique is pushed to its limits, stretching not only what each step looks like but also what dancers can do. For example, when working on articulation of the feet, a dancer begins by practicing battement tendus. In this step, the dancer presses her foot along the floor as the leg opens, arriving in an open position with a stretched foot and ankle and then closing back to either first or fifth position, with the weight distributed equally back onto both feet. In most traditional ballet training, this movement is followed by the practice of battement tendu jeté, a "thrown" battement tendu, which is the same step but comes off the floor to a height of forty-five degrees. The next iteration of this foot articulation is the grand battement jeté, which is practiced at the end of the barre work, in which the leg reaches maximum height at the end of the brush off of the floor. This preparatory barre work eventually progresses into the grand jeté, when the brush of the foot and leg take the dancer off the floor into a large, high-flying leap through the air. Without understanding first how to stretch properly through the feet and legs in a simple battement tendu, a dancer can never achieve the grand jeté with freedom and brilliance. Artistry and nuance and the freedom of expressivity in performance therefore are built on rock-solid technique developed through repetitive and logical training.

This fundamental reliance on progression and exponential progressive development allows—and, in fact, encourages—the genre of classical ballet to evolve while retaining some essential foundational characteristics (i.e., the seven basic movements of ballet: plier, étendre, relever, glisser, sautér, élancer, and tourner). This progression can be seen in a study in which Elena Daprati, Marco Iosa, and Patrick Haggard analyzed images from the Rose Adagio from *The Sleeping Beauty* as performed by the Royal Ballet between 1946 and 2004 and found that "despite the codified positions established by the choreography, there are systematic differences in elevation angles according to the year of ballet production."[1] In fact, this study finds that leg elevation has consistently increased over time and the back has been held more vertically during arabesque penché, demonstrating an increase in the physical performance of extreme virtuosity in the role of Aurora during this time.

This is true also for dancers throughout their careers, as the process of submitting one's body to this disciplined training is what makes a person able to become a professional ballet dancer. One cannot interpret the choreography of the classical repertoire until she or he has the proficiency necessary to move through the required steps with ease. The classical repertoire cannot exist without the dancers, individuals who have spent years working their bodies and minds so that they can best articulate and express the ideas of the balletic canon without an overemphasis on executing the steps. The experience of learning, practicing, and performing transforms the identity of the many female performers of ballet, making them literate in the syntax of the classical balletic vocabulary and immersing them within the historical and cultural world of the tradition.

Just as linguists such as Benjamin Lee Whorf and George Lakoff argue for a kind of linguistic relativity—that is, that people think according to their language and cannot conceive of ideas without first having words for those ideas—ballet provides an aesthetic landscape for both performers and audience members that is accessed through a language of learned-movement vocabulary. Seen through the lens of Saussurean semiotics, the danse d'école in which dancers are trained acts as a signifier, while the concepts portrayed through performance are the signified. It is the combination of the dancer and the dance that create the recognizable sign in performance. The ability to convey this sign language means that dancers must understand both the signifier and the signified, and for ballet dancers this complex process takes place only through intensive and repetitive conservatory-style training in ballet.

This is not purely a process of subordination. It is also a process of transformation. And although this is not a utopian process in which dancers learn only positive, healing, and emancipatory messages, it is a process that transforms a person's identity. In learning to convey ideas through classical movement vocabulary, dancers become adept and authoritative communicators. Even members of the corps de ballet who do not attain ballerina status within their companies become dancers, not just by taking a paycheck issued by a ballet company, but by doing the labor of training, rehearsing, and performing ballet. This discursive practice implies a process of identity formation. The process of becoming/being a dancer results in individuals' understanding and defining themselves through and by the physical and artistic practices in which they engage.

In addition to developing expertise and authority through dancing and performance, women have often taken on leadership roles within the ballet world. Even within the conservative genre of ballet, there are many examples of female producers and choreographers who have shaped the path of American dance history. Despite their contributions to the field, however—as performers and as pedagogues, coaches, choreographers, and artistic directors—many of these women have fallen through the cracks of dance history. In a desire to streamline and mythologize the history of dance, scholars have constructed a linear narrative of Western European classical dance that traces direct lineage from the court of Louis XIV to the neoclassical work of artists and choreographers such as Christopher Wheeldon and William Forsythe. Certain trends in choreography have also been deemed better than others. For example, as Andrea Harris argues in her article about the female choreographer Ruth Page, women's choreographic practices have been "marginalized—or worse, historicized as second rate—by the ghosts of an exclusionary critical discourse that continue to haunt our archives."[2] She argues that during the 1930s, the critics Lincoln Kirstein, Edwin Denby, and John Martin not only worked to establish dance as a serious American art form but also determined how ballet was to be viewed, interpreted, and evaluated. In establishing categories of genre and aesthetic function, they also created gendered aesthetic hierarchies that privileged the abstract modernist choreography of George Balanchine.[3] Part of this process was the exclusion of other voices from what would come to be known as "American ballet."

In addition, funding structures such as the Ford Foundation have shaped the cultural identity of American ballet, giving preference to certain aesthetic and leadership styles. By funding certain companies for making certain kinds of work, these funding structures shape what kinds of work are produced and how that work is shown. Dance history and historiography, however, need to account for the complicated actualities of cultural production, including the contributions of women and the complex web of interrelated cities and regions from which ballet in the United States has emerged.

In this more accurate historiography, dance is not an evolutionary progression in which tradition is handed from one man to the next, from one city to the next. Rather, dance is better envisioned as a web of activity in which many diverse artists are working concurrently, in many places. By breaking apart the embedded hierarchy and linearization in traditional ballet and dance history that have privileged certain male choreographers in specific geographical sites (Saint Petersburg, Paris, New York) as more valuable and significant than their sisters in the field, this approach also responds to more recent feminist critiques of the academy in which a canon is both established and perpetuated by excluding many other voices of interest. This book presents an introduction to a dance history that responds to these critiques. In presenting a more full and accurate history of ballet, however, we also need to account for the perspectives of ballerinas themselves, certainly, and to account for the dance leadership work of female producers and choreographers. Catherine Littlefield and Barbara Weisberger, both of whom are important female artistic directors, are protagonists in the narrative that is at the heart of this book, as are countless other female leaders in the ballet field, including Ninette de Valois, Agnes de Mille, Bronislava Nijinska, Ruth Page, Lucia Chase, and Anna Pavlova.

This book tells the story of ballerinas and female producers by examining the American premiere of *The Sleeping Beauty* in 1937, as well as the ballet's restaging almost thirty years later, in 1965, and then thirty-two years later than that, in 1997 (with a restaging in 2002). The 1937 restaging was produced by Littlefield; the 1965 restaging, by Weisberger. The 1997 restaging was produced by Roy Kaiser, a dancer in Weisberger's company who became the artistic director. In that case, although the production was not innovative, it offered an opportunity to hear the ballerinas talk about their role as dancers in shaping what audiences saw happening onstage.

Littlefield and Weisberger come from the world of the studio and, interestingly, from the stage, a topic that is discussed later. Despite their rigorous traditional dance training, however, these women were not silent, docile creatures (the stereotype of women trained in classical ballet). They directed dancers with strong voices and opinions; communicated with boards of directors about fundraising and marketing; and provided visionary leadership for the institutions they drove. Their ballet training provided them with a strong physical presence. This embodied confidence also carried over into these women's abilities to command attention and respect from both dancers and administrators. I also touch on the work of Lucia Chase, who directed American Ballet Theatre between 1945 and 1980, who made her own classical premiere dancing the role of Aurora in Mikhail Mordkin's production of *The Sleeping Beauty* in 1936 and produced the full-length ballet for American Ballet Theatre in 1975.

Dance History from the Stage: Shifting the Gaze

The second claim at the heart of this book is the necessity of shifting the frame from which we look at, write about, and make meaning of ballet. For many reasons, which I outline in more detail in Chapter 5, dance history typically has been written from the outside in. The criticism and scholarship of dance writers has been invaluable to establishing ballet as a genuine American art form, however much of the significant work has not been done by dancers. Although a few collections of dancers' writings exist, non-dancing scholars have produced most of the academic research on ballet. Ironically, this most physical and immediate of the performing arts has often been analyzed, interpreted, and evaluated from the perspective of the gazing yet static audience member, not from the sweating, moving, dancing body of the performer. Traditionally created by historians and critics trained in the arts of writing, analysis, and interpretation of the dramatic and performing arts, dance studies has been informed by but not shaped by dancers. Grand narratives have emerged in dance history painting a trajectory of ballet's emergence in France, dramatization in London, technical perfection in Russia, artistic experimentation in Paris, and modernization in New York. The principal—and male—actors in this narrative are Louis XIV, Jules Perrot and Jean Coralli, Marius Petipa, Michel Fokine, and Balanchine. Dance has been envisioned as flowing from the ballets of one mythic man to another. This conventional narrative leaves out, and in no way fully accounts for, the many small streams and rivulets that flow from the river of ballet history and the many other people and places for whom and in which ballet flourished.

An unfortunate gap exists between the lived experience of the ballerina and the lived experience of the ballet historian and critic. Academic writing and academic dance practice tend to see ballerinas as instruments of male choreographers and in the case of feminist criticism, as having even less agency—that is, as objects of the male gaze on display for audience members and as female bodies disciplined by the political and social control of the capitalist patriarchy. But there is more to the story than this, and there is a different feminist analysis, which I narrate in this chapter and the following chapters. These conventional perspectives understand what a dancer is and what a dancer does as shaped by a reigning concept in which the choreographer is primary and the dancers are interchangeable. When one strives to account fully for the lived experience of dancers, however, new critical questions can be posed, such as "What does the ballet dancers' embodied understanding of learning and performing the repertoire add to the current narrative surrounding ballet?" I believe that listening to the voices of female dancers and female producers and choreographers creates a discrete intervention in the current historian-driven and male-focused writing in dance studies.

Briefly look to recent dance history for an example of how the story of ballet changes when ballet dancers speak and we listen to their voices. The furious incident around the dance writer Alastair Macaulay's skewering of Jenifer Ringer comes to mind. Macaulay is a dance critic for the *New York Times* and former theater critic for London's *Financial Times* and *Times Literary Supplement*. For decades, his opinions have shaped the values and trajectories of dance companies producing ballet. In the winter of 2010, Macaulay reviewed an opening night performance of *The Nutcracker* danced by the New York City Ballet. He wrote in the *New York Times*, "This didn't feel, however, like an opening night. Jenifer Ringer, as the Sugar Plum Fairy, looked as if she'd eaten one sugar plum too many."[4]

This statement, so insensitive and distant from actual audience experience, was also ignorant of Ringer's struggles with a long history of eating disorders. The article provoked a huge wave of controversy both inside and outside the dance realms. Ringer even appeared on NBC's *Today* show to defend herself against Macaulay's attacks. The result was that many audience members, as well as members of the dance world, felt that the attacks were both unfair and written from the point of view of the out-of-touch bystander. Ringer herself stated on national television that she was not overweight and that her "womanly curves" should be celebrated. One of the thousands of bloggers who commented wrote, "I can think of two scenarios where criticizing a dancer's weight would be fair: when the performer's physical condition impairs his or her ability to dance (not the case with Ringer), or when a performer's body type is an important component of the character they inhabit onstage. Macaulay would be right to complain if Ringer were playing the role of a concentration camp inmate, for example, but she wasn't." In addition to appearing on *Today* and on *Oprah*, Ringer was the focus of an article in *Working Mother* on how she balances her family and career.[5]

The outcry was so great that Macaulay had to publish a follow-up article in the *Times*, entitled "Judging the Bodies in Ballet,"[6] in which he defended his comment and perspective. The time is ripe for dancers' opinions to matter more in the construction of meaning around ballet. Just as people sought out Ringer's response, audience members are ready to hear what dancers think about the ballets they perform, stage, and produce. Dancers do live and work in a particular culture. Many of the shared meanings of the ballet community are understood by participants but not by outside observers such as audience members. Writers and historians can build a bridge from the stage and studio to the audience. On the one hand, this would probably increase ticket sales as the genre would feel less like an elite, boring, and stuffy institution that "regular folks" do not understand. On the other hand, this approach would also open ballet up to new conversations and new criticism. This does seem to be the trend in popular culture: in 2012, *Breaking Pointe*, a documentary reality television program that follows the lives of certain dancers in the well-established regional company Ballet West, and *Bunheads*, a situation comedy following the daily intrigues of a ballet school, debuted on television. The huge popularity of films such as *First Position* (2012), *Black Swan* (2010), *Mao's Last Dancer* (2010), *Billy Elliot* (2000), *Center Stage* (2000), *The Turning Point* (1977), and *White Nights* (1985), as well as books such as *Dancing on My Grave*, *A Winter Season*, *Holding On to the Air*, and *Once a Dancer* is testament to Americans' desire to get into the lived world of the ballet dancer.[7] What has been sold so far to the non-dancing public as the world of the ballerina has been carefully selected to present a skewed picture that panders to the commodity of glamorous but self-destructive beauty. The women at the heart of this book, however, are smart and assertive, and like

Ringer, they are articulate and intelligent about their work and about the aesthetic field in which they operate.

Shifting focus so that women are front and center especially makes sense in the world of ballet because women are most often the central characters onstage. Women are literally at the center of the stage and outnumber their male counterparts by the hundreds. Even if professional dance companies evenly split their contracts to create companies of equal numbers of men and women, the women perform more often onstage and in larger roles. In addition, pre-professional dance schools show a huge discrepancy in the number of male and female students, making it far less competitive for male dancers to attain a professional contract with a dance company. As any audition demonstrates, ten times more women than men typically try out for the few coveted company spots offered each season. This female-driven focus is especially the case in *The Sleeping Beauty*, in which women are the main characters. Prince Désiré does not drive the narrative action onstage; Aurora, the Lilac Fairy, and Carabosse do, and they are all female. A powerful female fairy (Carabosse) curses Aurora. A different powerful fairy (Lilac Fairy) remits the curse, and although the passive, unthinking insensitivity of Aurora's father at not inviting Carabosse to the baptism angers the fairy and causes her to condemn Aurora to death, it is Aurora's own choices that result in the curse's coming to fruition. Aurora is also part of the aristocracy and has a considerable amount of political power. The original ballet made strong reference to the court of Louis XIV, the Sun King, and in representing his court in the performance onstage, it directly links Aurora to the divine monarchy of the French Renaissance.

Dances performed by women are at the architectural center of the classical repertoire. To take an example from *The Sleeping Beauty*, the Rose Adagio revolves around Aurora, who stands center stage and takes ownership of the stage with her authoritative presence and regal demeanor. Aurora performs solo variations in all three acts of the ballet, the only character with this much solo stage time. Her variations contain the thematic core of the entire ballet, and they draw on choreographic material in the (female) fairy variations from the prologue of the ballet. For example, in her first act variations, Aurora begins with balances in first arabesque and attitude derrière.

She then goes on to perform rond de jambe en l'air en dehors with her gesture leg while simultaneously hopping en pointe with her supporting leg. Aurora then performs a series of pirouettes en dehors, followed by runs en pointe with hops in attitude devant and derrière. Finally, she completes her variation with a manège of piqué turns en dedans. This material is inherited from her godmother's prologue variations and incorporates the movements of her matriarchs into her solo work as she grows from girlhood to womanhood over the course of the ballet.

For example, from Candide (Candor), she inherits her hops en pointe in attitude. From Coulante or Fleur de Farine (Wheat Flour), she takes her pas couru, or runs en pointe. Miettes qui Tombent (Breadcrumb Fairy) also performs the hops in attitude and pas couru en pointe that Aurora incorporates into her first act variation. The Canari qui Chante (Canary Fairy) gives Aurora the soft flowing port de bras that accompanies her delicate and precise footwork. Violente (Force, who is also known as the Finger Fairy) bequeaths to Aurora sharp and clean rond de jambe en l'air en pointe, and the Lilac Fairy gives Aurora strong balances followed by a lovely faille through to a well-established first arabesque, as well as a strong series of pirouettes en dehors. Aurora's technique grows in stature along with her character; the technical and spiritual/emotional qualities of Aurora are bound together in a way that makes them inseparable. The classical choreography demonstrates the changes in Aurora in each act. Her first act variation emphasizes her delicacy and perfection, and she looks to her parents for affirmation. Her second act variation demonstrates the yearning, searching quality a woman explores in her maturation. She looks to find herself and she shades herself, literally and figuratively, through both the port de bras that accompanies her slow, drawn-out relevé lents en écarté and the suspension and tension she embodies in her slow fouettés to arabesque. She constantly shifts from directly facing the audience to more of a profile view from the audience's perspective. Her body is shaded by both her physical positioning and its illumination by stage lights. Even her final pose in arabesque tendu croisé derrière is on a bent knee, low to the ground, and she reaches away from the audience, her focus down and toward the ground and out through the wings. She in no way confronts the audience or other performers with her gaze. However,

Aurora's third act variation gives her the opportunity to claim her maturity and perform confidence in herself as a woman. She displays an open and playful sense of femininity, flirting with the gaze of the audience, and demonstrates extreme power in her jumps in arabesques that finish en pointe facing the audience in a balance in attitude derrière en face. As she travels across the stage, rolling the invisible orange of prosperity between her fingers, she opens herself to the audience and the court, majestically presenting her strength and her power. She shows that she has grown into herself as a woman and her new role as queen. Aurora's nuanced performance of the movement vocabulary allows the audience to understand her transformation and maturation.

Accounting for the lived experience of dancing, Aurora also allows readers and audience members to understand her not only as a delicate and ethereal emblem of femininity but also as a finely tuned athlete who has trained with discipline and rigor for a minimum of ten years to become proficient enough to perform the role with a professional dance company. This is a significant change, as we do not associate athletes with the kind of passivity that is usually attributed to ballerinas. Aurora's choreography is exceptionally demanding technically, and it is this challenge that dancers most often discuss when they describe their experience of dancing the role. The physical and emotional demands of such difficult choreography make the Aurora role one that transforms the bodies and careers of the women who perform it. Surmounting such challenges allows them to become confident figures of authority within their dance companies and in their own bodies, learning how to negotiate the strictures and demands of tradition while simultaneously learning how to develop and articulate their personal voices in the performance of canonical choreography.

The Importance of Place: American Ballet and Location

This book argues that women have been important contributors to ballet history, even though they are absent from traditional histories written on the topic. As important producers and interpreters of the genre, ballet dancers are intelligent and well-trained artists whose perspective has much to offer those interested in making meaning of the work these dancers and choreographers craft. In addition to bringing women's creativity back to the center stage of ballet criticism, this book revolves around the importance of place and the consequent importance of a decentralization of dance history. In the linear and progressive structuring of dance history, places have been inserted into a hierarchy of importance so that certain regions or cities have become more worthy of being placed in that history than others. In widening our historical lenses, we must take in more of the map of the ballet world as it actually exists, not restricting dance history to the large urban centers of prestige and prosperity. Around the women at the heart of this story are their communities of smaller cities. Without the network of family members, funders, students, and dancers with whom they lived and work and intimately knew, these women would not have been able to make their important contributions to American ballet. Place matters a great deal.

This decentralization of the meta-narrative of ballet history happens partially as a result of including women's creativity in dance scholarship. It also is important because the past fifty years have seen ballet in the United States become a regional phenomenon. Companies in Boston; San Francisco; Washington, DC; Seattle; Salt Lake City; Miami; and sometimes Philadelphia produce some of the finest ballet in the world. While New York City continues to be a central location producing ballet of very high quality, the companies there often have an international flavor. Although it is called "America's National Company," American Ballet Theatre has principal dancers who were trained in academies across the globe. The reality of working within the professional world of ballet in the United States, however, is one of dispersion throughout the country. For example, one ballerina who was a member of American Ballet Theatre and a renowned teacher in the city's most respected schools, affiliated with companies such as Alvin Ailey and Mark Morris, recently relocated from New York City to Oklahoma City, where she took on the directorship of a fine academy of classical ballet affiliated with the Oklahoma City Ballet. In no way was this a demotion for her. In fact, the students and dance artists in Oklahoma are of such high quality that the woman (my friend) feels fulfilled and challenged in her new work environment. The ballet world in New York City is indeed one to which top-level performers flock from around the world. This community, however, is only part of a web that both receives dancers from around the nation and the world and sends trained and experienced dancers throughout the nation and world.

Failing to see the many centers of American ballet is a failure to see much of what Americans know and understand as ballet. Raymond Williams and the cultural studies theorists of the British school of thinking on popular culture would urge dance writers to turn to the reality of ballet in its actuality, and the majority of ballet performances in this country take place outside New York City. In this regard, Philadelphia, the setting of such interesting historical female-driven ballet production, should be seen as an important node on the web of sites that constitutes the international dance community.

Tangled into this story of hearing ballerinas and accounting for the work of female producers and choreographers is a story about one of the cities in the web of ballet history: Philadelphia. Not merely the forgotten little sister of New York City, Philadelphia ballet has had a significant history. As Clive Barnes wrote in the *New York Times* in 1972, in ballet the Philadelphia Story is rather a good one.[8] This story speaks to the simultaneity of history and the ways in which a less compartmentalized view of that history demonstrates how artists and events rub against each other, influencing each other's development. This is the story of the performing venues, their locations, and shifting significance within the context of the city of Philadelphia over the sixty-five years spanning the three productions of *The Sleeping Beauty* in question.

In bringing in this perspective, I want to remind readers that this book is not a comprehensive study of ballet in Philadelphia between 1937 and 2002; nor is it a regional study. To the contrary: what it does illustrate is the kind of more greatly textured dance history that can emerge when we bring in the ways that place and history and sociopolitical context witness and influence the production, performance, and reception of ballet. As the nearest large city to New York, Philadelphia has its own specific importance. It repeatedly has been the testing ground for artistic ideas in dance and theater, and if a production is successful in Philly, it often takes off on the larger international stage of New York. Still in use, the Academy of Music and Robin Hood Dell have borne witness to the important performances of not only Littlefield and Weisberger, investigated in this book, but also countless others. This way of creating ballet history celebrates the particularities and details of the specific stages and studios where *The Sleeping Beauty* was rehearsed and performed between 1937 and 2002 and facilitates a greater appreciation for the physicality of dance history and how it is located in bodies moving together in specific geographical and spatial and physical locations.

Any discussion of location and sites of importance touches on an element of the approach to American dance that needs revision. American dance is often framed in certain ways that highlight the unique Americanness of the dances, as in the following quote from Martha Ullman West: "From the pioneer experience came Martha Graham's *Frontier* and *Appalachian Spring*, and several ballets including Eugene Loring's *Billy the Kid* and George Balanchine's *Western Symphony*."[9] American dance is seen as dance set in an American context, with American themes and American performers.

While much important American work does reflect these American themes, this approach fails to follow the ways in which European forms have evolved and shifted in their new American context, adapting to the new communities in which they are learned and performed. Oddly enough, Catherine Littlefield is not listed as one of the top one hundred America's Irreplaceable Dance Treasures, although many European dancers and choreographers of her era are. And although women's work has been considered vitally important to the emergence of American modern dance, and despite their active presence in establishing the form, American women are noticeably absent from most histories of ballet. Going to the specific places in which ballet was performed and describing the particular work of women within the field of ballet is one way to enrich the current narrative of ballet as a genre created and led by men's genius in only the most international of European and American cities. It is also a way to create ballet history afresh.

Shifting the Discourse of Dance Studies

The implications of these three shifts—from the audience to the stage, from men to women, and from New York to the many American cities in which ballet flourishes—are clear. The fourth part of this book's argument challenges the current understandings of ballet that have led to misconceptions about the genre and resulted in ballet dancers and academics looking at one another from across a vast divide. Precisely because of the nature of training, with conservatory-style, repetitive work as a foundation for proficiency in ballet, and because of the short time span of a ballet dancer's career, ballet dancers rarely receive postsecondary education. Therefore, the language they often use to describe their experience is quite different from the language used by those trained in dance departments who study notation, analysis, critical theory, and dance history. A female-centered history of dance must take a different approach from traditional dance historiography and reimagine the dance field as a whole. Much attention has been paid to choreographers, and even to producers and impresarios, as responsible for the major contributions of the dance field. In addition to considering female creators (such as Littlefield) and producers (such as Weisberger), a new approach to understanding creativity and artistry allows the contributions of dancers to surface as significant achievements throughout dance history. Disciplinary divisions have plagued the field of dance scholarship since it entered into higher education in the 1920s, due to—and despite—the pioneering efforts of visionary artists and educators such as Margaret H'Doubler. Dance departments are divided among scholars, artists, and teaching faculty; dance curricula also uphold these false divisions, which are based on the Cartesian binary split between mind and body, male and female, and rational and creative thinking. Such thinking, however, denies the ways in which dance as a genre and specific dancers operate. The women at the heart of the dance field, and at the heart of this story, are people who merge creative and rational thinking, as well as the disciplines of pedagogy, choreography, and history. Truly accounting for the creative and articulate contributions of performers and teachers is a first step in writing a multilayered and multidimensional dance history that can accommodate the work of the female dancers at the center of the field.

Some of the divide in academic dance studies can be attributed to the important political efforts of first- and second-wave feminists and their counterparts within the dance field, as well as modern dance's gendered critique of ballet. For example, Isadora Duncan embraced a natural and unencumbered femininity, advocating freeing women's bodies from the painful corsets and pointe shoes used in ballet. Martha Graham and Doris Humphrey also turned away from the strictly codified and what they saw as repressive and regressive strictures of ballet technique in their choreography, which was inspired from a place of personal and artistic protest against what they felt were outdated and old-fashioned modes of expression. Early dance departments such as those at Bennington College and the University of Wisconsin were places of experimentation and conceptual freedom, not training conservatories meant to furnish large ballet companies with dancers. Thus, the academic dance world developed as a site that fostered artistic and political rebellion against regressive and restrictive tradition. In addition, as dance studies has grown within higher education, it has borrowed methodologies from many older, better-established disciplines, including anthropology, phenomenology, cultural studies, and history.

Ballet immigrated to the United States. Therefore, an American balletic tradition is only about as old as an American modern dance tradition. The state of the genre in the 1920s and 1930s was not what we now imagine when we think of ballet. Without established companies that could support them, dancers with ballet training supported themselves by performing in vaudeville shows, movie halls, and musical theater reviews meant to entertain a public that was not educated in the balletic tradition. However, the women at the heart of this book envisioned a uniquely American form of ballet, and their vision has made the current state of the art possible.

In addition, in the postmodern world in which we now live, boundaries between genres have eroded, and the stratification of artistic genres has morphed into a web of interconnected techniques in which a dancer must be versed. Challenges to become truly inclusive are pushing university programs and conservatories alike to provide access to and training in a full spectrum of genres to their students. Dancers may still focus on one area of specialty; however, a world in which dancers train in only one discipline is no longer an option.

Ballet is a significant component of this more broadly based approach to dance studies, and the artistry and history embedded in the technique are significant topics for research and essential for solid dance training. Learning historically derived choreography allows students to embody aesthetic trends that emerged from distinct historical periods. Learning passages from *The Sleeping Beauty*, for example, allows students to research the ballet's performance history, linking them physically and conceptually to the history of their field. The balance and aplomb so central to Enlightenment philosophy and discourse are physically experienced in the choreographic text of Aurora's variations. Within the ballet world, the choreography of Marius Petipa is part of every student's education. To use just one contemporary example, in 2012, at the internationally acclaimed Jacob's Pillow Summer Ballet Intensive, college students studying in the program learned variations from the classical nineteenth-century repertoire because, as Anna-Marie Holmes, the school's director, put it, "It is good for them."[10]

It is only as a trained ballerina and dance professor with nearly three decades of experience in the worlds of ballet performance and academic criticism that I am finally able to appreciate the layers of dance history that live within my own body, passed on to me in the studio by master teachers of the tradition: teachers such as Sonia Arova, Clara Cravey, Margarita de Saa, Tensia Fonseca, Melissa Hayden, Allegra Kent, Rosemary Miles, Larisa Sklyanskaya, and Maria and Marjorie Tallchief. This history, learned in the studio in classes and rehearsals, is retained in the muscles of my body, emerging when I begin to dance or teach. As with the histories of many women in other artistic disciplines, this knowledge has been passed from woman to woman and in many cases was never recorded on paper. As many women's historians have noted, the work of women in all fields, not only creative disciplines, is often undocumented and difficult to bring to light.

This book is one attempt to create a venue for the illumination of these histories and their importance, creating a way to present academic analysis and scholarship that honors and observes the actual ways in which dance history is passed on. Ballet is documented and carried within the dancers who learn, perform, coach, and teach the repertoire and in what and how they work together. When a young woman learns the first act variation from *Beauty*, she is learning physical steps. However, if she is coached well, she is also learning creative, interpretive skills along with layer upon layer of sociopolitical history. First, she must understand how Aurora enters the space at her sixteenth birthday. She must convey the youthful energy inherent in both Tchaikovsky's score and Petipa's choreography, as well as the etiquette and social protocol expected of young women in the nineteenth century, when the ballet was originally created. Next, she performs the simple piqué in first arabesque. At its most bare, this is unabashedly simple academic technique. But the quality with which the dancer springs into the pose and melts out of it and the strength and clarity of her technique also make the beginning of this variation one of the most beautiful and nuanced in the classical repertoire.

Although many dancers now augment their learning of choreography by consulting dance videos, that extra process is not what I describe here. Instead, I am speaking about how one dancer envisions and communicates the classical repertoire to another dancer. This process of imagining and transferring the living history of classical dance is an act of creative scholarship that has not been documented fully or honored by writers distant from the process of setting and staging classical ballets.

Although the tasks of writing a history of women in ballet and of classical ballet in the contemporary dance world are too large for the scope of this book, I hope it will set a precedent for such studies. I have chosen *The Sleeping Beauty* as the ballet at the center of the study to work as a metaphor for the classical balletic genre. Just as Aurora sleeps for one hundred years, reawakening after the sleeping curse has run its course, ballet sleeps until it is reanimated by the dancing bodies of performers who resuscitate the form in each restaging of a canonical work.

For many girls and women, ballet is an opportunity to train and strengthen their bodies and to become proficient in a public and physical demonstration of mastery. Ballet classes are a place where young women learn to harness their physical capacities, challenging themselves to push the boundaries of what they can do. The classical canon of ballet is a world of work that revolves around the strength developed in classes and rehearsals. The performance of principal roles in *The Sleeping Beauty, Swan Lake, The Nutcracker, Paquita, La Bayadère*, and *Le Corsaire* is possible only if a dancer has attained physical, emotional, and mental toughness and vigor.

The gendered, feminized bodies of young women in ballet have been relegated to the role of support or objectified symbols of men's desire in the thinking of many historians and critics. But the perpetuation of tradition—so central to codified and structured techniques and genres such as classical ballet and African dance—is carried within the bodies of performers and teachers. Without these windows to the past, which both look back and reenvision tradition, these art forms would be lost. This book shifts the current discourse of dance history: it is not just about including the history of women or making sure that we place international centers like New York within the web of dance creation throughout the nation's cities, and it's not just about shifting the focus from the critic in the audience to the dancer's perspective onstage. All these things come together in shifting the discourse to one that places equal emphasis on performers, teachers, audience members, critics, choreographers, and producers of dance and repositioning dance history to acknowledge all of these roles as equally imaginative and significant in the survival and reanimation of classical ballet in each context of its performance. In order to do this, I craft a historical narrative about the female-driven emergence and development of classical ballet within the United States, and connect that historical narrative to the voices and experiences of performers who can speak directly to how that history, living within their muscles and bones, shapes their understanding of what they do.

This shift in discourse more accurately reflects what the ballet world already knows, that ballet dancers are bright, dedicated, hardworking and organized artists whose skills account for much more than mimesis. It also helps to bridge the divide between the professional practice and scholarship of ballet. Professional dancers often speak with trepidation about the detached practices of dance scholars and the futility of teaching ballet within the world of academia, while academics often speak of ballet dancers with disdain as emptyheaded automatons plagued by eating disorders and other infantilizing emotional issues. By theorizing a new understanding of the ways that dancers, even within the *corps de ballet*, can be articulate and creative artists, this book is a step toward closing some of those artificial divisions and the resulting misunderstandings between the disciplinary divides of the dance world.

2.

From Saint Petersburg
to Philadelphia

Reviving and Reanimating Classicism in America

The Academic Purity, Simplicity, and Long-Reaching Power of *The Sleeping Beauty*'s Choreographic Vocabulary

The Sleeping Beauty has long been established as the jewel of ballet's classical canon. It is one of the longest ballets in the classical repertoire at close to four hours and four acts long, and it includes a huge cast. The choreography at the heart of the ballet is simple and straightforward. It reflects the classicism of Marius Petipa and his drive to codify technique. His characters are conveyed through the nuances of the classical steps they perform and establish a new type of performativity with a technical base. Much like what Merce Cunningham did for contemporary dance, Petipa did for ballet. Although he used narrative as a structural framework on which to hang his choreography, his ballets are truly about the beauty and fascination of ballet technique. The ballet has an almost scientific approach to beauty that is based on progression and exponents and in which form follows function and classical steps embody fairy tale characters.

For all of these reasons, dancers are transformed by the experience of performing Aurora, the protagonist of the ballet. The difficulty of the role, as well as the sheer presence required to maintain the attention of the audience for three long acts, pushes a dancer to become an authoritative and commanding presence. Many dancers speak of Aurora as taking them from dancer to ballerina; after performing the part, they take on a new leadership role within their companies and even in their own conception of themselves as dance artists. In addition, ballet companies seeking to establish themselves as true players in the field of professional dance have often turned to *The Sleeping Beauty* as a testing ground of their classical proficiency.

The performances examined in this book actively negotiated their relationship to the original production of *Beauty*, and although many well-researched books have been written about the original ballet, I have here included a brief description of the premiere production because of its importance in the later Philadelphia restagings.

The Premiere, 1890

On January 15, 1890, *The Sleeping Beauty* premiered at the Maryinsky Theater in Saint Petersburg, Russia. Before the curtains rose, Pyotr Ilyich Tchaikovsky's booming overture heralded the splendor of the ensuing ballet. The ballet's audiences were stunned by the magnificence of the production and astonished by the classicism and majesty of the ballet, which quickly established itself as a benchmark performance to which all later classical ballets would be referred.[1] From that date forward, *The Sleeping Beauty* commanded a special position in dance history and became the centerpiece of a vital tradition from which twentieth-century ballet emerged.[2] Despite the fact that the ballet was not initially well received by the Saint Petersburg public, its style and form have generally taken over to represent what the international ballet community understands as "classical," in that they draw from classroom technique as taught to dancers in pre-professional academies. Instead of relying on improvisation and dramatic stage effects, such as lighting and other special effects, Petipa drew on the classical and virtuosic vocabulary of ballet in his choreography for the ballet not by using pantomime and props but, instead, by developing each character and the narrative arc of the work through the specific steps danced by each performer and how the steps grew and developed in complexity and nuance throughout the dance.

In addition, relationships between characters were established through the sharing of certain choreographic elements or step combinations. The idea of the abstract vocabulary of ballet having narrative capability and the ability to convey character and style makes *Beauty* unique in its craftsmanship. The challenging nature of the choreography comes from Petipa's bare-bones approach to technical vocabulary, exposing the architecture inherent in the basic positions and actions of the balletic language to tell a story through moving images onstage. The demanding nature of this choreography, and its un–Romantic exposure of physical execution, made it a ballet that required dancers' training and performance to evolve into a form requiring perhaps fewer dramatic acting skills and more athletic and virtuosic proficiency.

Petipa, the resident choreographer and ballet master at the Maryinsky Theater, choreographed the ballet at the height of his career, and the piece is famous for its perfect fulfillment of Petipa's strict academic style and classical aesthetic sensibilities of harmony, order, balance, and clarity.[3] Dance critics and historians often cite *The Sleeping Beauty* as Petipa's masterpiece, the ballet in which he crystallized and codified classical ballet in its purest form.[4] The ballet is built on grandiose spectacle; elaborate and opulent design and sets; virtuosic choreography; and an ordered, symmetrical, and balanced aesthetic sensibility.

As the ballet historian Tim Scholl has stated, "Writers on *The Sleeping Beauty* have called the ballet a lexicon of nineteenth-century ballet."[5] Other authors have also commented on the academic style that Petipa created and perfected within his masterpiece ballet. In 1990, Arsen Degen commented that Petipa "fostered a strictly academic style that provided the rigorous framework needed to contain the outbursts of emotionalism so typical of the Russian soul."[6] In the same article, Degen went on to discuss Petipa's structured and formal choreographic approach, describing the way in which Petipa worked—composing according to a strict formulaic blueprint that relied heavily on classic works from the past.

Vera Krasovskaya also has written extensively about Petipa's choreographic approach. She comments, "All was obedient to the rules of alternation of pantomimic mise-en-scène and dances: feeling was regulated by form and the drama served as a foundation for effective spectacle."[7] This regimented method of creation was an accurate embodiment of Petipa's militaristic aesthetic. This aesthetic, in turn, can be seen as a manifestation of the philosophy underpinning Russian government of the late nineteenth century. *The Sleeping Beauty*—and, likewise, most of Petipa's choreography—is an artistic representation that capitalizes on the same aesthetics as that of the troops of the Russian Army. Petipa intentionally and politically created images and wove a performative aesthetic intended to please Tsar Alexander III, who personally financed the Imperial Ballet and to whom Petipa thus was directly accountable.[8] To satisfy his royal benefactors and his own artistic vision, Petipa created an aesthetic expression that spoke to the values of the autocratic regime that supported him.[9]

Petipa's benefactors—the imperial family and a clique of aristocratic balletomanes—did not attend the ballet to experience artistic experimentation. Instead, they sought simple entertainment, often with an ideological bent. Tsar Nicholas I, for example, was convinced that beauty was a sign of strength. The uniformity and subordination he developed in his troops were the same qualities that he desired to see in ballet.[10] Petipa responded to this imperial aesthetic by training a corps de ballet that became a model of Foucauldian discipline. The unprecedented uniformity and precision of Petipa's corps de ballet was, therefore, a reflection of the values of the Russian aristocracy of late nineteenth-century Saint Petersburg.

Petipa's choreography was built on the theme of hierarchy, a value that he deeply instilled in the consciences of his dancers. As Lynn Garafola has noted, "In Petipa's ballets the corps framed the ballerina, inscribing her into an etiquette as strict as that of the Imperial court; she ruled the stage as absolutely as a tsar. Around her, in order of precedence, lesser ranks danced: coryphbeés, in groups of eight; demi-coryphbeés, in groups of four; *demi-soloistes*, in pairs; soloists and premières danseuses, in lesser principal roles."[11]

The training of Petipa's dancers, then, as well as the staging of his ballets, directly reflected the high value placed on order, control, symmetry, and equilibrium both at the Maryinsky Theater and in tsarist government bureaucracies. This regimented vision of beauty reached perfection in *The Sleeping Beauty*. With amazing skill, Petipa created a magical city that evoked King Louis XIV's Versailles—a place and time of civilized order.[12] His utopian vision of harmonic stability pleased audiences with beautifully organized and sometimes kaleidoscopic images. Petipa worked out most of these stage groupings at home. Nicholas Legat was a principal dancer with the Russian Imperial Ballet from 1888 to 1914 and the successor to Petipa. As ballet master, he taught and passed on the legacy of the Petipa repertoire. Legat stated, "He used little figures like chess pawns to represent dancers, arranging them all over the table. He would spend long hours studying these groupings and write the successful ones in his notebook."[13]

Petipa's aesthetic values emerged from this ideology of militarism, aplomb, strength, precision, and hierarchy. They were reflected in his approach to creation, as well as in the Russian court around him, the structure of the ballet company, and the military parades so favored by Tsar Alexander III. Petipa composed nothing in front of his dancers; he simply explained to them how each step was to be performed.[14] Although some roles were improvisational and certain dancers were allowed to compose sections of their own variations, Petipa coached his dancers (especially the corps de ballet) in autocratic style. His formulaic approach to creation enabled him to compose more than sixty full-length ballets, in which he employed an enormous number and variety of dances. It also ensured that what was represented onstage strictly conformed to Petipa's ideas of beauty and grace.

The Sleeping Beauty not only emphasizes an Apollonian love of order through its classical choreography. It also supports conservative values through the theme and origin of its narrative. Ivan Veselovsky, the director of the Imperial Theatres, looked back to the age of Louis XIV as a utopian society based on order, balance, and civilization.[15] He was obsessed with Enlightenment codes of order, balance, and rationality, which he believed were values that should be inculcated into the Russian citizens in his audience.[16] It was his idea to base the meaning and context of Petipa's *The Sleeping Beauty* on the utopian French court featured in the fairy tale *Le Belle au bois dormant*, by Charles Perrault.[17]

It is not a surprise, therefore, that Petipa, a man deeply entrenched in the culture of tsarist Russia, would find one of Perrault's didactic tales a suitable framework for his choreography. His aesthetic of order and hierarchy flowed perfectly into the themes and content of the French story. The multiple layers of meaning within the ballet all point to a golden age of enlightened monarchy. Writing about the ballet, Alastair Macaulay comments, "Primarily [*The Sleeping Beauty*] is about Versailles and the spirit of Louis XIV."[18] Macaulay also claims that the message of the ballet is clear: "It is about the continuance of the classical ideal (Apollo) by way of the Sun King and the emergence in France of ballet—and by implication, as crystallized in Tsarist Russia."[19] Sally Banes also comments on the use of Perrault's tale: "It was a way to claim elegance, propriety, courtliness, luxury and political power as Russian attributes just as French ones."[20] It is quite clear, therefore, that both the choreographic and the thematic content of *The Sleeping Beauty* paint a picture of Versailles as a utopian society based on controlled, graceful order and balance. This vision of equilibrium, in turn, is based on a romanticized picture of the French courtly tradition and monarchist cultural-political regime.

Scholl argues that Petipa actually included many archaic elements in his choreography to connect the ballet more firmly to the French baroque style. They can be seen in the court dances and farandoles in the second act of the ballet and in the court dances and sarabande in the final act.[21] Scholl also points out the baroque style of the processionals, or entrées, that conclude the ballet, writing that these processionals, which give structure to the work, date to the early eighteenth century.[22] Macaulay also writes about baroque ingredients in the choreography of *Beauty*. He claims that three positions characterize Aurora throughout the ballet: the croisé tendu devant, the effacé attitude derrière, and first arabesque. He argues, "The tendu front we associate with the minuet and the eighteenth century; the attitude with the 1820s neoclassicism of Carlo Blasis; and the long-stretched line of the first arabesque with the late nineteenth century."[23]

On technical aspects of *Beauty*'s choreography, the Russian ballet master Fyodor Lopukhov comments, "The foundation of the choreography of *The Sleeping Beauty* is openness: in poses it is *effacé*; in movement it is *en dehors*."[24] For example, all of the pirouettes Aurora performs in her first act birthday variation are en dehors—that is, they turn out from the body and are a gesture of generosity and munificence. All of her movements are displayed for the audience to see. Aurora's choreography feels in the body like a flower blossoming. The movements open the body out to the audience and a larger self. Like many other writers, Lopukhov claims that the brilliance of the ballet lies in Petipa's complete investment in the choreography. The logic and beauty of the dance steps are what give characterization to the dancers, and the story that the dance tells is complete. "Here is where Petipa proves his greatness," he writes, "and it is time people realized—those who confuse realism in ballet with naturalism—that realism in choreography is manifest in movement itself, for which there need be no explanation."[25] This is perhaps why the ballet is seen as a crystallization of Petipa's classical approach, leading writers to make claims such as "*The Sleeping Beauty,* the strongest and most perfect of Petipa's works, sums up the choreographer's long, difficult, persistent search for ballet symphonism."[26]

With its academic structure and orthodox aesthetic, *The Sleeping Beauty* conveys the conservative values of the Russian aristocracy. These values can also be seen in the grand size and scale of *Beauty.* The sumptuous sets and grandeur of the production are a significant part of what makes the ballet famous—and famously difficult to replicate for contemporary ballet companies. In his book *Balanchine's Tchaikovsky,* George Balanchine writes, "*Sleeping Beauty* was done magnificently. The curtain went up[;] onstage there were lots of people, all dressed in opulent costumes. . . . [W]hen they prepared the premiere of *Sleeping Beauty* at the Maryinsky, they spent fifty thousand rubles on the costumes alone—an enormous sum! *Sleeping Beauty* must be an extravagant spectacle."[27] It is exactly this issue that has plagued *Beauty* in its many restagings in Philadelphia and elsewhere, for much of what critics discuss about the ballet, especially regarding the many failed attempts to revive it, involves the impossibility of a contemporary company putting on such an extravagant production. Without imperial treasuries—and large audiences to sustain them— modern ballet companies are forced to pare down and streamline this huge ballet. When these shortenings and modernizations do occur, however, they are rarely met with approval.

For example, the ballet critic David Vaughan has written, "I take it as my premise that *Beauty* is the greatest of all ballets, and not just a masterpiece of ballet, but of Western art. The real question, then, is if a thing is worth doing, is it worth doing badly?"[28] Mary Clarke expressed similar consternation when she wrote about the 1993 restaging of *Beauty* by the English National Ballet: "*Beauty,* above all, must be grand in manner; prettiness is not enough."[29] These reviews, like many others I have read, find the revival inadequate because of its failure to live up to the majestic opulence of the original work. But authenticity, not only in staging but also in dancing, is enormously difficult—if not impossible—for modern companies to attain.

Scholl, a Russian studies scholar and professor at Oberlin College, as well as the author of several articles and books about Russian ballet, has stated that *The Sleeping Beauty* is fundamentally about its choreographic content. Going directly to the core of Petipa's choreography, he believes, can best access the "authentic" version of the work and give modern viewers the most direct connection to the essence of what the ballet is about. "*The Sleeping Beauty*, one century later," he argues, "is the rose adagio, the garland waltz, the grand pas de deux, the bluebird's pas de deux. A production of *Beauty* based squarely on the dancing may represent the most enlightened attempt to bring *Beauty* back alive."[30] Writing about his own restaging of *Beauty*, Balanchine said, "Ballet isn't a museum. . . . [E]very museum has rooms where people don't stop, they just look in and say, 'Ah, it's boring in here, let's go on.' Ballet can't survive like that."[31] In other words, ballet is alive and forever evolving. Balanchine's work was an attempt to combat the idea that ballet is a rarefied museum, an attempt to modernize, Americanize, and make relevant the classical danse d'école of the Russian school.

Balanchine's commentary is directly related to Macaulay's claim that "classicism not only evolves; it migrates."[32] The contemporizing of classical ballet through restaging is exactly what the women at the heart of this book achieved, with degrees of success and failure. Indeed, the historical emergence of *The Sleeping Beauty* migrates from an Italian fairy tale to the French court, the Russian court, Philadelphia stages of the Great Depression, and beyond. This tale of emergence itself is hardly singular. Such comments, highlighting the complexity and plurality of dance history, create a theoretical window for viewing the balletic canon. As artists undertake restagings of these works, they actively create dance history, reenvisioning and reinscribing classicism in each rehearsal and performance. The fact that much of this work was done by women outside of New York City is testament to the richness of American ballet history, as well as to the need to paint a larger picture that accommodates the labor these women undertook, allowing ballet to evolve and migrate throughout the United States.

The Project: Discovering Dance Matriarchs

The Sleeping Beauty has always held a central place in my consciousness. Many important moments in my dance history center on the
learning, performing, and, now, coaching the choreography from
the ballet. During my transformation from performer to historian,
I looked to the ballet as a vehicle or lens for answering some of my
questions about ballet history. I dug through my dance history texts,
following footnotes and chasing reviews, to understand the performance history of this canonical work. In discovering this history,
I came to understand that it paints a useful, detailed picture of the
larger context and specific ways in which ballet developed in the
United States and demonstrates the interconnected web of activity
that allowed a new dance genre to emerge: *American* classical ballet.

After its premiere in 1890, Petipa's *Beauty* was performed again in
Moscow in 1897 and 1914. In 1916, Anna Pavlova performed a shortened, forty-eight-minute version of *Beauty* in New York City. Serge
Diaghilev's Ballets Russes staged and toured with the ballet again
in November 1921. That production, the ballet's first presentation
in the West, was called *The Sleeping Princess*; it was choreographed
by the often overlooked Bronislava Nijinska (a brilliant choreographer and pedagogue, the sister of Vaslav Nijinsky, and a teacher of
Maria Tallchief) and performed at the Alhambra Theatre in London. Léon Bakst created the décor for the production.[33] A strong
link existed between two productions, in that Carlotta Brianza, the
original Aurora in Petipa's *The Sleeping Beauty*, performed the role
of the evil fairy Carabosse in Nijinska's *The Sleeping Princess*. The
Ballets Russes performed shortened versions of *The Sleeping Princess* again in 1922 and 1923, although never in its complete form. In
1939, Ninette de Valois produced the ballet for the Vic-Wells (now
Royal) ballet at London's Covent Garden.[34]

Although European companies toured Europe and the United
States with shortened versions of *Beauty*, and the British Vic-Wells
performed Nicholas Grigorievich Sergeyev's version of the ballet
in England in 1939,[35] a full-length American version of *The Sleeping Beauty* was yet to be choreographed, produced, and performed.
This is indicative of the lack of independent ballet companies in the
United States. During this time period, there was very little distinc-

tion among vaudeville, Broadway, burlesque, and ballet, and trained dancers had to participate in all of these genres to make a living. Mikhail Mordkin, a former principal dancer in the Bolshoi Ballet and a dancer with Diaghilev's Ballets Russes, came to New York City in 1924 and established himself as a teacher at that time.[36] Mordkin presented his version of *Beauty* on December 9, 1936. All of Mordkin's performers but one were students in his New York school, and he adapted all of the choreography he had learned to suit their abilities.[37] Because of Mordkin's limited resources, his version is relatively unknown, except for one important fact: The performance marked the professional debut of Lucia Chase, the financial backer and eventual director of American Ballet Theatre from 1945 to 1980. Her performance of Aurora not only secured her authority as a dancer but also established the Mordkin Ballet as a legitimate school that enjoyed a few years of (often criticized) performances in New York, as well as in Philadelphia and Scranton, Pennsylvania; Newark, New Jersey; Wilmington, Delaware; Baltimore; and Washington, DC, before being disbanded and absorbed into American Ballet Theatre (then known as Ballet Theatre) in 1939.[38]

In 1937, however, America saw its first professional, full-length version of *The Sleeping Beauty*, performed to a live, uncut Tchaikovsky score. It was performed by the Philadelphia Ballet Company under the leadership of Catherine Littlefield, who choreographed a new version for the restaging. Such a significant performance in 1937 is certainly noteworthy. However, during my graduate studies in the late 1990s and early 2000s, and in my professional dancing career during the early to late 1990s, I had never heard of Littlefield or her company. Intrigued, I decided to pursue the story of how this important ballet's American premiere had fallen through the cracks of dance history. The existence of a producer like Littlefield and her company's success challenge the meta-narrative of dance history, which often attributes the genesis of American ballet to George Balanchine and New York City. Telling Littlefield's tale widens the history of American ballet so it can include the important work of women and their distinct communities.

The Sleeping Beauty awoke to its new context in Philadelphia during the Great Depression, and the shape it took reflected the context of both its production and its reception. The Philadelphia Ballet

Company performed both in Philadelphia—at the Academy of Music and the Robin Hood Dell—and at New York City's Lewisohn Stadium. Littlefield, however, had very limited resources. Even though thousands of Philadelphians attended the performances put on by Littlefield's company, she had a tiny budget and a limited number of classically trained dancers with whom to work. Nonetheless, scraping from the students and professionals dancers available to her, all of whom she had trained, Littlefield assembled a cast of more than one hundred dancers onstage.

An American company created pared-down sets and costumes for the production. These Depression-era sets reflected an American understanding and aesthetic style as much as they fit Littlefield's constrained budget. Lee Gainsborough created the costumes for Littlefield's *Beauty*, and Jarin Scenic Studio developed the sets. The costumes were described in the newspaper as "perfectly in accord with the spirit and character of the ballet and . . . models of good taste."[39] The sets were described as of "similar superior quality."[40] A photo of Littlefield's tutu that ran in the *Philadelphia Evening Bulletin* shows that it departed from the traditional costume in that it had short, shoulder-length sleeves that draped over the upper arms, a decorative brooch at the center of the bodice's neckline, and a very short starched skirt.[41] The lighting for the production was borrowed from the Curtis Institute of Music, which had more and better technical equipment than the fledgling Philadelphia Ballet Company. The scenery was created with contemporary technology and involved an unfolding backdrop and a large spidery web that the prince had to rip aside to reach Aurora.[42] A lack of rehearsal time contributed to the challenges Littlefield faced in staging the ballet. For a performance at Robin Hood Dell, an open-air performance venue in Philadelphia's Fairmount Park, the company had only one day of rehearsal. Despite these difficulties, Littlefield brought the ballet to huge and receptive audiences and did much to educate American audiences in classical ballet.

After discovering Littlefield's work, I decided to pursue *Beauty*'s performance history further. After leaving Russia in 1918 with twenty-one scores of Russian ballets recorded in Stepanoff notation, Nicholas Sergeyev, a former dancer and company manager of the Maryinsky Ballet, traveled through Europe helping European companies stage *Beauty* and several other ballets. In 1939 and again in 1946, he revived *Beauty* for the Vic-Wells in London. That production was taken on tour to New York City in 1949, where it was performed at the Metropolitan Opera House. Sergeyev then revived the ballet for the Imperial Russian Ballet, or Maryinsky Theater, which is now known as the Kirov Ballet, in 1952. Other choreographers staged *Beauty* for the Stuttgart Ballet in Germany and the Royal Danish Ballet in 1957.[43]

In the early 1960s, the work began to sweep through the international ballet world. Finally, in 1965, Barbara Weisberger, artistic director of the newly founded Pennsylvania Ballet Company, took on the challenge of producing the evening-length ballet for her fledgling company. Although it was less successful than Littlefield's production, the 1965 restaging was nonetheless significant both in what it tried to do and in how it was received. Although it was not warmly reviewed by critics, it did establish the legitimacy and technical proficiency of the young Pennsylvania Ballet Company, and it offers another important chapter in the history of North American ballet as it developed into a regional art form funded by the National Endowment for the Arts in the 1960s.

In particular, Weisberger's production of *The Sleeping Beauty* demonstrates the power of funding machines such as the Ford Foundation and the power of George Balanchine and his penchant for abstract and architectural dance, with the pull of Broadway, jazz, and ballerinas' sex appeal, in establishing ballet as a well-established institution throughout the United States. As Alex Ewing wrote in his history of American Ballet Theatre, "The entire ballet world was astounded in 1963 when the Ford Foundation announced it was giving $7,765,750 to a small, highly selective list of ballet companies and one ballet school."[44] George Balanchine's School of American Ballet received half of the funds. The rest of the money was distributed to four smaller companies. Although Ewing (Chase's son) claims these grants went to all Balanchine satellite companies, his mother's American Ballet Theatre was not a nonprofit company at the time the Ford Foundation began its initiative. Ballet companies that were not officially institutionalized as 501(c)(3) organizations with tax-exempt status recognized by the federal government were dependent upon individual giving and the generosity of wealthy patrons and sponsors for support.

The Pennsylvania Ballet was one of the Ford beneficiaries, and Weisberger was one of Balanchine's close associates. Her ability to stage *Beauty* can largely be attributed to her favored position in the eyes of the power broker McNeil Lowry of the Ford Foundation and her special relationship with George Balanchine as his first child student at the School of American Ballet.[45]

The 1937 and 1965 productions of *Beauty* in Philadelphia clearly demonstrate the significant contributions of Littlefield and Weisberger, as well as of the Philadelphia dance community, to the history of ballet in the United States. These women had an impact on the ballet world during their time, and the details of their lives and labor contribute valuable insights into their perspectives on the field. These women were not only producers but also performers, and their ideas about the classical canon and how to bring it alive helped to establish a new understanding of American classical ballet. This understanding bridges the views from audiences and critics, whose reviews make up almost all of the primary documentation that survives from these performances, and augments that story with voices that emerge from the lived bodies of performers. These two chapters use stories from the lives of Littlefield and Weisberger to broaden and deepen the picture not only of who they were and how they made the choices but also of how American ballet developed as a genre between 1937 and 1965. These chapters act as what Brenda Dixon Gottschild called a "biohistory" in her book about Joan Myers Brown, another important Philadelphia artist, and the establishment of the primarily African American modern dance troupe Philadanco.[46]

In 1966, *Beauty* was staged for La Scala in Milan and the German Opera in Berlin. In 1970, Ben Stevenson staged it for the National Ballet of Washington. Lucia Chase, co-director of American Ballet Theatre, finally produced a full-length version in 1976. Various other regional and major companies performed *Beauty* throughout the 1970s, 1980s, and 1990s, with Helgi Thomason producing the work for the San Francisco Ballet in 1990 and the Boston Ballet performing different versions of *Beauty* in 1976, 1977, 1978, 1979, 1980, 1993, 1996, 2001, 2005, 2009, and 2013. With the explosion of regional ballet and the advent of video technology, the mid-1990s saw *The Sleeping Beauty* in the repertoires of hundreds of companies around the world and well known by virtually all loyal devotees of the ballet. American Ballet Theatre claimed that its staging was close to the original, as it took the Royal Ballet's staging, inspired by the company's original Sergeyev production of 1946, set and coached by Mary Skeaping, ballet mistress from the Royal Ballet and director of the Royal Swedish Ballet.[47]

None of the choreographers or producers of these ballets, however, could claim to have produced an *authentic* reconstruction of Petipa's famous premiere. This changed when the Kirov Ballet undertook a historic "reconstruction" of the work in 1999 and repeated this production on tour in 2002. The reconstruction was controversial and highly publicized. I attended a performance of the work on Sunday, February 17, 2002, at the Kennedy Center for the Performing Arts in Washington, DC. Locally, in 1997, the Pennsylvania Ballet also took on a new production of *Beauty*. It did this as the company reemerged from a period of great financial difficulty and tumultuous artistic leadership. I attended both the 1997 production and its restaging in 2002 at the Academy of Music in Philadelphia. During that time, I was doing a great deal of thinking about the gendered history of the *Beauty* productions done in Philadelphia by Littlefield and Weisberger, and those stagings were on my mind as I sat in the audience at the Academy of Music.

The 2002 production of *Beauty* by the Pennsylvania Ballet kept the choreography, staging, sets, and one of the three Auroras from the 1997 cast intact. As the ballet and the role of Aurora had already taken a prominent role in my consciousness and research by this time, I decided to take the opportunity to interview the Pennsylvania Ballet Auroras about their lived experiences performing *The Sleeping Beauty*. The tidy thirty-year spacing of the three productions seemed serendipitous, although this last production was directed by a man, the artistic director Roy Kaiser, who as a younger man had danced for Weisberger when she still directed the company. What was truly irresistible was the opportunity to fully incorporate the dancerly perspective by interviewing the ballerinas who danced Aurora.

My choice to conduct interviews with dancers living and working in my community also came from a theoretical commitment to illuminate the agency of the ballerina, getting beyond an understanding of her work as that of translation. These dancers were doing more than merely repeating choreography, channeling the ideas of Marius Petipa or Janek Schergen, a former Pennsylvania Ballet dancer who staged the work for the company in 1997. Accounting for women's history in ballet means that, not only in work produced by women but also in ballets in which women play central roles, historians must allow the voices of women to shape our historiographical process. Like choreography, history is created and shaped to reflect the tone and tenor of a moment, and I wanted the understandings and style of the ballerinas so important inside the field of ballet to shape how I wrote about and depicted the work they performed. In an interplay of dancing, writing, watching, and listening, I sought to bring their physical and emotional experiences of being Aurora, of inscribing the classical, of embodying the canon into this text. This new approach to writing ballet history seeks to bring the dancing to life, closing the gaps between the written and danced worlds of *Beauty*.

Significance

The protagonists of this book, the stagers and stars of the Philadelphia performances of *The Sleeping Beauty* danced in 1935, 1967, and 1997/2002, were important not only in terms of their autonomy and visionary artistic leadership during the emergence of classical ballet in the United States but also in terms of their roles in the passage of dance vocabulary from generation to generation and the iteration of a uniquely American style of classical ballet. This book's examination of the labor of these women, both on and off the stage, brings their significance and perspective to center stage and adds to our developing story of American ballet, especially outside New York.

It is worth repeating that this book does not claim to be a comprehensive study of *The Sleeping Beauty*. In truth, as a dancer trained in classical ballet who also holds a doctorate and a position as a professor of dance studies, I am amazed by the rich and important history of classical ballet linked to the community in which I live and work that is not widely known, recorded, and analyzed by the academic dance establishment. The contributions of the women about whom I write are intimately connected to my dance history. As I was beginning to research her production of *Beauty*, Weisberger contacted me to ask whether I would teach in the ballet program she was beginning to develop at the Peabody Institute in Baltimore. While discussing the opportunity, our phone conversation wandered to *Beauty*, and I knew I was uncovering information that should be shared. I also discovered that Weisberger had chosen Melissa Hayden as her first cast Aurora. I had studied with Hayden at the Chicago City Ballet School (a school run by Maria Tallchief and her sister Marjorie) in the mid-1980s and had learned from her the fairy variations from the prologue of *Beauty*, bringing me further into the folds of the history I sought to uncover.

I acknowledge the subjectivity of history within the postmodern context. With transparency, I have allowed my presence within this story, as well as my investment in the genre, to permeate the walls of historical truth. I do not claim objectivity. This is why I situate and explain the argument of this book—disclosing my interdisciplinary approach, which moves between historical and philosophical approaches—and how the stories I tell work to bolster my perspective. Borrowing theoretical tools from the world of cultural studies, I examine dancing bodies in specific geographical and historical locations, demonstrating the importance of women's work within the ballet world in the United States within a period of sixty-five years.

Many works have been written about how ballet reflects the racist, patriarchal, and authoritarian ideologies of the liberal Enlightenment. I do acknowledge that ballet is certainly not a feminist dream. Catherine Littlefield, for example, created many racist and problematic representations of people of color in some of her work and excluded African Americans from her company and general school classes.[48] In fact, the same year her company premiered *Beauty*, it also premiered the blackface ballet *Let the Righteous Be Glad*. This ballet, which was shown at the Constitution Celebration at the Academy of Music, began with stylized "voodoo dances in the African jungle" and moved on to the hold of a slave ship and then the world of the Negro spiritual.[49] These problematic issues, however, do not discount the importance of these women's achievements, for nothing is a feminist dream, even genres shaped and formed out of an impulse to encourage and develop feminine power. Despite the reality of ballet's challenges, individuals within ballet have used the studio and stage as a creative space and resisted hegemonic cultural forces in their own public, expressive, and physical artistry in performance and in life through small but sustained acts of resistance to the status quo. The very presence of women in the field of ballet is in itself a resistance to a masculine hegemony.

In demonstrating physical prowess in a public arena, the ballerina is a symbol of more than dominant discursive productions of femininity. She challenges those norms through her artistic nuance, her physical strength, and the obligatory reverence she must be paid by audience members and fellow dancers alike. The ways in which dancers negotiate their performance of gendered characters teaches us much about the ways this is done offstage, as well.

The Sleeping Beauty is a construction that revolves around the fairy tale trope of the damsel in distress. The fairy tale has gone through many incarnations as story and cultural myth. In Chapter 5, I trace the various representations of the sleeping beauty character in the work of Charles Perrault (as well as in other versions of the literary tale), the librettists of the Maryinsky Ballet, and the original choreographer of the ballet, Marius Petipa, as well as in the paintings of Edward Burne-Jones and other artists of the Pre-Raphaelite period. Juxtaposing these representations against the dancing bodies of the women who have performed the ballet's central role, this chapter demonstrates the ways that ballet dancers have created and continue to create articulate expressions of strength and authority in their dancing of the fairy tale.

For example, while *La Belle au bois dormant* (1697), drawn from Charles Perrault's complete collection of fairy tales, *Histoires ou contes du temps passé*, paints Aurora's character in one way, the choreography Aurora dances in the ballet tells a different story. The 1890 ballet by Petipa and Tchaikovsky looked to the court of King Louis XIV as a utopian vision of stable prosperity, a respite from the anxieties facing a Russian aristocracy and intelligentsia on the brink of huge social and political change. The choice of story for the libretto was informed by the desires of the ballet's collaborators for a world in which order and symmetry took prominence over the chaos and violence of revolution. The embodiment of these themes, however, takes on a highly kinetic and physical power in the choreography and movement vocabulary of the nineteenth-century classical ballet.

Now we look to *The Sleeping Beauty* as a metaphor for classical ballet itself. Falling asleep in the heyday of Russian academic classicism, Aurora awakes to find herself in Philadelphia during the Great Depression. How she must adapt to her new surroundings is indicative of the changes ballet underwent as a genre in its new context. The ballet resides in the bodies of its performers. Once awakened, it is enacted and embodied in rehearsal and on the stage. Performers of the work, therefore, reinscribe the classical, bringing Aurora alive in each new presentation.

3.

Catherine Littlefield and
The Sleeping Beauty's American Premiere
(1937)

The Sleeping Beauty Awakens to Find Herself
in Great Depression Philadelphia

Philadelphia in the 1930s was in the midst of the Great Depression. Reeling from the trauma of World War I, anxious about the growing instability in Europe, and profoundly affected by the Stock Market Crash of 1929 and the resulting shortages across the country and the world, Philadelphians, like all people across the urban industrial U.S. Northeast during this time period, faced a bleak urban landscape of poverty and unemployment. The city was bearing the brunt of the country's economic downturn, and the country was bearing witness to the rise of fascism and the spread of World War II.[1] Although Philadelphia did have a thriving arts community, including the Philadelphia Orchestra, which was led by Leopold Stokowski and was called "incomparable" and Philadelphia's "chief contribution to civilization" by the *New York Herald Tribune*,[2] the city also experienced widespread poverty and suffering.

In addition to the development of ballet during this time, Philadelphia witnessed the work of early modern dancers. Charles Weidman, head of the influential Humphrey and Weidman dance school, regularly taught classes at Temple University in the newly formed Tyler School of Art. His star pupil, José Limon, was a frequent guest instructor and performed at Temple University regularly throughout the 1930s.[3] The Robin Hood Dell, a ten-thousand-seat open-air amphitheater built in 1930 in West Philadelphia, witnessed many important dance performances throughout the 1930s. Easily accessible by public transportation, the venue saw visits by Limon, George Weidman and Doris Humphrey, Irma Duncan and her dancers, Michel Fokine's Ballet, and Sandor Harmati and his American Ballet between 1930 and 1935, when Catherine Littlefield's company began performing there.[4] During those years, thousands of Philadelphians visited the Dell: Called the "Salzburg of America," the venue was widely acknowledged as "an indispensable part of summer life in the city of Philadelphia."[5]

The orchestra held regular seasons there beginning in 1930, once the city's budget had been depleted by the Great Depression and no work was available over the four summer months. When not performing at the Academy of Music from May through August, the orchestra took on running Robin Hood Dell as a cooperative venture. Ninety members of the Philadelphia Orchestra who became known as the Robin Hood Dell Orchestra played every day for eight weeks initially, eventually moving to four performances a week in later years. Robin Hood Dell Concerts was formally incorporated on April 25, 1935, "to provide summer orchestral concerts, operas, ballets, and other musical events of the highest standards."[6]

Ballet and opera were the most popular attractions during these summer seasons, consistently attracting large crowds, even though the orchestra shell was not designed for dance performance and rehearsal time with the full orchestra was limited. As early as 1932, a newspaper article stated, "The largest audience of the Philadelphia Symphony Orchestra's . . . season in Robin Hood Dell turned out last night for a well-rounded program featuring Catherine Littlefield and the Philadelphia Grand Opera Company Ballet Corps."[7] About the eventual showing of *Beauty* at the Dell, the paper stated, "Entrances, side aisles and banks accommodated several hundreds who could find no seats. Several hundred were turned away" (see Figure 3.1).[8]

As audiences for dance grew within Philadelphia, dance schools spread across the city, and more dance companies performed in venues such as the Academy of Music and Robin Hood Dell. During this time of development for dance, Philadelphia underwent additional cultural changes. Although a time of artistic growth in Philadelphia,

Figure 3.1. Philadelphians out for an evening of ballet at the Robin Hood Dell, 1933. (*Philadelphia Evening Bulletin* Photo File, Special Collections Research Center, Temple University Libraries, Philadelphia, PA.)

the 1930s also saw poverty and unrest. Philadelphia was the third largest city in the United States. City workers staged strikes against companies that forced them to work in unhealthy and inhumane conditions.[9] Unemployment soared while the city's economy collapsed. By the spring of 1932, four in ten of the city's workers were totally unemployed, and two more in ten were reduced to part-time work.[10]

In 1930, approximately two million people lived in the city of Philadelphia.[11] In 1934, three years before the premiere of *The Sleeping Beauty*, eight in every one thousand homes in the city had no running water; three thousand homes had no heat; and seven thousand homes were considered unfit for occupancy.[12] A housing survey taken the same year showed that almost twenty-four thousand families were sharing quarters to make ends meet.[13] Littlefield and her company felt the impact of these trying times. Littlefield's company was short-lived, largely because by 1941 most of the male dancers had resigned to enlist in the armed services.[14] These times of hardship, however, also saw the emergence of a uniquely American form of classical ballet that combined elements of popular and elite dance forms and blended them into a new genre that suited the context of its emergence. Littlefield's production of *The Sleeping Beauty* of 1937 is one example of this new genre of American ballet. It is a piece that demonstrates Littlefield's artistic vision of what ballet could and would look like on the uniquely American stage.

How did a girl from modest means, growing up in Philadelphia, a depressed city without professional ballet, envision and produce this new genre of American classical ballet (see Figure 3.2). Details from Littlefield's life history help to explain her creativity and imaginative genius. Catherine Littlefield was born in 1905 into a theatrical family living in West Philadelphia. The influences of her family, her training, and her community all contributed to how she envisaged dance as a performing art.

The Littlefield family attended the Philadelphia Opera, and all three children—Catherine, Dorothie, and Carl—were encouraged to participate in the performing arts. But her mother's training and background most strongly influenced Catherine Littlefield's dance training and choreographic style. Caroline Littlefield was Catherine's teacher and coach and played a significant role in her personal and professional life. Littlefield's mother taught her ballet technique. This made her professional artistic life a possibility in a very real way. Her mother supported her later training and performance career; she also began the creative endeavors that Littlefield would finish in her own career. When Littlefield established an independent ballet company in the city of Philadelphia, it was in many a ways the fruition of her mother's hopes and dreams.

Caroline Littlefield had wanted to be a dancer but was forbidden by her parents. Forced to turn to other creative disciplines, she pursued a dream of becoming a concert pianist and studied at the Philadelphia and Paris conservatories. She also volunteered as a supernumerary for the Philadelphia Opera. Compelled and enchanted by the dancers she saw on the opera's stage, she began training with Romulus Carpenter, the Philadelphia Opera Company's ballet master at the beginning of the twentieth century. However, she began train-

Figure 3.2. Catherine Littlefield posing for a studio portrait in her Aurora tutu, 1936. (*Philadelphia Evening Bulletin* Photo File, Special Collections Research Center, Temple University Libraries, Philadelphia, PA.)

ing too late in life to achieve true virtuosity. Despite her lack of proficiency, dance was her passion, and she did eventually perform with the Philadelphia Opera Ballet, dancing a solo in *Fairy Doll*.[15] Her major contribution to the dance field, however, was as a teacher, not as a performer, of dance. When a community organization sought to develop its social programs by instituting ballet classes for local women, Caroline Littlefield took on the running of the school.[16] In 1908, she established her own dance academy, the Littlefield School, across the street from the Academy of Music at 1415 Locust Street.[17]

Caroline Littlefield was not the only dance teacher in Philadelphia. In fact, in 1926 the Yellow Pages listed eighty-five different dance teachers. Few, however, offered serious ballet instruction by teachers trained in a well-established curriculum.[18] "Toe-dancing" was offered alongside ballroom, acrobatic, aesthetic, interpretive, and tap dancing at many of these schools. During this period, Florence Cowanova was one of Philadelphia's most commercially successful and widely advertised dance teachers. Reminiscent of Isadora Duncan's claims about the spiritual benefits of dance as an art form, Cowanova's approach, which catered to the city's socially prominent families, was to tout the values of dance training as "a diversion and physically restorative." She went on to claim, "The mere self-discipline of smiling as one dances, which is a part of the art of ballet dances, does wonders for many a girl and woman of negative, pessimistic or over-repressed nature."[19] Other well-known Philadelphia dance teachers were Al White, a popular tap teacher; Ethel Phillips, a former dancer in the Chicago Grand Opera Company, Broadway musicals and comedies, and vaudeville; and Billy Herman, who taught acrobatics.[20]

The Littlefield School distinguished itself from all other ballet schools in Philadelphia as an influential force in the development of American ballet. It produced dancers such as Lucille Bremer, Karen Conrad, Douglas Coudy, Jane Deering, William Dollar, Norma Gentner, Miriam Golden, Joan McCracken, and Jack Potteiger.[21] The teachers at Caroline's Littlefield School taught many forms of dance, including social, folk, ballet, acrobatics, and tap. The school's reputation grew when students performed well at local concerts for charitable causes. Caroline—or "Mommie"—Littlefield's success in putting on these charitable performances led the managers of Philadelphia music halls to engage her to stage dances for their productions, as well. In the mid-1920s, after she arranged and directed a ballet from

Aida for a spring music festival held at Franklin Field, an outdoor space attached to the University of Pennsylvania, the Philadelphia Civic Opera asked Mommie Littlefield to direct ballet for all of its productions. These successes eventually led to opportunities from many of the city's well-known opera companies, including the Philadelphia Opera Company, the Philadelphia La Scala, and the Italian Opera Company.[22] By the late 1920s, the Littlefield School had grown to more than four hundred students, with students ranging in age from twelve to twenty-four.

International Influences of Classical Ballet

As the Littlefield school grew, Mommie began to take a back seat, and her daughters, Catherine and Dorothie, took on more of the teaching load. Catherine Littlefield's teaching style was influenced by not only her mother's approach but also the approaches of international dancers she saw in performance and studied with. At ten, Littlefield saw Diaghilev's Ballets Russes perform at the Metropolitan Opera House in New York. She was in the audience at the Academy of Music for Anna Pavlova's last Philadelphia performance in 1920.[23] In the 1930s, Littlefield also watched the companies of Serge Denham and Vassili De Basil perform in Europe.

In addition to watching performances of international ballet performers, Littlefield had studied with international coaches throughout her career. Each summer she traveled to Paris to train with Lubov Egorova and Olga Preobrajenska (see Figure 3.3). Egorova was a well-known former member of the Maryinsky Ballet and Diaghilev's Ballets Russes and had a studio at the Place de la Trinité. Preobrajenska had been a prima ballerina with the Maryinsky and was so well known that almost every major mid-century Western ballet dancer visited her for lessons. While in Paris, Catherine and Dorothie also studied with Léo Staats. Staats was someone who also bridged the boundaries between classical and popular dance. He was trained at the school of the Paris Opera Ballet. He performed in the company and then was named ballet master of the Paris Opera Ballet in 1908. Between 1926 and 1928, however, he was the first permanent choreographer for shows at the Roxy Theatre in New York City.[24]

Littlefield traveled to New York to study with another Russian émigré, Mikhail Mordkin.[25] Mordkin, formerly of Moscow's Bolshoi

Figure 3.3. The worldly Catherine and Dorothie Littlefield returning to Philadelphia from Paris after a summer training under the influential teacher and former Russian ballerina Lubov Egorova, 1936. (*Philadelphia Evening Bulletin* Photo File, Special Collections Research Center, Temple University Libraries, Philadelphia, PA.)

Ballet, also performed with Diaghilev's Ballets Russes and partnered with Pavlova. He eventually returned to Russia, becoming ballet master at the Bolshoi, where he stayed until 1924, when he went to New York. There he formed and danced in several touring companies and taught ballet in New York and across the United States. He was also a founder of what eventually became Ballet Theatre and later became American Ballet Theatre.[26] Mordkin had a huge influence on another important Aurora, Lucia Chase. She performed Aurora in Mordkin's version of *Beauty*, which was danced to recorded music in her hometown of Waterbury, Connecticut, in December 1936.[27]

Littlefield also studied intensively with Luigi Albertieri,[28] an Italian dancer and ballet master. A favorite pupil of Cecchetti, Albertieri performed in the London premiere of Luigi Manzotti's *Excelsior*. He was premier danseur of the Empire Ballet in London, a choreographer at Covent Garden (1895–1902), and ballet master of both the Chicago Lyric Opera (1910–1913) and the New York Metropolitan Opera House (1913–1927). In 1915, Albertieri opened a school in New York, where Fred Astaire was one of his most promising pupils and where Littlefield took classes.[29] Yet another important teacher of Littlefield's from the international ballet world was Ivan Tarasoff, who sent his own son to study and perform dance with Littlefield's Philadelphia Ballet Company later in life.[30]

Littlefield, then, is a prime example of the kind of transnationalism that pervaded dance in Philadelphia during the 1920s and 1930s. A local girl who stayed in her local city, she also studied with the most well qualified international coaches of her time. She learned from them a unique mixture of Russian, Italian, French, and American styles of dance, with a focus on clean, clear technique and the basic foundations of the danse d'école.

Littlefield's exposure to the training and performance of these international dancers was part of a larger trend in early American ballet. Like the other influential choreographers and dancers of her time, Littlefield was an artistic descendant of both the Russian Imperial Ballet and its modernist successor, the Ballets Russes. As Jennifer Homans commented in her history of ballet, "Performance by performance, class by class, over many years, these itinerant Russians passed on their tradition. Not only the steps and techniques: they brought to their lessons the entire Imperial orthodoxy of Russian ballet, and it was in their sweaty encounters with students that the long process of transplanting ballet to American minds and bodies began."[31]

Local Influences, Popular Dance, and Hybridity

Littlefield taught more than just the tradition of the Russian Imperial Ballet. Although her classical training undergirded Littlefield's craft, her aesthetic vision and ideas about dance as a performing art were also shaped by the popular dance of her day. In the 1930s, Americans sought entertainment to escape from the bleak realities of life during the Great Depression. Popular venues for an evening out were Hollywood films, musical theater, and mixed bill revue shows that including comedians, magicians, and dancers who were trained in tap, soft shoe, and ballet. Classically trained ballet dancers had no professional American ballet companies with which they could work. Instead, they went from job to job, dancing in operas, in musical theater, or in revue shows. This was a necessity for American dancers, classically trained or not, before the establishment of American ballet companies in the 1930s and 1940s. As Lynn Garafola explains, "Although Americans filled the lower ranks of the Metropolitan Opera ballet, most ballet-trained dancers found work on the popular stage—in Broadway musicals and revues and in the ballet troupes attached to the Radio City Music Hall and the Roxy. . . . Many shuttled between the commercial and concert realms."[32]

As she matured and sought professional employment in the dance field, Littlefield had to look for work outside of teaching classes at the family's dance school, and she performed in many operas and musical revues. As her talented counterparts across the country did, Littlefield took part in the Ziegfeld Follies, where eventually she would become a star. Between 1920 and 1925, she performed in musical theater productions across the country and took on leading roles in Broadway shows, performing in New York and on the road.[33] Littlefield also found employment at the Roxy Theatre, the palatial movie hall in New York City, where dancers performed before the screening of films.[34] George Dorris describes the context of such dancing: "One of the stranger moments in theatre history was the flourishing in the 1920s of the American movie palaces with their elaborate 'prologs.' As part of a program lasting around two hours, the patron could sit in baroquely spectacular surroundings and see a varied stage show featuring music and dance in addition to a film."[35] It was in this context of opportunity for classically trained dancers that Littlefield developed the vision she would eventually bring back to Philadelphia and use to create the American premiere of *The Sleeping Beauty*.

"Free and Fresh": Littlefield Develops Her Style of Classical American Ballet

Littlefield identified as a performer, teacher, and choreographer. Each facet of her artistry influenced the other. Unlike many artistic directors from the world of ballet who cast, taught class, and coached rehearsal from a chair, Littlefield continued to perform actively throughout her career. Her experiences onstage and in class were the ground from which she imagined performance and from which she imagined the genre of classical ballet as a whole. When Littlefield returned to Philadelphia in 1926, she announced that she would devote herself to developing ballet in her native city.[36] She took a strong teaching role at the Littlefield School and began staging her own works for large groups of dancers who performed at movie theaters around Philadelphia. Around the same time, Mommie Littlefield was appointed ballet director of the Philadelphia Civic Opera and installed Catherine as the principal dancer of the opera company, where she would lead a corps de ballet made up of dancers from the Littlefield School in a well-received season. The success of this first Littlefield-dominated season led to many more, which from time to time included special all-ballet performances. The dancers were called "The Caroline Littlefield Ballet," and they performed a range of productions, including *Carmen*, *Aida*, *Giovanna*, and *Lakhme*, as well as *Fairy Doll* and *Carnival Ballet*.[37]

Catherine Littlefield trained the dancers in the opera company to be quick and strong, and they performed to acclaim both in revue shows and on the classical theater stage. By the end of the 1920s, the Littlefield School had earned a citywide reputation for bringing out the best in dancers in class and in performance. The school was known throughout the northeastern United States, and in fact throughout the entire country and even abroad, as producing well-trained professional dancers able to give top-quality performances in large venues. The Mastbaum Theatre at Twenty-First and Market Streets engaged Littlefield to supervise the staging of its ensembles, then under the direction of the manager Robert Alton. When teaching her own classes, Littlefield used set or memorized Cecchetti barre work, along with center exercises that focused on pirouettes, adagio, and allegro. Emphasizing speed and mental alertness, her entire class lasted only an hour, and students were given minimal time to work out the combinations before having to execute the choreographed sequences in groups. Littlefield's teaching was drawn from her own training, and it placed a strong emphasis on confidence, quickness, strength, and clarity.[38] Littlefield also added to the traditional training of her instructors, making it her own. She described the style she taught as "modern in the best sense of the word—I mean that it is free and fresh in approach and viewpoint. We use classical ballet technique, but only as a means to the end of unhampered esthetic expression."[39] The results of this approach were significant. Her dancers were frequently noticed for their fresh American style, as a review published in 1935 noted the dancers for "the technical accomplishments of the group but also . . . a certain character and spirit which distinguish their organization from other groups of dancers."[40]

In 1928, in her new capacity as teacher and coach, Littlefield took over the role of ballet mistress of the Philadelphia Grand Opera Company. By 1930, the Littlefields' opera ballet company was renamed the Philadelphia Grand Opera Ballet and included a corps of one hundred dancers, in addition to the soloists.[41] Over the next few years, Catherine and Mommie Littlefield remade the primarily student-based group of the opera ballet into a professional troupe. To accomplish this shift, Catherine Littlefield took over the bulk of the choreography for the operas and the stage ensembles. Her talent was immediately noticed by the conductor of the Philadelphia Orchestra, Leopold Stokowski, who asked her to choreograph ballet segments for the world premiere of a performance by Carlos Chavez, with scenery and costumes by Diego Rivera.[42] Despite Littlefield's artistic success, by the early 1930s the Philadelphia Grand Opera Ballet faced mounting financial deficits. By 1933, the financial hardships of the Great Depression had caused the opera company to close its doors. Littlefield was again forced to find employment. She moved to New York City, where she worked temporarily at the Roxy Theatre, choreographing, rehearsing, and performing in dance productions.

After fourteen weeks of performances at the Roxy, she returned to Philadelphia to continue her teaching.[43]

Establishing an Independent Ballet Company

Soon after she returned to Philadelphia, in June 1933, Littlefield married Phillip Ludwell Leidy, the son of one of the major supporters of her former employer, the Philadelphia Grand Opera. The marriage provided Littlefield with a secure financial base from which, in 1935, she would gather advanced students from her school and build an independent ballet company. Despite her newfound financial support, however, Littlefield continued to struggle to form an autonomous ballet company. She had trained all of the dancers with whom she wanted to work and was so successful at training them that soon after the inception of her company, a large group of her most advanced dancers were hired away to New York. Lincoln Kirstein and George Balanchine selected at least eight of Littlefield's best dancers for Balanchine's new School of American Ballet in New York City.[44] The *Philadelphia Record* recorded this bittersweet success: "Eight of the 12 scholarships available at the American Ballet four years ago went to Catherine Littlefield's girls. Her sister, Dorothie, was the only American teacher on the faculty of the American Ballet. Of 18 dancers taken to Hollywood for a ballet feature, four were from the local troupe."[45]

The Philadelphia Orchestra invited Littlefield to choreograph and perform ballet interludes for opera presentations for the 1935 summer season at Robin Hood Dell. In the 1930s, these summer seasons were a vehicle for presenting some of the most influential dance artists in the country. Littlefield became intimately involved in the work at the Dell and presented there each summer. The management also invited the Littlefield Dancers to present an all-ballet evening on July 17, 1935. Now to be known as the Littlefield Ballet, the company gave its inaugural performance in November 1935,[46] with sixteen dancers and an apprentice company that allowed the group to expand to forty dancers when necessary. The company danced with a uniformity of training and style that reflected the training and aesthetic vision of the Littlefield School. Only two months after its first performance at the Robin Hood Dell, the company became the Philadelphia Ballet, a momentous event for Littlefield and for the city. The program for a December 1935 performance announced the thinking behind the change:

> The company is fully cognizant of the great responsibilities which the use of the name "Philadelphia" entails. Under the personal direction of Catherine Littlefield and her corps of assistants, your company will strive to continue to present the dance and music public of Philadelphia the best in the classical and modern-classical dance. New ballets will be produced from time to time with music specially written for the dance, and it is hoped in the very near future among other things to present what the management sincerely believes to be a true "American Ballet." The aim of your company will be to give performances not only in large but also in small auditoriums at popular prices [i]n order to develop in all sections of the city and its vicinity a ballet-conscious public.[47]

Philadelphia was thrilled to announce its own ballet company. Writers for local papers touted the company as a local treasure. Lacking a home theater, the company performed around the city. During its first season, it danced everywhere: at Reading High School, Olney High School, Temple University, the Bellevue-Stratford Hotel, the Academy of Music, and Robin Hood Dell, as well as the City College of New York's Lewisohn Stadium.[48]

Following the first season of the Philadelphia Ballet, Littlefield and her husband went to Europe to vacation. Littlefield used the trip to study new scores for the ballet company and to confer with European designers for her big vision: a new production of *The Sleeping Beauty*. During the vacation, Littlefield also made plans for her company to perform abroad, in Paris, London, Deauville, and Brussels, the following season. Before embarking on the company's first European tour, however, Littlefield choreographed the first American production of the jewel of the classical canon, *The Sleeping Beauty*.[49]

The Sleeping Beauty Premieres in the United States (1937)

On February 11, 1937, *The Sleeping Beauty* premiered at the Academy of Music in Philadelphia. The production was the first American performance of the full-length version of the ballet and was a result of Littlefield's international training and connections. It is certainly an important piece of the web of ballet as it emerged in the United States. Drawing on the initial success of the Philadelphia Ballet,[50] Littlefield decided to choreograph the entire full-length ballet (with the exception of the pas de deux in the final act) for her company's second season. The choreography was attributed to Marius Petipa, as it had been set by Madame Lubov Egorova, with whom Littlefield had studied in Paris the previous summer.[51] Littlefield stated that she created the steps "in the style" of the original work by Petipa.[52] No film recording or notation of the production survives, but many newspaper reviews do, and they document the ballet's performance and allow us to reconstruct details about its historic reception. These reviews revolve around Littlefield's attempt to create a ballet that was authentically traditional. The push-and-pull between discussions of American freshness and the classicism of European tradition takes on a prominent status in the discourse that circulated around the work. Littlefield's imaginative artistic vision and ability to negotiate these tensions allowed her to set the national stage for the emergence of a new American professional ballet. That she did this from a regional setting is of much note.

At this point, it is important to discuss the idea of reconstruction. This is a much debated issue in the worlds of music, dance, and theater and is obviously quite relevant to this discussion, although outside the purview of the story I am telling here. Obviously, with a genre as ephemeral as dance—one performed by living, breathing, changing people that disappears the moment after its performance— we must question whether any dance can truly be reconstructed. What, therefore, does it mean to restage a work "in the style of" an original? Littlefield made no claims of "authenticity" in her work. Rather, she wanted to share what she had learned from artists such as Egorova and Mordkin with the people of Philadelphia, making the established canonical work accessible to large audiences for reasonable prices. She sought to build an audience for ballet in Philadelphia, as well as to develop a group of well-trained dancers capable of performing the demanding works of the Euro-Russian canon alongside more contemporary, American-style choreographic projects.

In keeping with these desires, Littlefield did her best to mount a ballet that reflected the grandeur of the imperial-style ballet. Reviewers reported that Littlefield's *Sleeping Beauty* costumes were sumptuous. They cited the European woolens and furs used (though other critics remarked that "the production would naturally have been enhanced by richer costuming").[53] Jarin Scenic Studio designed and executed the sets. Alexander Smallens conducted the eighty-five-musician Curtis Symphony Orchestra, which accompanied the first presentation.[54] One hundred students from the Littlefield School augmented the Philadelphia Ballet Company for the production. With all of this support, no deletions were made from the full score of the ballet. One hundred miles away from New York, it was the Philadelphia Ballet that became the first American company to dance a full-length ballet performance of *The Sleeping Beauty* with a professional cast and live orchestra.[55]

Littlefield's husband invested $10,000 to cover the costs of mounting the ballet.[56] This was a tremendous cost in the midst of the Depression, and it signifies the weight that Littlefield and her husband felt the ballet carried. They hoped their success with *Beauty* would win them the support of outside bookings, as well as the financial backing of investors within the city. This, indeed, was the result of their huge undertaking. Many critics spoke about the company's triumph in staging the ballet and welcomed the Philadelphia Ballet to the international ballet scene. By embarking on the elaborate and traditional work, Littlefield succeeded in establishing her company as an authoritative institution worthy of the ballet world's respect. John Martin of the *New York Times* wrote about the Philadelphia Ballet, "With all due allowances, it has done a good job of this tremendously ambitious project. It gives a consistently better account of itself at each of its presentations and shows that its approach to its work is soundly based, and that it is not concerned with faddism and sensation. The very fact of its revival of this ballet in the old romantic tradition testifies to this in a degree, and the straightforwardness of both the choreography and the performance add further evidence."[57] And commenting on the company's performance of the ballet at the Hollywood Bowl in Los Angeles, Dorathi Bock Pierre wrote, "If there is a doubt in anyone's mind that an American ballet company cannot match any European company, the Littlefield Ballet should make them change their opinion. . . . [T]he choreography showed [Littlefield's] love of the traditional ballet, with a fine sense of theatrical pageantry and democratic ideal."[58] The *Philadelphia Inquirer* expressed a similar sentiment: "The Philadelphia Ballet, which is to the dance art in this city and America what the Philadelphia Orchestra is in its field, added a few more feathers to its already well-decorated cap with the American premiere of Tchaikovsky's fairy tale, 'The Sleeping Beauty.'"[59]

Much of Littlefield's labor was concerned with legitimizing her work. She wanted to prove her pedagogical lineage and the classicism of her training and the training of her dancers. In choosing a canonical piece with the cultural status of *The Sleeping Beauty*, Littlefield signaled her understanding of this tradition and claimed her place in the trajectory of dance history. Littlefield balanced the fresh-faced Americana of her young company full of truck drivers and waitresses with the cultural capital inherent in producing a work that holds such status within the canon. In addition to creating and producing pieces such as *Barn Dance*, a work of jolly Americana that would become part of not only this company's repertoire but also that of American Ballet Theatre, she had the knowledge and skill to produce a work of significant international magnitude and prestige.

Critics responded to her call to classicism. They noted Littlefield's relationship to Petipa. An article in the *Philadelphia Evening Bulletin* acknowledged that "the choreographic style is strictly in the classic manner, and Miss Littlefield has wisely made no attempt to modernize it."[60] The critic's emphasis on the importance of capturing the late nineteenth-century style of the ballet is an example of the typical interest of the time in the ballet's historical and aesthetic continuity. Similarly, a critic in *Dance Magazine* wrote that Littlefield's "choreography is in the best classic tradition . . . and as should be in *The Sleeping Beauty*, the most outstanding dance is the *grand pas de deux* of Act III, credited in the program to Petipa as reconstructed by Egorova."[61]

Dance critics' desire for authenticity was complicated by many reviewers' more modern reactions to the ballet. The ballet's length and antiquated aesthetic also challenged audience members and critics who had more regularly attended mixed bill review shows and Hollywood movies. It is also important to remember that American modern dancers had made significant headway during this time. The

1930s saw the emergence of an entire genre of indigenous American modern dance led by Martha Graham, Doris Humphrey, Ted Shawn, Anna Sokolow, and other artists. Critics such as Edwin Denby and John Martin contributed to the development of a discourse around the work of modern dance. Institutions such as Bennington College and Jacob's Pillow emerged as centers of artistic experimentation where the new dance was created and generated. It is indicative of the field of professional dance during this time period that Humphrey, Irma Duncan, José Limon, and the Fokine Ballet—American modern dancers and European-born ballet dancers—also performed at Robin Hood Dell, the open-air performance venue where Littlefield's company performed *Sleeping Beauty* twice during the summer of 1937.

As an American-born ballet dancer, Littlefield sought to establish her work as different both from that of other American artists working at the time and from that of European dancers abroad. This had been one of her principal reasons for taking on *The Sleeping Beauty* project. In an article entitled "Sleeping Beauty Given at Stadium,"[62] Martin acknowledged the difficulty of Littlefield's project: "Miss Littlefield has not at her disposal either the spectacular facilities or the human material to do justice to the work."[63] Although, Martin—along with 5,500 members of the audience at Robin Hood Dell—found value in the Littlefield version of the ballet, he questioned the feasibility of a young American company performing a work of such grandiosity, spectacle, and opulence.[64] But in a later review of the production, he wrote, "In the reviving of an old work of this kind, . . . it is almost essential to preserve something of its stuffiness in order to give it its true flavor."[65] For Martin, the ballet was a historical piece, a didactic poem that instructs its audience by representing an older society with its own aesthetic sensibilities. Like Littlefield, he wavers between his desire for tradition, and his desire for contemporary compelling work. He expanded on his feelings about the ballet, writing, "Here is really a grand old work, a ballet with a large B. Its lovely score, its foolish fairy-tale plot in which nothing ever happens, the inherent quality of bravura which its scenarist and composer have instilled into any possible choreographic arrangement, all proclaim unmistakably the year 1890 in which it was created."[66]

Martin is correct in that the ballet represents a stable culture of opulence and order. But that world is one of fantasy derived from people who were facing the bleak circumstances of poverty, industrialization, modernity, and chaos. I want to make a strong parallel between the onstage world of *Beauty* and the world of opulence and grandeur in the films of actors such as Fred Astaire, Ginger Rogers, Joan Crawford, Greta Garbo, and Shirley Temple that were so popular in the 1930s. People facing poverty, social change, and the stresses of war found comfort in depictions of rich and beautiful people living lives of ease and prosperity. As a matriarch of American classical ballet, Littlefield wanted to use her well-trained dancers to depict the old and lovely world of the classical ballet. She wanted to take her audiences to a place of calm and secure beauty. Her dancers carried on the grand tradition of the art form even while allowing for subtle shifts and changes. It was a nuanced project; Martin sensed this sophisticated reconciliation of aesthetics and approved of Littlefield's approach. In fact, he cited the portion of the ballet that had been "reconstructed" as the highlight of the work: "The choreography of the present production is newly designed by Catherine Littlefield, with the single exception of the grand pas de deux of the last scene which, thanks to the memory of Lubov Egorova, is believed to be the original composition of Marius Petipa who gave the ballet its first choreographic setting in 1890 for the Imperial Ballet in St. Petersburg. . . . [T]his bit provides the evening's most brilliant moments."[67]

Littlefield, however, billed her company as not only a bastion of classical Western European tradition but also as a fresh, modern American troupe. One of her publicity statements described the company as "the first purely American ballet company to translate into the American idiom the glamorous traditions of a thrilling stage art . . . an art finding an exciting renaissance in the superb vitality of young America."[68] In this regard, from her perch in Philadelphia she participated in a larger trend in the emerging American ballet scene. As Lynn Garafola has discussed, it was essential for dance companies in the United States to "uncouple the aspiration to creative excellence from wealth and social snobbery" to gain popularity with American audiences.[69] Littlefield's vision of American ballet was that it would be exciting and accessible, as well as grounded in proper technique. "Miss Littlefield frequently said that she did not believe that ballet had to be dull or slow," noted the *Philadelphia Evening News*. "'We gave it pace and life and snapped it up without sacrificing technique or true ballet tradition,' she said."[70] This she did not only through her training and hiring of American dancers but also by creating a diverse repertoire of newly choreographed ballets and traditional Russo-European works such as *Beauty*.

In a *Philadelphia Evening Bulletin* article describing the company's return from a European tour, Littlefield is quoted as saying that the Europeans "called us America's national ballet."[71] Littlefield used American-born and American-trained (Philadelphia-trained) dancers. One article reviewing *Beauty* remarked on the novelty of an all-American ballet company: "In the performance, over 100 dancers will appear in various scenes of the ballet. All of these except two are Philadelphia born. This in itself is a remarkable thing because coming as many of them do from foreign-born parents it would be natural to suppose that . . . they had come to Philadelphia as youngsters from the national home of their parents or might have moved here during their younger days from some other city in the United States."[72]

Littlefield balanced her company's reputation for American youth, newness, and freshness of approach with a demonstration of her company's solid grounding in tradition. She created a diverse repertoire that included new and old works of choreography. She encouraged the development of a uniquely American style of performance. Janet Gunn, a newspaper critic for the *Chestnut Hill Herald* and the *Philadelphia Examiner* wrote, "If there is an all-American rating for contenders in the art of dancing, this company holds it by an overwhelming number of points."[73] How did Littlefield convince American audiences of her company's worth? By making ballet exciting. Bridging the popular dance stage and the classical ballet academy, she forged an identity for her company that embraced both its classicism and its modernism. Littlefield's hybridization of ballet as a high art and a low art allowed ballet to gain a foothold in the United States as it emerged in the 1930s, as did her negotiation of these realms of cultural discourse. *The Sleeping Beauty*, as performed by the Philadelphia Ballet Company, became a metaphor for ballet itself as it awoke inside the confines of the United States.

Conclusion

Although her legacy was not acknowledged in the canonical treatment of American ballet, in producing *The Sleeping Beauty* Littlefield successfully legitimized and established American classical ballet. Her work allowed American ballet to enter the international dance scene as an important contributor, which, in turn, gave the genre longevity and a future in the shifting sociopolitical configurations of the post–World War I world. As the *Philadelphia Evening Bulletin* reported:

> Together with the company's American premiere of Tchaikovsky's "The Sleeping Beauty" last week [the company's polished performance] brought the group yet wider recognition as the leading organization of its kind in the country. No one argues that "The Sleeping Beauty," was a faultless production, but there has been general agreement that for technical finish and for its qualities as a composition it represented an extraordinary accomplishment. In the work of the company and in the interest and enthusiasm displayed by the audiences at each of the two performances one sensed the sturdy healthy growth of the organization and a public awakening to the potentialities as well as to the accomplishments of American dancers under capable supervision.[74]

Littlefield was successful in merging the traditional ballet of her teachers with her newer American understanding of the art form. *The Sleeping Beauty*, like the modern American career woman, underwent significant change in 1930s America. Littlefield reestablished the underpinnings of the classical aesthetic of order, symmetry, and balance that are at the very foundation of classical ballet; this was part and parcel of educating the American ballet audience and of proving the technical excellence of the Philadelphia Ballet Company.

Taking on such a large and audacious production also cast Littlefield in a new role: She was not just a choreographer and rehearsal assistant and teacher; she was an artistic director and impresario of grand scale. Along with Bronislava Nijinska, Ninette de Valois, Ruth

Page, Agnes de Mille, and Lucia Chase, Littlefield redefined the role of women in the ballet studio. Women's role was no longer to support but to create. Through the vehicle of the classical repertoire, Littlefield established herself, her distinctly American ballet company, and the genre of classical ballet. The Philadelphia Ballet Company was recognized as "one of the country's foremost dance organizations."[75] It was a genuine American ballet company that brought ballet to larger and more diverse audiences. True to her vision, Littlefield would "give performances not only in large but also in small auditoriums at popular prices, in order to develop in all sections of the city and its vicinity a ballet-conscious public."[76]

The personal and professional influences on Littlefield led her to a place where she was able to make these important contributions to dance history. To close this chapter, I outline these influences on Catherine Littlefield, painting a picture of the extraordinary life circumstances that allowed her to envision and develop this new hybrid genre of classical American ballet.

Littlefield's vision influenced the course of classical ballet in its early years in the United States. As one critic said of her company, "The Philadelphia Ballet stands for American creative efforts and it is this that has won it fame."[77] In 1936, Littlefield somewhat prophetically predicted, "There is a great future for ballet in this country, and eventually large cities will have repertoire ballet organizations of their own as they now have symphony orchestras."[78] Her contributions should be added to those of the other, male artists who worked in the same time period of the 1930s to create a richer and more complex picture of the development of classical ballet in the United States. Although scholarship exists illuminating the history of early American ballet, much of this work centers on the birth and emergence of the New York City Ballet under George Balanchine and Lincoln Kirstein. Many dance history texts draw a narrative of American ballet that follows genius from Petipa, working in Russia in the 1890s, to Michel Fokine and Vaslav Nijinsky, working in Paris in the 1910s and 1920s, and George Balanchine, working in New York in the 1940s–1960s, ignoring both Littlefield and the primacy of Philadelphia as the center of American ballet during the 1930s. The conventional narrative minimizes the accomplishments of many women who were working in the United States paving the way for the professionalization and decentralization of professional ballet in the United States. In 1937, the well-known dance critic Arnold Haskell, the distinguished authority on ballet, wrote, "[Michel] Fokine, [Léonide] Massine, and [George] Balanchine have been working for considerable periods in America. But it has taken an American woman to produce the first American works for American dancers to find favor both in Paris and London."[79] Unfortunately, dance history afterward forgot about Littlefield's work and legacy.

The work of the Philadelphia Ballet Company and its large-scale production of *The Sleeping Beauty* attest to Littlefield's importance as a strong foremother of classical ballet and to Philadelphia as an important artistic hub with an active cultural life throughout the twentieth century. The Philadelphia story suggests that the New York–centered meta-narrative of ballet history has been unstable, especially for the 1920s.[80]

In 1937, following the home premiere of *The Sleeping Beauty*, the Philadelphia Ballet Company embarked on the first European tour by an American ballet company. The company captivated audiences in Paris, London, and Brussels.[81] The following year, Littlefield and her company went on to perform for Franklin D. Roosevelt, receiving recognition both nationally and internationally for their distinctive American style of well-polished ballet. In 1939, the Littlefield Ballet, a select, reorganized group of dancers drawn from the Philadelphia Ballet Company, became the resident company of the Chicago Civic Opera. This further emphasized the national scope of Littlefield's work, even as she created ballet in the direst economic circumstances.[82] Although the loss of men to the armed forces during World War II and inconsistent funding in 1941 finally forced the company to disband, Littlefield continued to be active in choreography. In these later years, she veered toward popular dance, choreographing for Broadway musical revues, ice skating shows, and *The Jimmy Durante Show.*

It is unfortunate that, despite the success of the Philadelphia Ballet under Littlefield's leadership, the time was not right for the city to sustain its own company. This inauguration of a uniquely American ballet lasted only a few years. In presenting a more complex and nuanced narrative of American ballet that takes innovations outside New York more seriously, it is worth considering that Catherine Littlefield and George Balanchine were contemporaries. They respected each other, and the history of ballet has erased the ways in which Littlefield helped Balanchine develop and train American talent in a new American style of classical ballet. The United States is a country in which disparate communities have been places of generative creativity and inspiration and are intricately connected with the creative work done in hubs like New York. Littlefield's work in Philadelphia is an extraordinary demonstration of the work of women's creativity and vision in ballet production, as it is a demonstration of the importance of one of those communities.

4.

AURORA STREAMLINED AND
ACCELERATED

Barbara Weisberger and the Second
U.S. Production (1965)

Philadelphia in the 1960s

F ollowing the premiere of Catherine Littlefield's *The Sleeping Beauty* in 1937, during the Great Depression, the full-length ballet was not performed again in Philadelphia until 1965, when it was again produced during a significant moment of American cultural and political ferment. In fact, Philadelphia was without a formally established professional ballet company between 1942 and 1963. Despite *The Sleeping Beauty*'s growing popularity in the thirty years between productions, and the continued establishment of American professional ballet, no American company took on a staging of the full-length production during this time period. As were so many Americans, Philadelphians were experiencing the transitions and dislocations that accompanied the transformations of American society that created, sustained, and followed the Civil Rights Movement, the emergence of the Vietnam War, and the women's liberation movement. In 1960, Philadelphia was the third-largest city in the United States, with a population of 2,002,512.[1] The city faced housing shortages, political and racial polarization, and increases in crime and labor unrest.[2]

Throughout the 1960s, Philadelphia (again, like many North American cities) experienced riots against police, as well as storefront looting and destruction. In August 1964, only months before the Pennsylvania Ballet's new production of *The Sleeping Beauty*, more than two thousand people in North Philadelphia fought with police, resulting in the deaths of two Philadelphians and the injuring of 339.[3] A rising protest movement developed that focused on civil rights for African Americans and other minorities. By 1965, for example, more than one thousand police were detailed to Girard College, a historically African American boarding school for children of single-parent homes, where large groups of protesters decried the institution's failure to comply with the U.S. Supreme Court ruling enforcing nondiscriminatory entrance policies.[4] Fighting between the Black Panthers and the Philadelphia police extended throughout the 1960s and 1970s. Gang warfare rose to a new level, reaching forty-one gang killings in Philadelphia in 1969.[5]

Philadelphians encountered the complex psychology of modern existence when they experienced the fears and paranoia that accompanied politics and cultural life over the decade. It is important, however, that many of the city's residents also clung to older ways of life even during the dramatic transitions of a new age. Anxiety accompanied the growing violence and tension that developed throughout the 1950s and 1960s. Seeking to gain control over children, adults expanded such supervised activities as Scouting, school sports, and chaperoned dances. Traditional values were enforced, with Little Leagues becoming fixtures in the emerging suburban landscape, while in the city people cooperated with the police in the Police Athletic League.[6]

Amid these changes, and accompanied by city residents' desire to rebuild after the deterioration brought on by years of economic depression and local government corruption, Philadelphia's Pennsylvania Ballet gave birth to yet another incarnation of *The Sleeping Beauty*. Before examining this performance, however, I first turn to the birth of the company and woman who produced it. For all of its problems, the Pennsylvania Ballet can still call itself "one of the premier ballet companies in the United States."[7] Despite many financial difficulties, the organization celebrated its fiftieth anniversary season in 2014, a major achievement in a world in which both individual and government support for the arts has dwindled. The company also represents a case study or iconic example of the regional type of company that now characterizes much of the balletic genre in North America. The Pennsylvania Ballet, along with many other companies that proliferated during this period, developed a distinctive style and aesthetic in response to the preferences of limited funding sources, as well as the tastes of a small and loyal audience base. For example, the support of McNeil Lowry of the Ford Foundation and the initiative to sponsor local arts organizations in the 1960s were instrumental in creating the Pennsylvania Ballet; however, the company's emergence is in many ways attributable to Weisberger's personal and pedagogical connection to George Balanchine.[8]

Barbara Weisberger and the Pennsylvania Ballet

Barbara Weisberger, the founder of the Pennsylvania Ballet Company, began studying ballet with Marian Lehman in 1931 at the age of five in her native Brooklyn, New York. Three years later, in 1934, when Weisberger was only eight years old, Lehman took her to audition for George Balanchine's newly formed School of American Ballet. Weisberger was accepted and became the first child to study at the school. There she took classes with William Dollar, Erick Hawkins, Charles Laskey, Heidi Vosseler, and Dorothie Littlefield. More than half of this class came from the Littlefield School of Ballet in Philadelphia, and it was these dancers in Balanchine's top level at the school who would become the first instantiation of the New York City Ballet. It was only six months after Weisberger arrived, however, that Balanchine established the short-lived American Ballet. With this transition, he could no longer offer a child a steady schedule of classes, and Weisberger was still too young to join the company. Weisberger therefore began training with Margaret Curtis at the Metropolitan Opera House,[9] where she stayed until the age of fourteen.

In 1940, Weisberger and her family moved to Wilmington, Delaware. Wilmington is about a forty-minute train ride from Philadelphia, and at the suggestion of Balanchine, her former teacher, Weisberger began training under the strict regimen of the Littlefield School of Ballet. When the United States entered World War II in 1941, the Littlefield Company, Balanchine's company, and American Ballet Theatre (ABT) were all disbanded or temporarily suspended operations because of lack of funding and a lack of male dancers. Few performing opportunities existed at this time, and Weisberger enrolled in classes at the University of Delaware, transferring to Pennsylvania State University in 1943. After graduating in 1945 with a teaching certificate in speech therapy, she married and taught elementary school in Philadelphia. Her marriage lasted two years, after which time she returned to her parents' home in Wilkes-Barre, Pennsylvania, and began teaching at a local ballet school. It was there that Weisberger found an outlet for her passion for dance—in teaching. In 1975, she told Olga Maynard that her "life changed because I discovered that working with dancers brought me as much joy as I had found in dancing."[10]

In 1949, she married the Wilkes-Barre businessman Ernest Weisberger and began the path that would allow her to make her mark on the American ballet community. She opened a school whose enrollment quickly grew to more than two hundred students. She then drew dancers for her company from that school. Though limited by the small population of Wilkes-Barre, Weisberger made every attempt to present her students with as many performing opportunities as possible. Reflecting on her experience there, she stated that everything she did in Wilkes-Barre was preparation for the company she would later found in Philadelphia.[11]

Expansion and Decentralization of Professional American Ballet

In the 1950s, the American ballet world began a process of decentralization, in which professional dancers, choreographers, and teachers in noticeable numbers migrated away from New York City because of the city's inability to sustain all of the artists who wanted to work there. This led to a period of tremendous growth and institutionalization of ballet as a widespread American art form. As stated in earlier chapters, dance activity was, in fact, taking place in the nation's other cities. Although ballet did exist outside New York City, as demonstrated by Littlefield's Philadelphia Ballet Company, the companies were small in number and not supported by any organized government or national philanthropic initiative.

Philadelphia, for example, was without a permanent ballet company after Littlefield's Philadelphia Ballet Company folded on December 8, 1941, the day after the Japanese attack on Pearl Harbor.[12] Many Philadelphians, however, provided the foundation of both the New York City Ballet and ABT. Karen Conrad and Miriam Golden, both trained by Littlefield, as well as William Dollar, Edward Caton, and Jack Pottieger all joined ABT and had successful performing careers with that company in the 1940s.[13] ABT, however, did not initially establish itself as uniquely American. Throughout the 1940s and 1950s, the short-lived success of Littlefield's uniquely American ballet company fell from memory, and ABT struggled to establish an identity for itself apart from its Russian stars. In 1942, speaking about this trend, Linton Martin argued, "What can be done by our own choreographers in this direction has already been brilliantly and successfully demonstrated in this city by Catherine Littlefield with truly professional prestige, and by some others in varying degree." He also protested about ABT's repertoire, "Ballets that were labeled 'American' seemed anything but that . . . because almost everybody but Americans had a hand in devising them."[14] Relying on the tried and true strategies of the Philadelphian ballet promoter and impresario Sol Hurok, ABT modeled itself on the Ballets Russes in both repertoire and casting. The company used Americans to fill the corps de ballets and international stars to dance principal roles and hired a sprinkling of fresh American choreographers while using the works of European and Russian artists. In 1943, Arthur Bronson of the *Philadelphia Record* claimed, "Americans Have 'Discovered' the Ballet," pointing to ABT's mostly American dancers and Lucia Chase's desire to "streamline the Russian technique."[15] (Chase was the driving force behind the ABT's financial and artistic existence from the company's inception through the 1980s.)[16] The press, however, continued to debate the degree to which this was true. Regardless, by the 1960s, New York City clearly could not absorb and sustain the many talented dancers trained and nurtured throughout the country. Thus, for Balanchine, Lincoln Kirstein, and McNeil Lowry of the Ford Foundation, an emphasis on building professional ballet throughout the country became a priority.[17]

In addition, funding structures were beginning to change. In the 1930s and 1940s, impresarios such as Sol Hurok of Ballets Russes fame were able to present artists and make a profit. In Philadelphia, the impresario Emma Feldman established the All Star series in 1933, bringing international companies to the city. This umbrella group merged with the Forum, created by Edward W. Bok in 1921, and became the Philadelphia All Star–Forum in 1962; it continues to operate in Philadelphia as a promotional company bringing stars to perform in Philadelphia at the Academy of Music and other venues.[18] Over the course of the 1950s and 1960s, however, the personality and force of an experienced and talented impresario were no longer enough to sustain an artist's or company's survival. Nonprofit status as well as external support from government subsidies and private and corporate donations became necessary for the ongoing survival of ballet companies.

As part of this national trend, an important organization formed and drove the effort toward the proliferation of professional American ballet. This movement was led by Weisberger and another woman who made a major contribution to the development of American ballet, Dorothy Alexander. In 1956, with the support of Weisberger and other entrepreneurs/teachers across the country, Alexander proposed the idea of the Regional Dance Association and its accompanying festivals. In 1959, the Scranton and Wilkes-Barre Ballets co-hosted the first Regional Ballet Festival in the Northeast.[19]

In 1960, Balanchine attended the second festival, which took place in Erie, Pennsylvania. While there, he renewed his relationship with Weisberger and urged the dancers and company leaders to bring ballet to every town in the country. Not long after, Weisberger took part in one of Balanchine's teaching seminars in New York. At the seminar, Balanchine spoke about how so much dance talent was being wasted because there were not enough jobs for all of the dancers in New York. Joining the movement toward decentralization, he urged the teachers there to create outlets for the dancers they trained. Around the same time, the father of one of Weisberger's dancers urged her to come to Philadelphia, calling the city a "desert" in terms of dance. That summer at a cocktail party at the home of Lincoln Kirstein, Balanchine again spoke about how new places must be established for dancers to dance. Weisberger asked, "Why not Philadelphia?" to which Balanchine replied, "Barbara, my smart ballerina, you must do it."[20] Weisberger later commented that she "recognized that it was a moment and that I had enough chutzpa to make it happen."[21] Thus began her vision of the Pennsylvania Ballet (see Figure 4.1).

Philadelphia in many ways was prepared for its own ballet company. The city maintained a lively arts scene throughout the 1950s

Figure 4.1. Barbara Weisberger and George Balanchine discussing the future of ballet in Philadelphia, 1961. (Pennsylvania Ballet Records, Special Collections Research Center, Temple University Libraries, Philadelphia, PA.)

and early 1960s, with regular performances at the Academy of Music. Academy audiences saw performances by the jazz greats Ella Fitzgerald, Duke Ellington, and Count Basie; by celebrities such as Dennis Day and Victor Borge; by performers of international music such as Brazilian bossa nova; by Italian opera stars such as Flaviano Labo and Franco Corelli; and by Eugene Ormandy's Philadelphia Orchestra.[22] These concerts were well attended and supported by a loyal audience of Philadelphians.

Philadelphians also saw a diversity of dance during this time. Each winter, beginning in 1948, for example, a Christmas ballet was put on by Wanamaker's Department Store. Wanamaker's also put on Easter ballets, including an interpretation of Lewis Carroll's *Alice in Wonderland*. Using casts of up to thirty-five dancers and incorporating scenic technology such as "black lights," projected effects, vivid scenery, costumes, and masks, as well as the choreographic talents of Thomas Cannon, a former member of the Littlefield Ballet, these performances brought ballet to thousands of Philadelphians.[23] The Philadelphia Civic Grand Opera Company also maintained a corps de ballet. In 1951, the group performed choreographic arrangements to Jules Massenet's "Thaïs," as well as Nikolai Rimsky-Korsakoff's "Scheherazade," among other pieces, at the Academy of Music.[24] In 1956, the *Philadelphia Inquirer* published a three-page photo spread on the Ballet Guild, a cooperative school and performing group founded and run by and for ballet dancers. These dancers all studied with the well-known choreographer and pedagogue Antony Tudor when he came to Philadelphia to teach in 1950. Despite their limited budget, in 1955 they rented two floors over a garage at 1528 Waverly Street and continued to engage Tudor to teach occasional lessons, although the dancers also took turns teaching class. The best of these dancers (who could not be paid for teaching and performing, however) left Philadelphia to pursue paid professional work.[25]

Philadelphians, along with the rest of the nation, also began to interact with ballet through the growing influence of television. In April 1957, for example, the Royal Ballet broadcast a full-length *Cinderella*, danced by Margot Fonteyn, with Frederick Ashton and Kenneth Macmillan in the roles of the wicked stepsisters on television.[26]

Throughout the 1960s, the dance scene in Philadelphia further opened up to wider influence. In 1960, Les Ballets Africains, under the directorship of Kante Facelli, performed for a week at the New Locust Theater.[27] In 1963, a panorama of American dance entitled "America Dances," incorporating ballet, modern dance, and hoofing, was performed at the Academy of Music. Conceived by Walter Terry and choreographed by Todd Bolender, the show presented a cross-section of dance crazes in America and showcased Norman Walker, Ruth St. Denis, Nathalie Krassovska, Thomas Andrews, and Rochelle Zide, among other dancers.[28] In 1964, Philadelphia was visited by six touring dance companies: the Ballets de Madrid, the Chilean National Ballet, the Kirov Ballet, Ballet Folklórico of Mexico, the Royal Ballet, and the Moiseyev Dance Company.[29]

All of these companies performing in Philadelphia, however, were amateur groups or, if they were professional, did not use the talented dancers who were being trained in the city and surrounding area. Weisberger recognized this and decided to remedy the situation not by looking to external sources for talent, but by building a school and company in Philadelphia for Philadelphians. With Balanchine's blessing and his promise to lend dancers, costumes, choreographic works, and moral support, Weisberger set out to establish herself in a town where she was relatively unknown. Stella Moore, an active supporter of dance in Philadelphia as a member of the Pennsylvania Council for the Arts and the Association of American Dance Companies—as well as both the national and the Philadelphia dance chairman of the National Society of Arts and Letters and, eventually, a member of the National Endowment for the Arts advisory council for dance—warned that this would be a tricky situation for Weisberger.[30] Moore, originally an important advocate for Weisberger and her ballet company, would leave the company's board, along with some other socially prominent Philadelphians, as soon as the company experienced minor difficulties.[31] Therefore, after making contacts with people in the community, Weisberger decided to join forces with the Philadelphia Lyric Opera, an established institution in the city. Weisberger initially called her company the Philadelphia Ballet Company. However, she changed the name to the Pennsylvania Ballet because of legal difficulties with a man who ran another ballet school in Philadelphia, who threatened board members and their families over his territorial claim to the name Philadelphia Ballet.[32] As school director and artistic director, and with the help of Balanchine as artistic advisor, Weisberger pulled together an ensemble of dancers from the School of American Ballet, the New York City Ballet, national auditions, and some of her Wilkes-Barre students.[33]

Balanchine went to Philadelphia and met with local sponsors. At that time, he also promised the assistance of Ballet Society, Inc., the fostering agent of the New York City Ballet, to act as intermediary recipient of tax-deductible donations until the new Pennsylvania Ballet Company became eligible for federal tax exemptions. He also volunteered to teach occasional classes upon request and offered ten ballets to the company, in addition to costumes, musical scores, and dancer exchanges.[34] By 1963, with that support and the guidance of Moore, who had chaired the dance committee of the Philadelphia Art Alliance since its establishment in 1944,[35] Weisberger fulfilled her true passion for teaching by opening the School of the Pennsylvania Ballet, which she established as a 501(c)(3) to ensure eligibility for funding as an educational organization. Initially, two dancers who had trained at the School of American Ballet—Barbara Sandonato from

Westchester County, New York, and Patricia Turko from Pittsburgh, Pennsylvania, agreed to work in performances of the Lyric Opera and teach in the school as permanent staff members.

The school's early faculty worked without a salary. The initial faculty (Weisberger, Michael Lopuszanski of Ballet Trianon, and Evelyn and James Kenny of Devon Festival Ballet) had their own schools. Guest artists such as Janet Reed of New York City Ballet and Franco Jelinic of the Yugoslavia State Ballet and Joffrey Ballet supplemented the regular faculty.[36] Weisberger has commented, "I remember when the landlords padlocked the studio doors for non-payment of rent."[37] Sandonato and Turko were paid $20 a month. Turko has said, "We lived on faith."[38]

After the school's inception, Weisberger received the support of the Ford Foundation and used its gift of $45,000 to pay her teachers, hire professional dancers, and take care of overdue bills. In addition to the unconditional gift of $45,000, the foundation promised $250,000 more—conditioned on contributions of $500,000 from non–Ford Foundation sources—as well as continued support for a ten-year period.[39] The difficulty Weisberger's company faced in its efforts to raise the matching funds, however, limited the size of Ford grants for which it qualified in later years. With the help of additional grant money received in 1966 and 1969, however, the company managed to stay alive.[40] With the additional $250,000, Weisberger decided to show the community what the new company had to offer and began planning a debut performance.[41] Although the Pennsylvania Ballet was incorporated in 1962 through its establishment of the School of the Pennsylvania Ballet,[42] it made its official debut in July 1963 at an outdoor amphitheater on the Paoli estate of C. Colkut Wilson III, the president of the Pennsylvania Ballet's board. The company performed a contemporary program that included Weisberger's *Symphonic Variation* and *The Green Season* and Balanchine's *Pas de Dix*. The audience exceeded eight hundred people.[43]

The historic Ford Foundation grant had a huge impact on ballet in Philadelphia, as it did on ballet in the other cities with recipients. In December 1963, the foundation announced its allotment of the largest sum any foundation had ever given to any art form at one time. The regional dance grants program was described as "a historic 10-year plan designed to strengthen professional ballet in the USA."[44] Seven individual companies received grants, including the Pennsylvania Ballet, which received $295,000. The entire dance world was astounded by these grants, which totaled $7,765,750. More than half of this amount was designated for Kirstein and Balanchine's School of American Ballet. The sum of two million dollars was earmarked for New York City Ballet, and much to the chagrin of Lucia Chase and ABT, the remainder was portioned out to four companies in Boston, Philadelphia, San Francisco, and Salt Lake City, directed by either New York City Ballet alumni or longtime Balanchine associates.[45]

Armed with a school and a stream of funding,[46] the Pennsylvania Ballet gave its first subscription series performance at the University of Pennsylvania's Irvine Auditorium in April 1964. The series continued with performances in October of that year and again in February 1965. During these early performances, the media kept a close eye on the company. For the company's second season, like Littlefield, Weisberger decided it should perform its first full-length ballet, *The Sleeping Beauty*. For Weisberger, performing *Beauty* was a symbolic step: It announced the company's establishment as a real force in the American dance community.[47]

The Sleeping Beauty (1965)

Premiered at a gala performance at the Academy of Music on November 26, 1965, Weisberger's version of *The Sleeping Beauty* was also choreographed "after Petipa," by Henry Danton and reconceived new choreography by Heinz Poll.[48] The creation and the reception of the ballet—the only full-length American *Sleeping Beauty* since Littlefield's in 1937—was fraught with tensions surrounding issues of historical and aesthetic continuity. Thus, in addition to providing an interesting way to look at the development of ballet outside of New York City, and a female ballet producer, the production presents a critical opportunity to think through the ongoing issues of authenticity in ballet. Despite desire among critics and audiences for conventional restaging and a return to tradition, any ballet company that existed in Philadelphia in the 1960s faced cultural, economic, and artistic demands that differed substantially from those faced by a Philadelphia ballet company of the 1930s or, certainly, from a Parisian company from the 1920s or an imperial Russian company of the 1890s. Believing that her company could uphold classical tradition while evolving to suit the needs of a contemporary audience and limited funding base, Weisberger tackled *Beauty* as a vehicle to demonstrate both her company's viability and legitimacy as an heir to long-standing balletic tradition and its importance in the evolving and changing American ballet scene.

Of all the traditional works, *The Sleeping Beauty* was always Weisberger's favorite ballet. Once her company was established in the Philadelphia community, she wanted to present a version of it that, according to Weisberger, was "not too pretentious . . . [and] within our means."[49] *Beauty* was to be the opener for the company's 1965–1966 season. Company records that note the performance and rehearsal schedule show that although *Beauty* constituted only six of sixteen different blocks of company rehearsal time, $20,510 was set aside for *Beauty*'s rehearsal in a total budget for the season of $36,510.[50] Company records show the high costs of producing and presenting the work. Documents show that salaries for dancers (without paying for Melissa Hayden, the one guest soloist from New York City)—twenty dancers paid $135 per show and twelve lower-ranking dancers from the school paid $120 per show, as well as twenty-six extras paid $5 per show—totaled $12,810, for just three performances. For those same performances, the orchestra would need $5,680; the stage crew would cost $4,116; and the costume mistress and dressers would require $1,000. Additional costs included fees for the designer, conductor, and choreographer, totaling $5,750; rental of the Academy of Music facility, piano, score, music stands, ushers, and so on, totaling $4,732.50; advertising and promotion, totaling $2,400; and costumes, shoes, and tights, totaling $7,000. Props, building, and painting cost $8,050, and production expenses, including insurance, crates, office help, and hauling, were $5,005. Overall, a three-show run of this streamlined *Beauty* was projected to cost more than $50,000—no small amount for a new company.[51]

In a telephone interview, Barbara Weisberger and I talked about the ways in which her *Sleeping Beauty* departed from the original Petipa version. She was very focused on the concept of authenticity, although she told me that although "our [Weisberger, Danton, and Poll's] adaptation [for the Pennsylvania Ballet] still had truth and meaning, we were not trying to emulate Western European productions of the ballet."[52] Weisberger was adamant about her desire to modernize the 1965 version of the ballet. Her insistence on the need to make these changes is to a large degree a reaction to the context of both the ballet's production and the ballet's critical reception. Although the collaborators on the 1965 *Beauty* wanted to create an accessible and current production, and many regional critics received the ballet well and viewed the work as a success, reviewers in major newspapers and dance publications outside Philadelphia were merciless in critiquing the work. It therefore quickly fell from the company's repertoire, and its failure shaped the eventual trajectory of the overall aesthetic and style that would mark the Pennsylvania Ballet.

Some critics called Weisberger's *Beauty* "a beautifully integrated production."[53] But others, such as Clive Barnes of the *New York Times*, harshly condemned Weisberger's attempts to modernize *Sleeping Beauty*. He wrote that the production was, "an object lesson in how not to revive a 19th century classic. It was a mixture of the authentic, traditional Petipa (borrowed from the Royal Ballet version) with totally uninteresting and unsuitable chunks of modern choreography. . . . As it was it seemed nothing but a chance missed and an evening wasted."[54] This reaction points to the struggles of the small company and to how Weisberger would work to define its identity as she moved forward. These issues take on national import when we examine how they point toward larger trends in American ballet as it has developed in the past fifty years. The now prevalent "mixed bill" evening of contemporary and classical ballets in many ways is maybe a result of companies such as the Pennsylvania Ballet turning away from the classics and toward contemporary choreographers and the Balanchine repertoire to sustain both audience interest and company budgets.

Although the members of the artistic team that produced this version of *Beauty* were quite outspoken about their desire to create something that diverged from the work's traditional staging, they also sought to build on ballet's earlier traditions, claiming part of the canonical Euro-Russian repertoire as their own. According to a review of the work in *Dance* magazine, "Great old ballets don't just fade away, they sleep. Someone picks up the challenge, revives them, and wakes us. Which is exactly what happened when the Pennsylvania Ballet presented its three-act *Sleeping Beauty* in Philadelphia's elegant old Academy of Music."[55] In its second season, the Pennsylvania Ballet sought to create something new, exciting, and original. *Beauty*, however, was not seen as the appropriate vehicle for that labor.

The company was based on democratic ideals of individualism and risk taking. Both the choreographic choices and the nonhierarchical, nondifferentiated ranking of the dancers reflected these values.[56] As they were for many small companies springing up across the country during this time, full-length classical ballets were a challenge for the Pennsylvania Ballet. How, then, did companies establish themselves as legitimate members of the ballet tradition? Many of these companies envisioned tradition as something malleable. The choreographer Heinz Poll stated that he wanted to update *Beauty* and make it accessible to modern audiences. He began with an understanding of *Beauty* as a complex and varied historical artifact. Unlike Barnes, Poll rejected the idea that an authentic version of the work existed. He told a writer for the *Philadelphia Inquirer,* "There are more variations to any fairy tale than there are in Tchaikovsky's music."[57] In the *Philadelphia Evening Bulletin*, James Felton remarked on Poll's efforts to streamline the ballet by cutting it down to two hours. To achieve this version, Poll removed from the original the long pantomime sections, as well as the third act, or Vision Scene. "If you ask me whether I changed the choreography of Petipa, I say, yes. Petipa and Tchaikovsky were human beings after all," Poll told Felton. "My aim is to make 'Sleeping Beauty' dramatically stronger. There should be no extra or unnecessary scenes, moves, gestures or bodies. Ballet should be believable. . . . [B]allet is a serious art form, not some kind of mushy frill."[58]

Clearly, it was not the intention of Weisberger, Poll, or the costume designer Thomas Skelton to capture the essence of aristocratic luxury embodied in Petipa's creation. Poll was informed by a modernist vision of beauty, which emphasized economy and a rigorous efficiency of movement and design. Like the architect Frank Gehry and visual artists such as Alexander Calder, Andy Warhol, and Marcel Duchamp, Poll had a choreographic vision that embraced the streamlining and popularization of life in the 1960s. Even the Philadelphia-based music and dance critic James Felton approved of the streamlining and shortening of the ballet and the desire to attend to the changing needs of a modern audience, remarking, "The legend of 'The Sleeping Beauty' will be danced on the stage of the Academy of Music this week, but mercifully for all except the arch-purists, not as the four-hour ballet marathon created by Peter Ilyich Tchaikovsky and Marius Petipa."[59]

Figure 4.2. Modern streamlining in action: the Lilac Fairy with the royal court, 1965. (Pennsylvania Ballet Records, Special Collections Research Center, Temple University Libraries, Philadelphia, PA.)

Here the critic consents to the changes in culture that have caused a shift in audiences' tastes. By the mid-1960s, America had developed a culture of speed, efficiency, and economy. People were used to traveling on the subway, watching syndicated television, and cooking instant rice; they no longer had the patience to sit through a four-hour-long ballet production. Two years after Martin Luther King Jr. made his "I Have a Dream" speech and President John F. Kennedy was assassinated, Americans carried with them both a cynicism about humanity and a desire for stability and peace that they did not find in their everyday lives.[60] In response to these changing tastes, the collaborators of the "ruthlessly revised" 1965 production of *Sleeping Beauty* worked to pare down the original and putatively timeless tale, reenvisioning it for its contemporary context.[61]

Part of this effort was a "functional streamlining" of the choreography and stage design (see Figure 4.2).[62] Accepting changes in not only tastes but also resources for ballet companies in the modern American context, Poll pointed out the smaller budget within which he was forced to work. Again, Felton reported, "Poll acknowledges that he is also making a virtue out of necessity. He is working with a young company, assembled by the company's director, Barbara Weisberger, that doesn't pretend to offer itself for comparison with older companies. The limited experience of his dancers and the relatively limited financial resources of the company have led him to adopt his concept of functional streamlining."[63] Another regional critic wrote, "'The Sleeping Beauty' was a modernization of the original. . . . [T]he changes suited the special talents of the Pennsylvania company much better than rigid adherence to the classic original. It was, in fact, refreshing to see new thought given to this ballet."[64]

Another result of this effort at streamlining—and budget cutting—was a reconceptualization of the ballet's costuming. In the 1965 production, Aurora wears the only tutu in the ballet. The fairy godmothers are traditionally bedecked in fabulous jewel-toned velvet tutus. In the 1965 production, however, they wear modernistic costumes that evoke a Spartan vision of beauty that combines athleticism, aerodynamics, and elegance. In a photograph from a 1968–1969 season souvenir program, the Lilac Fairy is shown leaping through the air in a gently curved assemblé derrière. Strips of chiffon float loosely from her neckline, accenting her body's sharp angles and strong muscles. The ballerina's lean, long limbs are covered by only a unitard, which shows through the loose strips of fabric, accentuating her strength and power even further. She wears a large triangular tiara in her tightly pulled-back hair. The headpiece emphasizes her verticality, regal stature, and height.[65] Her look is clean and athletic, similar to fashion models of her day. Here in Skelton's reenvisioning of the costuming, we can see the proposal of an expression of a modern American aesthetic sensibility.

Contact sheets from a photo shoot of the 1965 production show the entire group of fairy godmothers together onstage. The architectural and aesthetic differences between this group of women, all in minimalistic and aerodynamic costumes, compared with productions in which the fairies are in large "pancake" tutus cannot be underestimated. Even Carabosse in the Pennsylvania Ballet version wears the long dress made of strips of fabric. With dancers clad in these minimalistic costumes exposing so much of their bodies, the stage becomes a vehicle with which to see the dynamic physical prowess of the characters onstage and less a vista of baroque splendor and prosperity.

In addition, the Balanchine training of the company is evident in these photographs. Balanchine's neoclassical influence and the School of American Ballet training can be seen in poses such as écarté in which a dancer leans off-balance, allowing her pelvis to shift off the supporting leg over which she stands en pointe. In a grand jeté, the same dancer extends her arms beyond the "classical" nineteenth-century style line of the arms in fifth position en haut allongé, her arms and hands instead showing the force of her activity, flicking with energy and life into a hyperextended pose over her head that shows brilliance and force rather than composure in the jump. Photos of group work also show that the corps de ballet lacks the cookie cutter appearance of larger more classically trained companies. The dancers vary in size and shape, as well as in the exact appearance and style of their port de bras, and understanding of shape.[66] I do not attribute this to lack of rehearsal but, rather, to Weisberger's attempt to create a company of individuals, each with his or her own personality and ability to carry off soloist roles. Because of the contemporary repertoire of the company, in which dancers were expected to move in many ways and do more than required in the typical corps work for many classical ballets, these dancers have a less uniform, and less polished, appearance. In fact, Weisberger recently told me that the true foundation of her company was "love, a love of beauty." For her, that did not mean technical perfection or homogeneity of style. Rather, it meant "the physical ability to translate that beauty to an audience. . . . [Successful companies have] a beating heart that audiences can feel and see and respond to."[67]

Both the style and the size of the company, then, resulted in reaction like that of Daniel Webster, a *Philadelphia Inquirer* critic, who wrote, "It is a low budget production . . . and offers a version of the fairy tale that depends heavily on the skills of the dancers rather than stage magic. . . . The production raises the question of its suitability for a smaller company. The answer seems to be no."[68]

In Poll's desire to "prune the work to its essential meaning," he made changes in the formal choreographic content and structure of *The Sleeping Beauty*, removing the extended pantomime sequences that he saw as "Victorian" and "schmaltzy."[69] He also changed some of the narrative devices of the story. Afraid that audiences would no longer know what a spindle was, he dispensed with the spinning motif altogether. The artistic team in charge of *The Sleeping Beauty* decided that Aurora should instead by strangled by a scarf.[70]

Poll acknowledged the difficulties of staging the classic piece for a small company with limited resources. He told Daniel Webster, "I knew we couldn't do the Royal Ballet version—we didn't have all those people or those sets, and after all, why not do something different? Classics 100 years from now will be the things that are being tried today. Because something is traditional doesn't mean it is good."[71]

But despite these aims by the company's artistic director and choreographer, *The Sleeping Beauty* is a canonical work of immense importance to the genre of ballet. As a response or development emerging from an original, no restaging can ever fully dissociate from its grand origins. Tinkering with Marius Petipa's choreographic formulae certainly alters the traditional practices at the heart of *Beauty*. It is not, however, for me to decide, or even suggest, whether the 1890, 1937, or 1965 version was most successful or valuable or even whether I prefer one to another. Regardless, the collaborators brought classical ballet into the repertoire of the Pennsylvania Ballet. Even as Weisberger and Poll attempted to "revolutionize" *Beauty*, they negotiated a new relationship to classical ballet as a whole and a link between the Pennsylvania Ballet and the legacy of the Russian classical ballet tradition. For not only the stagers but also the performers and critics, the ballet was and continues to be inescapably connected to the 1890 Petipa version as its most significant execution.[72]

The irony of this tension of revolutionizing and the inescapable connection to the Petipa version is explicit in the themes of *The Sleeping Beauty* that are embedded in its choreography. As Alastair Macaulay has written, the ballet says that "classicism evolves."[73] Macaulay draws attention to the way that the academic dance steps at the heart of the ballet invoke dance history. He notes the recurrence of the tendu devant, effacé attitude derrière, and allongé first arabesque in Aurora's Rose Adagio. The tendu front recalls the minuet and the eighteenth century; the attitude derrière recalls the romantic neoclassicism of the 1820s; and the long, stretched line of the first arabesque embodies the late nineteenth-century aesthetic of Petipa.

In the enactment of her choreography, then, Aurora embodies the spirit of "classical-academic codification . . . and its subsequent development in her dancing."[74] As the audience witnesses Aurora—as a baby, as a young women, and then reanimated and ready to take the throne from her parents after her long enchantment—they also witness the metaphoric rebirth of ballet in a new time and place (literally and figuratively in the case of this production). Like Aurora, ballet does not die; rather, it sleeps and then reawakens with new emphasis. As a heroine, Aurora hardly ever mimes. Her inner life is expressed to the audience through the steps of her variations. As Aurora matures throughout the unfolding of the ballet, the structure of her choreography also takes on more shading, nuance, and complexity. If Poll moved away from this metaphoric structure in his choreography, he certainly altered the integrity of the piece. Weisberger's efforts, however, are still significant in what she sought to establish for her company. Weisberger envisioned tradition evolving. She believed that ballet in Philadelphia could be sustainable and could become a conversant expression that resonated with young audiences of theatergoers. She turned to the classical repertoire with a love of tradition but also understood the realities of making this tradition work in a contemporary context.

In addition, in tracing the choreography of the fairy godmothers from the prologue of the ballet, audience members can see the development of movement motifs in Aurora's variations when they are danced later in the ballet. As Fyodor Lopukhov wrote in 1975, "All of Aurora's variations are built on themes of variations in the Prologue. In the first act, it is as if the adult Aurora were showing how she has taken command of the gifts she received. . . . [W]e see compositional elaborations of the working elements."[75] Tchaikovsky's score also represents the emergence and development of the Aurora character over time. The adagios from each act stand as musical points of support for the action onstage. As Boris Asafiev has noted, "Cradle, girlhood, love, marriage. . . . [O]ne can, proceeding from them and studying the rhythm of the related scenes and dances, uncover, step by step, the wealth of construction in this wonderful ballet."[76]

Although they moved away from the "original" choreography for this production, Weisberger and Poll certainly understood and valued the choreographic and musical structure of the 1890 version. Despite their decisions to allow the transformation and modernization of the balletic piece, they did reference Petipa's choreography and left small portions intact. Much like the Littlefield production before

it,[77] the Pennsylvania Ballet production of *Beauty* left the fairy variations from the prologue and Aurora's variations, her Rose Adagio,
and her wedding pas de deux "unchanged" from the original. These
segments of the ballet are its most famous and therefore carry the
most cultural capital. They also contain the technical choreographic
content that most clearly expresses the abstracted narrative content
and development of Aurora's character. Aurora's dancing and that of
her fairy godmothers form the core sections of *Beauty* that take on
the same metaphor of tradition and authenticity that applies to the
larger ballet.

The negotiation of these tensions remains at the heart of ballet's
evolution in each new context in which it emerges. P. W. Manchester,
the well-known critic for the periodical *Dance News*, states, "When
it comes to construction [of] *The Sleeping Beauty* there are . . . two
legitimate ways of doing it. One way is to reproduce the Petipa choreography as closely as possible, having regard to the talent at your
disposal. This requires a great deal of preliminary preparation because the Petipa style cannot be acquired overnight. The other way
is to depart altogether from Petipa and re-choreograph an entirely
new version, again using the available talent to its best advantage."[78]
Manchester's problem with Weisberger's production is that Manchester felt Weisberger did not take a clear stance on which choice
to make. She neither departed altogether from nor attempted an authentic reconstruction of the original. Her "unhappy hybrid," from
Manchester's perspective, resulted in an unsuccessful diminishment
of the canonical work. It was primarily critics outside Philadelphia,
modeling their criticism on that of Clive Barnes and Manchester,
who argued that the 1965 production and the changes made to the
ballet in choreographic content, narrative structure, costuming, and
sets undermined the original purpose and beauty of the ballet. This
group of critical voices stated that the desired streamlining did not
modernize the ballet and make it more accessible. Instead, it detract-
ed from the simplicity and purity of earlier productions. Despite the
noted quality of the company's dancing, the Pennsylvania Ballet's
desire for contemporary freshness missed the mark with these critics, with a canonical text (*Beauty*) becoming a mistaken choice for
this kind of experimentation. In addition, the attempts to modernize
the ballet did not highlight the unique strengths of the company's

dancers. Rather than showing their personalities and fresh American training, *Beauty* demonstrated the insufficiency of the company's classical training; its lack of experience in performing a canonical repertoire; and its young dancers' limited ability to carry off such grand, iconic, old-fashioned choreography.

It is of note that even American Ballet Theatre, this country's most "classical" company, with the grandest scale and largest means at its disposal, struggled with restaging the ballet. Despite her desire to do so from the onset of her leadership, Lucia Chase of ABT did not attempt a full-length production until 1976, eleven years after Weisberger. When she did, it cost $350,000 for the sets and costumes alone, and her co-director, Oliver Smith, was quoted as saying, "This is the biggest thing we've attempted."[79] That production, derived from the imported 1946 version produced by the Royal Ballet, also included some "amendments to the production to keep up with the times."[80] Barnes and others in the press, however, praised the ABT production for its accuracy and authenticity, despite the double-edged claims that in places the ballet "was somewhat lifeless" and changes made were to the detriment of the work but could be "rectified . . . by re-establishing the status quo."[81] Chase, too, used the ballet to legitimate the work of her company and help the institution strike the necessary balance between innovation and tradition. It is significant that just as Littlefield balanced *Barn Dance* and *Beauty* and Weisberger balanced Balanchine and *Beauty*, Chase balanced Twyla Tharp's hugely important yet pioneering *Push Comes to Shove* and *Beauty*.

Weisberger expressed ardent frustration around the losing proposition of small American companies' reviving or perpetuating the classical lineage of the ballet profession. The company's struggles paralleled not only the genre of ballet's struggles in this country but also Weisberger's own professional history. Although she succeeded in not only mounting a production of arguably the most important ballet of the classical canon for the second time in U.S. history but also establishing her company as an artistically mature force on the American scene, the 1965 production was received with highly mixed reviews. These were led by two of the most revered critics of the time—Clive Barnes and P. W. Manchester—both of whom were British and both of whom "defended the Empire," or the royal tradition of classical ballet as a production of courtly life, as they criticized the new production's overt consolidation, reduction, and modernization of Petipa's lavish nineteenth-century aesthetics.

Furthermore, the critical discourse surrounding the 1965 staging points to a conservatism embedded in the balletic genre that continues to plague the art form's evolution in the twenty-first century. The negative discussions around the ballet, led by Barnes, are clear in their condemnation of Weisberger's attempts at modernization, despite her clear statements of intent.[82] In a review titled "Wrongheadedness," Barnes wrote, "There is no room at all for the Pennsylvania Ballet's pussyfooting approach, which tries all so vaguely, to combine a little of the original Petipa choreography—it is described as 'after Petipa,' but not so much gets within spitting distance—with ill-conceived modern choreography that looks vaguely German expressionistic. There was a shocking lack of seriousness here."[83] Barnes did not sympathize with the collaborators' conscious departure from the original or with their attempts to find a way to stage the ballet for a small company with young dancers and a limited budget. His anger at the young company's audacity is clear throughout the piece. He went on to state, "The story has been virtually eliminated, apparently in an attempt to remove some of the wicked mime element in the original that might have proved a corrupting influence on the young dancers." Demonstrating his devotion to the status quo and traditional format and protocol of such nineteenth-century ballets, Barnes argued, "The mime thus so boldly excised lasts all of two minutes and makes sense of a story that in this version is supremely nonsensical. It is little helped by the omission of the Vision Scene. . . . There could be sympathy for the worthy Philadelphian who stumped out at the end complaining to his wife, 'I didn't understand a word of it.'"[84]

In our interviews, Weisberger was adamant about her differences with Barnes. She especially continued to feel frustrated when confronted with the issue of authenticity in ballet restagings. As an advocate of the art form, she wanted to see ballet grow in popularity and relevance. For the art form to survive, Weisberger believed, ballet must become something real and accessible for American audiences. At the end of our last conversation, she asked me, "How relevant is classical ballet? Is it a dead language?"[85] She expressed her belief that ballets should not be museum pieces; instead, they should be "alive, vital, contemporary looks at traditional work."[86]

This brings up entire aesthetic realms of inquiry around issues of authenticity in dance. Her staging could have been a productive moment for the ballet community to have such a discussion. What happened instead was that her company moved entirely away from classical full-length ballets, performing a repertoire based on Balanchine, Antony Tudor, Glen Tetley, and other emergent choreographic voices. For the following season (1966), the company immediately moved away from the full-length *Beauty*, although it did not yet abandon the production. The company showed only the third act of *Beauty* and put it on the same bill as John Butler's *Villon* and John Tara's *Designs with Strings*.[87] For the 1967 season, during its first tour to City Center in Manhattan, the company performed Balanchine's *Concerto Barocco*, Tudor's *Jardin aux Lilas*, and John Butler's *Carmina Burana*.[88] Weisberger undoubtedly followed Barnes's opinions. Commenting on the company's New York debut, Barnes wrote, "The program for this first New York engagement very accurately reflects Miss Weisberger's approach to the building of a new ballet company." He went on to reference the earlier efforts at restaging classical work, stating, "Early on she attempted a full-length 'Sleeping Beauty' (shades of Littlefield) and it was, in my opinion, a disaster. . . . [B]ut soon she set about giving the company a character and personality of its own."[89]

The difficult task of bringing a canonical repertoire forward therefore was left for other companies to tackle. These issues, which continue to plague the dance community, are too large to be considered fully within the scope of this book. However, the story of how *Sleeping Beauty* was produced and received in the context of Philadelphia over the course of sixty-five years is an excellent case study of how restaging work can reanimate and resuscitate classical form and how other important elements influence the ballet's reproduction, circulation, and reception.

Barnes was not the only critic to see the Pennsylvania Ballet's *Beauty* as a failure. P. W. Manchester also condemned the streamlined Philadelphia ballet. She wrote in the January 1966 volume of *Dance News*, "The Pennsylvania Ballet's *Sleeping Beauty* is neither an honest attempt at Petipa nor a vigorous new creation to the great

Tchaikovsky score, but an unhappy hybrid. The program attributes 'new choreography and staging' to Heinz Poll and 'choreography after Petipa' to Henry Danton. However, Petipa is rarely allowed to raise his protesting head. . . . Whenever the two styles clash, it is not Poll who comes off best. . . . The choreography is repetitious and meaningless."[90] Manchester continues to protest the changing of the story. Furious about the substitution of the spindle with the scarf, she writes, "No well brought up child is going to be fobbed off with an article as uninteresting as a scarf."[91]

For these critics, the Petipa version thus floats in the mists of dance history and acts as an invisible and idealized sylph of a ballet. It perhaps stands as an impossible standard toward which contemporary versions must reach. Manchester and Barnes clearly articulated nostalgic desires that Weisberger's Pennsylvania Ballet could not satisfy. In 1965, the Pennsylvania Ballet Company was young. It was small in roster and budget. It was staffed by new dancer-interpreters from a wide range of national and cultural backgrounds, all of whom had grown up in the 1950s dancing Balanchine ballets. Their training, their coaching, and the rehearsal process, then, did not allow them to perform the Petipa work with the expected finish, but it did prepare them to dance something else—something more akin to Weisberger's production.

Barnes and Manchester, however, were not the only critics who commented on the ballet. Several critics, primarily from the Philadelphia area, saw the Pennsylvania Ballet's attempt at the classic piece as an ambitious and well-done undertaking. The stark contrast between the national (though led by British critics born and raised in a country with a national professional ballet tradition) and regional discourse (led by American writers who viewed ballet as "show biz" as it emerged from the burlesque and vaudeville circuits) is striking. Whether this difference in opinion emerged from the local critics' lack of dance background, and consequent lack of nostalgia for an original European production, or from their desire to support local efforts at building a ballet company is not necessarily of primary interest here. What is significant is the positive reception of the ballet by the regional community. Alexandra Grilikhes, a writer for the *Philadelphia Courier*, wrote a sympathetic and descriptive review of the ballet for *Dance Magazine*: "We find it little matters whether spells are cast by scarf or spindle. . . . [T]he vision scene—simplified as it was into an *Entre'Acte* in which the Lilac Fairy dedicated her cavalier to Aurora—held up too."[92] Grilikhes was not put off by the change of implement with which Aurora is put to sleep. Donal Henahan of the *Chicago Daily News* wrote, "Heinz Poll's tongue-in-cheek interpolations to the Petipa choreography struck a witty note, while the sets and costumes were craftily designed on an appropriately modest scale without making it all seem like a cheap imitation."[93]

For those clinging to a notion of authenticity, such as Barnes and Manchester, however, Aurora's dances—the ones left intact from their Petipa form—are the highlights of the performance. Barnes wrote, "The choreography, except where—chiefly in the role of Aurora, which is pretty accurately reconstructed—it follows the Petipa original, is a ghastly mess. . . . Melissa Hayden, a guest artist, danced Aurora in a very correct Royal Ballet style and wore an expression of gallant anguish appropriate to the captain of a fast-sinking ship."[94] Manchester similarly insisted on an authentic reconstruction of the ballet, expressing satisfaction with the traditional reconstruction of the Aurora role: "Petipa is rarely allowed to raise his protesting head. There is an occasional glimpse—not more—in the variations for the fairies who attend Aurora's christening; a little more in the dance of the court ladies in the birthday scene. There is most of all in the dances for Aurora. Guest artist Melissa Hayden, bless her heart, took the trouble to learn the Petipa Aurora and to dance the famous choreography as closely as she was allowed to within the confines of a production that constantly negates it."[95]

Not only did Barnes and Manchester show their bias toward the Royal Ballet style, which they most certainly understood as the status quo (both having been born in Britain). They also commented on the work of Melissa Hayden, the guest artist hired to dance Aurora.[96] This reaction to Hayden's performance was largely responsible for Weisberger's later insistence that the company hire no guest artists. The failed reception of the company's performance forced the Pennsylvania Ballet to develop its own style and learn to command the stage with the rich diversity of the young dancers' own personalities. Weisberger "never wanted to import stars," Claude Benner, director and president of the company's board, has said. "Her idea has always been to bring up her own people. After the disaster with Melissa

Hayden, Barbara has never brought in another star. And she's proved she's right."[97] When the *New York Times* critic Anna Kisselgoff asked Weisberger whether she wanted Margot Fonteyn and Rudolf Nureyev to guest with her company, Weisberger said, "I wouldn't humiliate my dancers that way. . . . I don't think any less of Fonteyn and Nureyev, but if we are to be a background for a guest artist, then we are killing something in ourselves. . . . My dancers are working their bloody heads off. Why give the cream to someone else? I would rather see a young company dancing up to its capability with integrity."[98]

This style indeed became a hallmark of the Pennsylvania Ballet, and the company's youth and freshness gained respect in the ballet world. Thus, in many ways, the harsh criticism from Barnes and Manchester helped Weisberger crystallize her artistic vision moving forward. For these critics, Aurora's dances—which in their minds remained faithful to the original—came the closest to an ideal reconstruction. This approach calls to mind Patrice Pavis's discussion of dramaturgy and the role of reconstruction: "For a long time criticism of the classics and interpretation of mise-en-scène have acted as if time had done no more than cover up the text with layers of dust; in order to make the text respectable, it was enough to clean up and get rid of the deposits which history, layers of interpretation, and hermeneutic sediment had left on an essentially untouched text."[99] Within her article on contextualization, adaptation, and historicization of theatrical texts, this approach, however, is discussed as insufficient to truly understanding the complex processes involved in making meaning from performances. Pavis concludes with the statement that text and context can never be fully separated. For the dance critics of 1965, however, context is not given its full due. Weisberger's intentions are not considered sufficient rationale for her adaptations to the canonical work. They argue for "authenticity," a problematic term in its subjective and variable meanings, and therefore find failure with a production that fails to reproduce the classical balletic genre unchanged—regardless of the context of the new dance's production and reception. This perspective devalues modern interpretations and individual interpreters and treats ballet companies as museums and the stage as a glass case in which to display reified moments of historical dance frozen in time. Even Lincoln Kirstein, one of the most influential men in the development of American ballet, wrote to Weisberger about the difficulty of presenting fresh work in the United States, where the only ballet people knew was imported from Europe:

> I think you have the best company outside of New York; very strong dancers and well trained girls, and certainly nobody works as hard or as loyally as your kids. I enjoyed the performance and was interested all the way through. I know what an enormous amount of work went into it, and how much more there was in the way of preparation that was not apparent. . . . I hope you are not too discouraged [by the Barnes review]. Of course Barnes was a very bad bit of luck, but he is English and has to defend the Empire even in Philadelphia.[100]

Mark Franko, dance historian and philosopher, has written extensively about the project of reconstruction and the art field's obsession with repeatability. He suggests that reinvention rather than reconstruction gets audiences and scholars closer to the essence of the dances they seek. In reading dancers as texts through the lens of postmodern theatrical theory, Franko suggests that the act of restaging choreography is an active theorizing of dance history.[101] For Franko, the essence of a work can be discovered only by understanding the historical and aesthetic context from which it emerged. From this perspective, the 1965 *Beauty* was a failure not because it failed to repeat the 1890 choreography faithfully, but because it failed to capture the aesthetic essence of grandeur, symmetry, and balance embedded in the 1890 work.

Even if a company were to reconstruct *The Sleeping Beauty* in its original incarnation, as the Kirov Ballet claimed to do in 1999,[102] many would argue that despite claims of "authenticity" or faithfulness to the Petipa choreography, each production of the ballet, no matter how traditional, constitutes a new version. Each time a ballet is danced, it is performed through the embodied interpretation of individuals who have grown up in a different cultural context from their nineteenth-century counterparts and even from the coaches and teachers who have passed the roles on to them in the studio. Each dancer, then, re-creates the ballet in each performance of the work. Despite this, *The Sleeping Beauty* has often been referenced as a supposedly "timeless" icon of the classical canon of the balletic genre.

This gives it mythological significance as the pinnacle of classicism. Thus signified, the ballet becomes an arbiter of powerful meaning for choreographers, dancers, and audience members.

Aurora's story replicates ballet's own life in Western dance history. As Aurora sleeps for one hundred years, she carries her "timeless" values and ideas about life through time and into the future. She reigns over a realm of peace, prosperity, calm, and order. Similarly, the ballet acts as a carrier of tradition, value, and aesthetic standards. Equilibrium, delayed gratification, and stability are the moral imperatives of Perrault's tale. Critics continually apply these themes to the ballet's choreographic content, evaluation, reception, and recreation. Petipa's audience valued the ballet's representation of order, grandeur, and wealth. Many who watched the ballet in 1890, as well as many who see it now, would undoubtedly agree that part of the ballet's attraction is its historical continuity. Audiences know how the story will turn out, and they expect to see certain elements of the story played out onstage. It is this expectation of stability, equilibrium, and order that the ballet encapsulates so well in its overall aesthetic presentation. M. E. Saltykov-Shchedrin, who attended the 1890 production, reflected on the ballet and on ballet's fundamental conservatism: "I love ballet for its constancy. New governments rise up; new people appear on the scene; new facts arise; whole ways of life change; science and art follow these occurrences anxiously, adding or sometimes changing their very compositions—only the ballet knows and hears nothing. . . . Ballet is fundamentally conservative."[103]

Although ballet changes over time, especially—as I begin to argue in the next chapter—due to the changing bodies, experiences, and philosophies of its performers, there is a tension between the shifting historical contexts of the ballet and the desire for the timeless vision of perfection and beauty that the ballet depicts onstage. In *The Sleeping Beauty*, audiences witness a vision of perfection, a place where an unattainable ideal of beauty, balance, and equilibrium can exist. Using the Rose Adagio as a metaphor for the visual and kinesthetic feeling of the ballet as a whole, an idea of stability and aplomb transcends the movement, creating an overwhelming sense of careful control.

I find Saltykov-Shchedrin's comment a useful point from which to enter an inquiry into the history of *The Sleeping Beauty*'s performance in Philadelphia. If the ballet is indeed a ritual enactment of social stability, if it is a formal and almost ceremonial return to equilibrium, then what does it say about a city's desires when the ballet reappears in the 1930s, the 1960s, and again in the 1990s? The tremendous critical outcry against the hybrid form of ballet attempted in the 1965 Pennsylvania Ballet production of *Beauty* can be attributed to the collaborators' failure both to capture the essence of the original work in their restaging and to stick with one aesthetic or theoretical concept throughout the evening-length work. Anticipating the controversial nature of modernizing a classic such as *Beauty*, Weisberger was advised to hire the British dancer and coach Henry Danton, an external expert on the Sergeyev version danced by the Sadler's Wells Ballet. Danton, however, pressured Weisberger to include the Petipa choreography in the third act of their ballet and to hire an outside guest artist to perform the role of Aurora. Therefore, Weisberger allowed the streamlined and contemporary vision intended by Skelton and Poll to fade away from the ballet's ending. Without grounding the work in the Versailles-style imagery evocative of a utopian society challenged by evil forces done in the original staging or capturing the symmetry and order inherent in the classical technique of the danse d'école throughout all four acts of the ballet, *Beauty* appeared out of context and without the expected meaning. Contemporary choreographic invention followed by traditional choreography without theoretical and aesthetic connection caused the entire work to give the impression of empty display. Despite these flaws, like the Russians and Europeans before them, Philadelphians turned to this ballet in times of distress because of its reassurances about continuity. However, the difficulty in finding a way to truly manage the negotiation of living tradition and the changing needs of the contemporary arts scene and its audience was poignantly demonstrated by the Pennsylvania Ballet's attempt at *Beauty* in 1965. The reception of the work and its lasting effect on the Pennsylvania Ballet's repertoire and casting profoundly influenced how classical dance evolved and changed as it reemerged as a cultural force in the North American dance world after World War II.

The philosopher Ralph Harper has written about *The Sleeping Beauty*'s reliance upon nostalgia. The mythological fable is about modern society's longing and fulfillment, he claims, and despite its depiction of court life, he states, the fairy tale is a product of modernity. "It was appropriate that, when all old values and beliefs were being discredited by revolution and by new confident bourgeois," he writes about Perrault's version of the tale, "some men should go back, surreptitiously to the past, for help in surviving a time when everything spiritual had disappeared but self-confidence . . . [f]or the fairy story represents permanent longings and convictions rather than history and change."[104] So although the ballet does, in fact, have unique meanings that emerge from the time and place in which it is produced and resuscitated, it is also a historical and aesthetic expression, a vessel of continuity, tradition, and stability. This can be seen particularly in the ways that the Aurora role was constructed and performed in all of *The Sleeping Beauty* productions examined in this book. It is this continuity of structure, content, and meaning that attracts audiences and dancers to the ballet, for individuals can lose themselves in the familiar tale that unfolds onstage during each performance.

Weisberger's work in Philadelphia continues to be felt today. Her presence is still significant at the Pennsylvania Ballet. A letter to the editor published in the *Philadelphia Inquirer* stated the following about Weisberger's 1982 departure: "[The] company has replaced its heart with ruled column ledger sheets."[105] But despite her sadness at being ejected from an institution that she built with her heart and soul, Weisberger still has high personal and artistic stakes in the success of the Pennsylvania Ballet, its dancers, and, especially, the School of the Pennsylvania Ballet. The city of Philadelphia owes her the establishment of its largest and longest-lived dance institution. The company celebrated its fiftieth anniversary in 2014, and despite critical opposition to Weisberger's tinkering with tradition regarding her production of *The Sleeping Beauty*, it was her "chutzpah" in doing so that allowed an expensive and Old World European tradition to survive in a primarily blue-collar city for more than half a century. After ousting its founding mother in 1982, the Pennsylvania Ballet has reclaimed a connection to her as the important creator of the company. Her contributions also make evident the limitations of a dance history that does not include her work in Philadelphia, for her contributions have shaped the direction of ballet not only in Philadelphia but also across the United States.

5.

Aurora Speaks

What Ballerinas Have to Say about
The Sleeping Beauty

Setting the Stage

At the end of the twentieth century, the Pennsylvania Ballet unveiled another production of *The Sleeping Beauty*—one that harked back to Marius Petipa's classic staging of the nineteenth century. In 1997, *Beauty* opened her eyes to a Philadelphia that was very different from the city in which she had awoken thirty years before. The radicalism and activism of the 1960s had given way to the postmodern disillusionment of the late twentieth century. By 2002, the year the Pennsylvania Ballet repeated its new production of *Beauty*, the United States and its citizens had suffered the blows of September 11, 2001, and the cultural transformations that accompanied that national tragedy. *Beauty* thus awoke again to a very changed world.

In October 2001, the United States began strikes on Afghanistan as part of President George W. Bush's war on terror. He identified and targeted nations in the Middle East as an "axis of evil" that relied on terrorist strategies to decimate the American people and their values.[1] As part of the new American hyperawareness about this terror threat, the country was on "terror alert" for many days in 2002, and heightened security measures were taken to prevent another massive terrorist attack. In addition, corporate scandals plagued the North American scene as companies such as Enron, Arthur Andersen,

Merrill Lynch, WorldCom, and Kmart were exposed as corrupt and unstable.[2] The religious world was also exposed: Throughout 2002, the Catholic Church was revealed as an institution that had covered up hundreds of cases of rape and child abuse committed by church leaders over several decades, many in Philadelphia itself.[3]

The entire world seemed to be a threatening and tenuous place. No aspect of Western culture felt like a safe haven of innocence. The moment brimmed with apocalyptic fears about the future of our world. It was not only the psychology and politics of Philadelphia that had changed, however. The landscape and physical environment of the city were also different.

Throughout the 1970s, 1980s, and 1990s, Philadelphia experienced the departure of big industry.[4] In 1991, as part of the federal downsizing of defense installations, the U.S. Navy ended its two-hundred-year ownership of the thousand-acre shipyard in South Philadelphia. At one time the shipyard provided ten thousand jobs to people in the city. People could walk to a job that had supported a large family. These stable, well-paying jobs provided neighborhoods with steady sources of income and community pride. All of that changed. Many other small factories closed along with the naval shipyard. As a result of these economic changes, neighborhoods and city politics became increasingly stratified. Social, economic, and political disparities widened, and the city increasingly displayed polarization among its neighborhoods and citizens.[5] What does a shipyard closing have to do with dance? This is the context in which *The Sleeping Beauty* again graced the stage in Philadelphia in 1997 and then again in 2002.

The Sleeping Beauty in the New Millennium

I attended the 1997 and 2002 stagings of *Beauty* as an audience member, and I followed the ballet's reception in the newspapers and the Philadelphia ballet community. In this chapter, I describe each of these productions of *The Sleeping Beauty* in terms of the details of its staging—including the choreography, sets, costumes, and rehearsal process—as well as the artistic director's, audiences', and dancers' responses to the work. Having introduced the social changes in the city outside the ballet stage, I go on to discuss the changes in the Pennsylvania Ballet between the earlier staging of *Beauty*, in 1965, and the new one, in 1997, to explain the changing context in which the ballet was rehearsed and performed.

This chapter, and my process of investigating the Pennsylvania Ballet's 1997 and 2002 stagings of *The Sleeping Beauty*, sets the stage and marks a methodological shift from the prior chapters because of the historical and geographical currency of the performances under examination. As *The Sleeping Beauty* continued to migrate through time and space, I finally came face-to-face with the ballet as a researcher in 1997. Existing in the same historical and geographical moment as the cultural manifestation under study allowed me to take intellectual action by spending time with, and asking specific questions of, the dancers I observed performing the ballet. As a result, I was able to probe the meaning of this ballet more fully.

In a special edition of *Dance Chronicle* published in 2012, the editors, Joellen Meglin and Lynn Matluck Brooks, asked the question "What might dance studies contribute to the debate on the status of women in ballet?"[6] The question is especially germane here; in seeking to answer it, I encountered *Beauty* and sought to acknowledge the agency and interpretive power not only of producers and choreographers but also of the women who translate and perform the ballet for audiences. Therefore, I added a layer of information to my exploration of these productions. In addition to the usual archival research, this chapter relies on extended oral history interviews and dance phenomenology. By focusing on the lived experience of dancers performing the ballet, I uncover the ways in which dancers act as important agents for the continued interpretation and embodiment of the classical canon in their performances of ballets such as *Beauty*.

In speaking to dancers and hearing their perspectives on dancing this role, I bridge a long-standing gap between scholars and performers, especially in the world of ballet. Although they are not trained in the language of the academy, the principal dancers in the Pennsylvania Ballet are exquisitely trained in the language of ballet. Their insights have much to contribute to an academic consideration of the value and potential contribution of their practice and experiences to the larger dance field. As we have seen, it is not only as producers and artistic directors that women have shaped the trajectory of ballet in the twentieth and twenty-first centuries. Women have also shaped the field and the art form in their coaching, rehearsing, and performance of the canon's pivotal roles. Any attempted objectification or abstraction expressed in choreography is compromised for audience members, choreographers, and dancers. The medium of dance performance is a living, breathing person with a beating heart and personal history. Despite any conceptual level of abstraction, when an audience sees two dancers onstage together, for example, it also sees a relationship between those human beings. Those human beings also literally have a relationship onstage in how they negotiate the interactions between their bodies through weight sharing, eye contact, and reliance on physical cues from one another. Because of this physicality, I am able to demonstrate in what follows how the studio and stage in Philadelphia in 1997 and 2002 acted as a productive space for female ballet dancers to exercise agency and creativity.

The Pennsylvania Ballet between 1965 and 1997

Although the United States experienced financial growth throughout the 1980s and 1990s, the professional ballet industry did not see the same development and success. Cultural changes in popular entertainment and the aging of traditional audiences for classical dance led to the diminishment of support for many smaller ballet companies across the country. The Pennsylvania Ballet in particular was plagued by financial and artistic problems throughout this period. By 1997, the year the company performed *The Sleeping Beauty*, it was in a state of disarray. The history of the Pennsylvania Ballet is one example of the trials and tribulations of keeping ballet afloat in a contemporary context. Of particular importance is the transnational flow of influence drawn from directors, coaches, and dancers who came to the city from across the globe. In addition, the instability and conflict that plagued the company throughout the 1960s, 1970s, and 1980s demonstrate the difficulty of keeping a traditional form of art making alive without the benefit of imperial treasuries and state-funded training academies.

Throughout the 1960s, the Pennsylvania Ballet increased its level of professionalism and gathered a devoted audience that regularly attended performances at the Academy of Music. Barbara Weisberger, the founder and director, made a conscious decision to use the works of George Balanchine as a base from which the company could grow; Balanchine gave his choreography to Weisberger and never charged her fees to perform his ballets.[7] Having a repertoire that included sixteen Balanchine ballets gave the Pennsylvania Ballet a certain degree of stability, as well as the flexibility to try out innovative and emergent choreographers' work. During this time, the Ford Foundation continued to support the Pennsylvania Ballet. In 1966, the company received $45,000 and was also promised $250,000 more with matching contributions from non–Ford Foundation sources, as well as larger sums of $1.2 million in 1968 and $2.9 million in 1971,[8] but the company was unable to secure these matching grants. Because of the low level of individual giving in Philadelphia, the company received only about $45,000 every two to three years, which left it to struggle and scramble for financial support and solvency. Elizabeth Kendall, the author of the Ford Foundation's 1983 report on aid to dance, included a reflection on the Foundation's support of Weisberger's original vision: "Not only one of the best American-trained teachers of her generation, Weisberger was also a person gifted with organizational talents and a grasp of what the nuts and bolts of a local ballet company might be, at a time when no one knew much about that."[9]

The Pennsylvania Ballet therefore entered the 1970s with an established repertoire and an expanded touring schedule. It presented varied performances. In addition to the choreography of George Balanchine, Antony Tudor, Michel Fokine, and Jean-Paul Comelin, the company presented dances by Robert Rodham (who not only was Weisberger's student but also eventually became ballet master and "resident choreographer" of the Pennsylvania Ballet under Weisberger's leadership).[10] The company performed this diverse repertoire in cities as varied as New York, Chicago, Pittsburgh, Oklahoma City, Baltimore, and, of course, Philadelphia, dancing more than two hundred performances a year, in nearly every state in the nation.

In the early 1970s, however, the Pennsylvania Ballet underwent a dramatic shift that foreshadowed the artistic and administrative changes that would wreak havoc on the company for the next thirty years (and perhaps continue to have a lasting effect on the company's administration). In their *Dance Chronicle* article, Meglin and Brooks noted that "while women have served as founding directors of many important ballet companies, once the companies become institutionalized (and enshrined as important cultural establishments in a city), men . . . often [have been] placed in charge."[11] Following that trend, the Pennsylvania Ballet's board of directors convinced Weisberger to take on an associate artistic director in 1972.[12] She hired Benjamin

Harkarvy, who would eventually take over her role as artistic director, while she moved into the more administrative role of executive artistic director. That spring, the Pennsylvania Ballet returned to City Center for its second New York season. The critic Clive Barnes described the company at the time as "one of the most secure and well-established ballet troupes in the country. . . . [I]t is dancing very well indeed."[13]

The Creeping Corporate Male Takeover of the Pennsylvania Ballet

The administrative changes that began in the 1970s, along with the company's growth, however, eventually led to artistic instability and financial difficulties. In 1974, Harkarvy was made the company's sole artistic director, and Weisberger became the administrative artistic director. Weisberger publicly discussed the situation in a *Dance Magazine* article in 1975. "My title clearly defines a bridge between the administrative and artistic direction of the company," she stated. "Our work is closely related, but for best operation, it became necessary to define separate functions. Bob, as always, maintains the rep[ertoire], now in the position of regisseur. Ben has already strongly influenced the company, as is obvious in its increased professionalism. Ben has influenced it in its style, and the quality of the dancing. The company—quite obviously—has taken a giant stride forward since Ben Harkarvy joined us."[14] However, this was the beginning of a spiral of decline into financial and artistic instability, as Weisberger lost her proximity to the dancers and the actual work being presented onstage. A board of directors more interested in financial solvency than in Weisberger's artistic vision slowly eroded her power, and conflicts between artistic and administrative staff began to arise. These disagreements began a series of shifts that weakened the company, as both a sustainable business and a world-class group of artists who consistently represented true national and international exceptionalism. Artistic disputes forced Rodham to resign. In 1977, the board of directors, who had gained more control, forced Weisberger to cede control of the company's school to Lupe Serrano and Mildred Keil and give additional artistic control to Harkarvy. In a situation that foreshadowed the ousting of Lucia Chase from the American

Ballet Theatre (ABT) in 1980 and her dancers' retaliation toward the company's administration,[15] Barbara Sandonato and several of Weisberger's other original dancers resigned in 1977, citing casting conflicts within the company. Massive financial and administrative problems beset the Pennsylvania Ballet, and by the summer of 1979, the company had lost all of its summer engagements.[16]

Throughout the 1980s, the company continued to crumble. In January 1982, the board of directors suspended all operations for the spring season. The administrative crisis could be traced to the shift of power from the artistic staff to the board. The situation, begun in the 1970s, worsened, and bitter conflict between Weisberger and the board ensued. The company was put on suspension, and artists' salaries were withheld. Finally, the board asked Weisberger to take a leave of absence without salary. Alienated by the very company that she had created and given only twenty-four hours to respond, Weisberger resigned.[17] "I am severing all my connections with the company," she told the press in 1982. "I wasn't just being asked to take a leave of absence. . . . [T]his was a power play. The issue was the organization of the company. I have been in the company's artistic leadership. It must have an artistic head, and I felt that to be asked to be a figurehead was an insult."[18]

After Weisberger's departure, much controversy arose both inside and outside the company regarding the status of the well-regarded upstart. First, George Balanchine wrote to the president of the company's board of directors, "Please be advised that I wish to withdraw my ballets from your company's [repertoire], effective at the end of your fiscal year. . . . These ballets were given to Barbara Weisberger many years ago to assist her in developing her company. Barbara and I had an understanding which had developed through the years, and now that she is no longer associated with her company, I do not wish my ballets performed or included in the [repertoire] of the Pennsylvania Ballet."[19] In addition, several dancers loyal to Weisberger also left the company, and the company's survival was questioned in the press. With all of this publicly reported on, a public debate ensued between the dancers and Weisberger and the administration alluded to an inability on Weisberger's part to manage the company's books. The difference of opinion that the company's priorities should be driven by vision and passion rather than by financial concerns are

clearly reflected in a letter David Brenner, chairman of the Pennsylvania Ballet's Board of Trustees, wrote to the *New York Times*:

> We have strived mightily for many years to follow the implied
> principle of the arts world that the artistic leadership of an
> organization must report only to its governing board. Our ex-
> perience has shown that not only does that not work, but that
> it becomes a divisive force in the day-to-day operations of the
> enterprise between the so-called "artistic side" and the "busi-
> ness side." In fact, they are thoroughly intertwined and the
> concept of separate artistic leadership is not valid. The prob-
> lem, and it is a legitimate one, is to find the appropriate leader
> who understands all facets of the company's mission and is
> able to bring them together as an effective operating unit.[20]

In our conversations, Weisberger spoke about her belief that the
artistic side must always remain at the forefront of an artistic director's plan. Obviously, balancing the books is a necessity for any organization's survival. It is her opinion, however, that the raising of
money is and should be the task of the board, while *artistic* directors
should concern themselves primarily with casting, repertoires, and
training of the company's dancers and pre-professional students.[21]
Following Weisberger's resignation, the Pennsylvania Ballet announced that Harkarvy would oversee all artistic responsibilities. His
tenure, however, did not provide the security the board sought. Suspi-
cious when he was denied a long-term contract five months later, he
resigned. Robert Weiss, a former principal dancer with the New York
City Ballet, replaced Harkarvy as artistic director. Peter Martins, another New York City Ballet dancer, was hired as the artistic adviser,
and Dane LaFontsee, a Pennsylvania Ballet dancer since 1967, became ballet master and assistant artistic director.[22]

Throughout the 1980s, the Pennsylvania Ballet Company continued to perform throughout the United States, modernizing and
expanding its primarily Balanchine-based repertoire to present original choreography by Robert Weiss, Paul Taylor, Merce Cunningham,
Lynne Taylor-Corbett, and Richard Tanner. Despite Weisberger's absence from the artistic administration, the company continued to
perform a similar repertoire, with the occasional classical excerpt

thrown in. Foreshadowing the company's "return to the classics" in the late 1990s, Martins staged the Bournonville classic *La Sylphide* for the company in 1985, and both critics and audience members received the piece fairly favorably.[23] Here, however, the company's lack of classical training once again came to the forefront with comments such as, "When you see American dancers suddenly take on the airs of the received Bournonville tradition, the results can be funny at best, infuriating at worst. . . . One sees dancing in the Pennsylvania Ballet production, and so even if not all the dancing was as effective as it might be . . . it was always credible."[24]

Because of worsening financial constraints, the Pennsylvania Ballet announced a joint venture with the Milwaukee Ballet in January 1987.[25] This merging of the companies provided year-round work for the dancers and allowed for a full performance schedule in both cities. However, it was an uneasy marriage, with only eight of Milwaukee Ballet's twenty-six dancers being invited to join the new forty-one-member troupe. Also, the Milwaukee Ballet lost its artistic director in the transition, and many members of the Midwestern ballet audience did not appreciate the neoclassical repertoire shown by the company. After the first year of the joint venture, the two companies continued to operate with financial deficits, and in March 1989, the union was officially terminated.

In 1990, Weiss also resigned as artistic director due to "irreconcilable differences" with "others in leadership" of the company.[26] Morale among the dancers was low, and six members of the company's forty-member board resigned to protest Weiss's ousting.[27] Amid the chaos, the dancer Jeffrey Gribler became ballet master and assumed many of the company's responsibilities of artistic directorship. In May 1990, the Pennsylvania Ballet announced that Christopher d'Amboise, another former New York City Ballet dancer, would lead the ballet as yet another new artistic director. D'Amboise described himself as "a keeper of the flame of classical ballet . . . committed to continuing the tradition I am a part of."[28] Still, administrative upsets continued to plague the company, and d'Amboise threatened to leave if the board's president, Patrick Veitch, did not resign. By March 1990, however, the financial situation was so grave that all operations of the performing company were once again suspended.[29] For the 1990 run of *The Nutcracker*, for example, the principal dancer, Lisa

Sundstrom, danced fifteen performances as Sugar Plum and Dew Drop in ill-fitting borrowed shoes because the company had not paid its bill to Freed of London and could not place a new order for the shoes needed by company dancers.[30] The Pennsylvania Ballet was not the only company in economic peril at the time. In 1991, the national service association committed to enhancing the infrastructure for dance creation and distribution, education, and dissemination of information, Dance/USA, found that twelve of the nation's major ballet companies faced million-dollar or multimillion-dollar deficits, and several others had six-figure debts.[31]

Not willing to simply pack their shoes up and leave, the dancers of the Pennsylvania Ballet took matters into their own hands in a remarkable move that commanded national attention. They decided to dance without pay and present an already scheduled Balanchine–Tudor program at the Shubert Theater. A volunteer group announced the launch of a two-week, grassroots fundraising drive dubbed "Save the Ballet."[32] A major publicity campaign was also initiated, with editorials in newspapers, a "Save the Ballet" phone line, and a tele-funding drive. Major figures from the world of the performing arts, including Mary Tyler Moore, Tony Randall, Chita Rivera, and Jacques d'Amboise, founder of the National Dance Institute (and the father of Christopher d'Amboise), contributed their time and enthusiasm to the company, giving speeches that encouraged financial support. Philadelphians rose to the occasion: in that two-week period, the Pennsylvania Ballet managed to raise $1.2 million from more than ten thousand individual contributors. At the close of the campaign, the Pew Charitable Trusts issued a challenge grant, and a continued flow of contributions, including grants from the William Penn Foundation and the Annenberg Foundation, brought the company's emergency fundraising efforts to a close by June 1991. In March 1991, Christopher d'Amboise was appointed president and chief executive of the company in addition to his responsibilities as artistic director.[33]

D'Amboise had strong ideas about his mission as director of the Pennsylvania Ballet. Chief among these was his desire to use the company as a vehicle for his own choreography. He bluntly acknowledged his lack of knowledge of and interest in the classics of the ballet repertoire, stating, "Part of my job as artistic director is to educate myself, but . . . I haven't had time."[34] In keeping with his desire to fashion the company into an embodiment of his personal vision and aesthetic, d'Amboise fired thirteen of the company's thirty-five dancers and ousted important board members from the executive board. Conflicts continued. By 1994, d'Amboise also resigned, saying he could not "maintain the artistic integrity of the ballet with the financial constraints the board had imposed for the coming season."[35]

Roy Kaiser and the Stabilization of the Pennsylvania Ballet

D'Amboise's successor, Roy Kaiser, brings us closer to the story of the turn-of-the-millennium staging of *Sleeping Beauty*. Kaiser, a former company member, was originally taken on as a dancer by Weisberger in 1979. He subsequently worked under the artistic directors Benjamin Harkarvy (1972–1982) and Robert Weiss (1982–1990) and was made a principal dancer by d'Amboise in 1990. Two years later, however, he retired from the stage, becoming principal ballet master and associate artistic director under d'Amboise, managing many of the day-to-day leadership activities of the company,[36] until he was appointed to his current position.

After he was unfortunately beset with back injuries, Kaiser retired from dancing and began regularly working with dancers, setting ballets, teaching class, and leading company rehearsals. When he took over, Kaiser inherited from d'Amboise a huge financial deficit that had plagued the company since the Harkarvy years. D'Amboise had left Kaiser with a $3 million mortgage on the new office and studio building, while the recession led to reduced ticket revenues and cuts in both national and local funding. In 1990, as the total debt reached more than $5 million, the board announced that the company's activities were to be suspended. Kaiser recalled all too clearly the shock the dancers and staff felt when they were suddenly told after class one morning that the company was going to close, at least temporarily.[37]

Kaiser's first mission, therefore, was to alleviate the company's fiscal troubles. He tried everything from a twenty-four-hour dance-a-thon and free performances to attract people to the Academy of Music to cutting the company's budget by curtailing the season. Beginning in 1995, the ballet began performing four instead of five programs per year, and dancers were paid for only thirty weeks instead of thirty-eight weeks of work per year. In addition, Kaiser introduced special programs, including children's matinees and singles' nights, in attempts to draw in new younger audience members.

Then Kaiser came up with the idea of increasing attendance at the ballet by adding classical works to its repertoire. He was the first director of the company who was not a choreographer, and he began looking to more traditional pieces drawn from the classical canon of ballet for the company. Long past the point in which an emergent regional company had to fight to be acknowledged as a legitimate institution, Kaiser's Pennsylvania Ballet was recognized by critics and audiences as a long-standing arts institution in the United States. "Kaiser, who was appointed on June 9 to a one-year term, will be the first director in the ballet's 30-year history to have no choreographic aspirations," Nancy Goldner wrote about Kaiser's takeover. "This means the ballet can no longer rely on its director to generate new work, that the [repertoire] must become more varied. It means that Kaiser must be more curatorial-minded than any of his predecessors have had to be."[38] Despite the fact that Goldner overlooks Weisberger's curatorial tenure, her comment does make an important point: Kaiser did not see the company as a vehicle for his own work. Instead, he saw it as his artistic home, a place that nurtured his creative aspirations as a dancer and administrator, and it was the company's prestige (not necessarily his creative genius) that he sought to build and solidify. In his first full season as director, Kaiser added Ben Stevenson's full-length *Cinderella* to the company's repertoire. Like Littlefield and Weisberger, for his second season as director, Kaiser produced Philadelphia's third version of the jewel of the classical canon: *The Sleeping Beauty*.[39]

The Sleeping Beauty: 1997 and 2002

In what follows, I examine the restaging of *The Sleeping Beauty* that premiered in 1997 and was repeated five years later, in 2002. The choreography for these two performances was kept intact, and one of the three dancers cast in the role of Aurora in 1997 repeated her well-reviewed performances in 2002. As part of a campaign to revitalize the Pennsylvania Ballet Company and reestablish and expand its identity after the financial instability and artistic confusion of the previous thirty years, Kaiser chose to tackle the legendary *Beauty* in an attempt to prove that the Pennsylvania Ballet was worthy of support by both the Philadelphia audience and the larger professional ballet and funding communities. Kaiser chose to stage *The Sleeping Beauty* for the Pennsylvania Ballet within generally accepted ideas of authenticity. Essential elements such as sets, costumes, narrative, and choreographic structure were maintained according to the general understandings of the nineteenth-century Petipa-based stagings of the work. Kaiser borrowed costumes and sets designed by Peter Cazalet for the Salt Lake City company Ballet West, and secured additional costumes from the Boston Ballet and Pittsburgh Ballet Theatre. The old-fashioned backdrops portrayed visions of palace interiors and forest vistas and played up the ballet's fairy tale theme.[40] Many members of the print media found these sets and costumes lackluster and hardly reflective of the sumptuous grandeur of the Court of Versailles. The critic Anne Levin noted that the "modest sets and costumes . . . leave something to be desired."[41] However, this view of the production was contradicted by others who remarked on its "ornate sets and lavish costumes" with delight.[42] Yet another critic commented that the costumes "transcend sumptuous. This is a riot of glitter and flowers and radiant colors and textures."[43]

I remember the costumes, if not the sets, as lovely and very ornate, although more indicative of twentieth-century than Versailles-inspired, Baroque-style costuming tastes. I specifically recall the striking array of vibrant jewel-toned tutus worn by the fairies in the ballet's prologue. The bright colors were reminiscent of the royal palette of earlier stagings. The pared-down and streamlined fit of the tutus, however—which emphasized the lean, sleek bodies and long, slender arms and backs of the dancers—was certainly reflective of twentieth-century developments in the ballet aesthetic. These costumes and sets did not rival those of a baroque performance, or even those of the Royal Ballet's famous production. Compared with the sparse aesthetic of the Pennsylvania Ballet's standard neoclassical works, however, the production appeared quite lavish.

The former Pennsylvania Ballet dancer Janek Schergen staged the choreography for *The Sleeping Beauty*.[44] He wanted to stay close to the Marius Petipa version while also adapting the work to modern audiences' new tastes. In her critique, Levin stated that Schergen's staging "plays it safe by following traditional lines—with mostly positive results."[45] She also remarked that the length of Schergen's staging of the work—almost three hours—made it "an endurance test for both the dancers and the audience."[46] Others also commented on the length of the work. One reviewer wrote, "The company made it through this *arduous* production, but without aplomb."[47] Yet another reviewer noted the old-fashioned aesthetic sensibility characterizing the lengthy work: "'Sleeping Beauty' is a stately ballet, not one that can rouse an audience to frenzy with splashy solos, but one that can be appreciated for the beauty and elegance of its unfolding."[48]

This insightful remark gets to a core issue in both this ballet's restaging and its reception: Its very aesthetic underpinnings reflect an earlier time in cultural and aesthetic norms and in political history. As discussed in earlier chapters of this book, the "way of seeing" inherent in the work is bound up in an autocratic demonstration of political and aesthetic conservatism.[49] This translates into an aesthetic production based on a slow and steady panoramic vision of beauty, without the jarring starts and stops a contemporary audience relies on to maintain interest in the action onstage (or on the screen). Audiences in nineteenth-century Russia, for example, were used to entertainment that took an evening to develop and allowed audiences to enjoy the luxuriantly slow progression of a ballet, opera, or symphony. Audiences of the 1990s, however, were used to television's and films' quick camera cuts and flashy visual iconography that delivered instant gratification and easy digestion of commodified images like those in the films that garnered the highest box office sales in 1997: *Titanic, Men in Black,* and *Jurassic Park.*[50] Contemporary audiences in 1997 and 2002 sometimes struggled with the slow pace of the nineteenth-century aesthetic Schergen worked to emulate.

Critics and performers also had conflicting views about the choreography. Although many reflected on the staging as traditional, others felt that Schergen's version strayed too far from Petipa's original work. Lewis Whittington, for example, commented that Schergen's "streamlined" production was "less affected" and "move[d] the evening-length program briskly."[51] Schergen himself commented that his version straddled the line between a slavish attempt at authenticity and a radical renovation of the old style. "The version I'm doing here is Petipa," he noted, "and its roots are strongly in that vein. I'm not adapting it for dancers that dance another style[;] I'm adapting them for Petipa."[52]

As they did for the other productions of *Beauty* examined in this book, questions about authenticity emerged as central in the criticism of and discourse around this production, and Schergen has important points to add to this debate. "There is no way to know exactly what *Sleeping Beauty* was 107 years ago," he noted. "I've seen so many adaptations that people have come to take as [the] Bible. One needs to sift through all the different productions, consider what is palatable to today's audiences and to what dancers now are capable of. You distill all that into a personal vision of the work."[53] In a telephone interview, he commented, "We really don't know what the original was. . . . [W]e can no longer do the original."

For Schergen, then, authenticity is possible even with shifting expectations and desires of changing audiences and dancers. His restaging does not depend on replicating the original. Instead, the staging is about translating the original for performance today. Schergen used the Benesh notations held by the Royal Ballet in England and relied on his own observations as a young artist who saw Beryl Gray's staging of the ballet.[54] "I didn't want to veer from what was generally accepted to be authentic," he said, "but I was not locked into a fact of authenticity."[55]

For instance, Schergen removed the Little Red Riding Hood variation from *Beauty*'s third act and the blind man's bluff game from the second. He felt that these pieces "slow[ed] down the story line and ha[d] just always been done for the sake of tradition."[56] By removing what he felt were antiquated pieces, Schergen attempted to streamline the ballet so it would be more palatable to modern audiences. Dealing with the realities of the aesthetic tastes of the 1990s, Schergen plainly stated, "Modern audiences would certainly be bored by some of the original choreography."[57]

Another major change that Schergen made was to remove the element of drag from the evil character in the *Beauty* story. Traditionally, company directors cast a man in the role of Carabosse to emphasize her ugliness, jealousy, and devastating power. However, Schergen did not want to use a man for the role because, in his opinion, "It can become a parody of the woman scorned if you're not careful. I wanted her [Carabosse] to be as gorgeous and powerful as the

Lilac Fairy." He commented that the part is "too hard for a man. It's not his life. But a woman understands what it's like to be offended and takes a different approach."[58] A man in drag also carries different connotations for contemporary audiences, and the performance of Carabosse illuminates social changes regarding gender as well as aesthetic tastes regarding ballet.

In addition, the realities of arts funding in the 1990s and 2000s made the types of productions witnessed one hundred years earlier in Russia impossible for the Pennsylvania Ballet in 1997 and 2002. Discussing the relatively small size of the Pennsylvania Ballet's thirty-two-member roster and the primarily neoclassical training of the dancers, the reviewer Barbara Malinsky stated frankly, "This production was not the perfect match for the company's strengths."[59] She was not alone in this observation. Anne Levin, a writer for the *Trenton Daily News*, wrote, "Mounting 'The Sleeping Beauty' was a challenge for the thirty-two member Pennsylvania Ballet, which mobilized every dancer, apprentice and a few students and teachers in the organization for this huge production."[60] On the disparity between the Pennsylvania Ballet's status as a midsize regional company and its attempt to perform a lavish production from the classical canon, Schergen remarked, "This company was never set up to do this kind of a thing. [The company's] mission and purpose was never to do full-length classics. That's not a good or a bad thing[;] it just is."[61]

Such comments illuminate important questions surrounding the vitality of the classical ballet canon and bring into question the feasibility of reconstructing classical ballets faithfully within the constraints of the twenty-first century capitalist culture in which we now live. The Pennsylvania Ballet continues to operate on the belief that restaging components of the classical canon is an important part of its mission to preserve ballet's historical and artistic traditions.[62] Standing as an example of American regional ballet, the Pennsylvania Ballet's attempts to keep the canon alive through restructuring and adaptation, with simultaneous attention to and retention of traditional legacies, demonstrate a common approach in American ballet historiography.

Analytical metaphors of drama and music are useful here. Shakespeare plays and medieval music, for example, are constantly reevaluated in terms of their ability to transcend time limits and remain relevant to contemporary audiences. Although performances of medieval music and Edwardian drama are based on recorded texts (musical scores and play scripts), the restaging of two-hundred-year-old productions is a commonplace practice in the worlds of music and drama. Ballet participates in this same tradition. The nostalgic appeal of an imaginary and idealized classicism inspires the perennial popularity of ballets such as *Beauty*. Discussing the appeal of the socially determined "masterpiece" and its associated cultural capital, one critic remarked, "After decades of the prominence of the neoclassical form, it may be time for a period of retrenchment, a luxuriating in the comfort of the narrative with its predictable triumph of good over evil."[63] Schergen remarked that "the ballet is based on the concept of the hundred year sleep, and everyone waking up in the court of Louis XIV. The change is the opulence of the court in Act III."[64]

Again, the discourse surrounding the reception and performance of *Beauty* revolves around ideas of authenticity and how traditions evolve as they travel across time and space. Here is where examining how dancers learn, practice, and perform the choreography gives us valuable insights into these perennial questions about authenticity and provides a series of new lenses and questions. It is through dancers' embodiment of choreography that the idea of classicism is brought into the world. Examining the specific ways in which *The Sleeping Beauty* resurfaces across time and space is one way to undertake a formal analysis of these questions. How living, dancing bodies perform tradition within the framework of a specific historical text (*The Sleeping Beauty*) demonstrates the concrete ways in which choreographers and dancers have approached this issue.

This bears an important restating of the usual way that ballet has been analyzed—that is, from the audience—and shifts it to what it looks like from the stage. In other words, I advocate that, along with examining ballet from the point of view of the audience (and the critic in the audience), we also incorporate the no less important view of the dancers onstage. This move makes it possible for scholars and researchers to understand more about what dancers mean when we speak about "classical," or "authentic," in regard to the balletic canon.

The Sleeping Beauty draws much of its essential identity for dancers, audiences, and critics alike as an icon that holds significant cultural capital. This identity relies upon the fact that the ballet is always understood as a reproduction of an original, authentic text and that this reproduction and referencing of the original are central to the ballet's meaning. As James Berger writes, "The uniqueness of the original now lies in it being the original of a reproduction. It is no longer what its image shows that strikes one as unique; its first meaning is no longer to be found in what it says, but what it is."[65] This is apparent in comments such as that of Joyce Mullins, writer for *Philadelphia Pride Weekly*, who emphasized the ballet's place within a framework in the classical canon: "It is *a fully pedigreed classic now*, and as such, whenever it is staged, expectations are high and companies are scrutinized unmercifully."[66] Regardless, *Beauty* is accepted throughout the ballet world as "the" example of a classic and as such has become significant to both audience members and performers. Again, Berger's *Ways of Seeing* is useful. He writes, "The bogus religiosity which now surrounds original works of art . . . is the final empty claim for the continuing values of an oligarchic, undemocratic culture. If the image is no longer unique and exclusive, the art object, the thing, must be made mysteriously so."[67] In this he refers to a cultural shift that took place with the invention of the printing press and camera. The same issue holds true for the effect of film technologies, for as art productions become available for mechanical reproduction, the original work becomes fetishized as a mythic prototype.

Many writers have commented on the conundrum of understanding traditional or classical art in the postmodern age. "The presence of the original is the prerequisite to the concept of authenticity," Walter Benjamin writes. He then goes on to comment on this original in the age of mechanical reproduction (for dance, this would be video): "The technique of reproduction detaches the reproduced object (in this case choreography) from the domain of tradition."[68] How, then, can restagings of canonical works manage to maintain any authenticity in performance? The physical labor of dancers passing choreography from one to another maintains continuity in dance. In learning from a dancer who has performed a role, younger dancers are able to inherit the choreography without the kind of detachment Benjamin mentions, as well as the falsity noted by Berger. Instead of Benjamin's "liquidation of traditional value of cultural heritage," dancers in the coaching and rehearsal process immerse themselves in living history, experiencing the "aura" or cultural moment by embodying a role developed over the course of a century or more.

The Pennsylvania Ballet's production of *Beauty* acted on this mythologizing push. Undertaking the staging of the large and well-known production was part of Kaiser's successful plan to draw audience members into seeing an imaginary dance of perfection and authenticity. Audiences' nostalgic yearning for an imaginary past did inspire ticket sales and mobilized the company's ability to "attract new audience members with popular, traditional works."[69]

Like the sets, costuming, and choreography for the work, however, the coaching of dancers for the 1997 production was only quasi-traditional. Unlike Petipa's or even Weisberger's dancers, the dancers for the Pennsylvania Ballet's 1997 production had only three weeks to prepare for the performances of this lengthy work.[70] Schergen came to Philadelphia, but unlike Petipa, who usually chose his own cast (under the influence of balletomanes and royal officials), Schergen did not choose his own cast. Instead, Kaiser, the company's artistic director, finished casting before Schergen arrived. Discussing the casting of Aurora, Schergen commented, "This is a very difficult role for a dancer. She has to do everything. It explores all aspects of classical technique. It really opens up a dancer to push outside her range."[71]

Such comments lead to the interesting debate surrounding the expressive dimensions of the Aurora role. Many writers have argued that ballerinas have little room for creativity and interpretation in their dancing and that they are victims of the objectifying male gaze of the audience and male choreographer. Most ballerinas and directorial figures inside the ballet world would disagree. "There is a lot of interpretive play for the dancers," Schergen said about the Aurora role. *The Sleeping Beauty* conveys most of its narrative through dancing, and not through pantomime, he believes, so the dancers must "speak with the body" in a way that makes the narrative and the choreography clear.[72]

His statement that dancers must speak with the body underlines the importance of the technical execution of *The Sleeping Beauty*. As stated earlier, ballet is a formal syntax that allows dancers to use the vocabulary of classical dance to formulate their own artistic voice. This expression relies on proficiency of technique and the embodiment of both conceptual and physical ideals of symmetry, aplomb, and grace, as well as nuance, dramatic character development, and subtle decision making. It is the technique itself that allows dancers to articulate and develop their artistry, manifested only in the well-trained bodies of its artist/performers. Once a dancer no longer has to worry about the mechanics of landing in a tight, nicely turned out glissade, for example, she can think about how she wants to turn her head from shoulder to shoulder; where and when to emphasize the weight of her body during takeoff and landing; and the dynamics, phrasing, and engagement of her arms and back to support the feeling of the transition of the glissade. Once all of this is worked out through a negotiation of the mind and body in rehearsal, a performance ideally becomes an expressive moment of transcendence, an authentic manifestation of an aesthetic idea.

However, technique is not artistry; it is merely the language that allows dancers to speak. Ballet training provides dancers and choreographers with a structure and lexis for the expression and articulation of artistic and creative ideas. It is a formal vocabulary, emphasizing clarity, geometry, and balance, and it is both historically and aesthetically derived from the Enlightenment project. By this, I mean the belief that emerged during the Enlightenment that people can understand and put order to the natural world (including the human body) through the use of clinical reason, science, and objective analysis. Because of its long performance history rooted in the world view of the Enlightenment court, as well as the complex contexts in which the genre has been studied and performed, ballet has produced and reflected a wide and divergent spectrum of gender and racial constructions onstage. While I acknowledge that many of these constructions have been, and continue to be, problematic, artists continue to embrace ballet as an aesthetic form that speaks with beauty and perfect balance of form. The elegance and harmony of ballet's structure and syntax, as well as the lived experience of dancers, speak to the complicated ways in which ballet acts as a vehicle for both men's and women's artistic expression. Through education rather than training—that is, through the transformation of self that takes place during the search for one's role within a certain discipline or vocation—the individual emerges with a point of view. In this way, dancers learn to shape balletic vocabulary into a personal language, allowing them to speak to the audience through performing fully, competently, and with the confidence of personal agency and expression.

The Sleeping Beauty is built on the aesthetic underpinnings of the classical ballet vocabulary, and according to Schergen, the need for a classical ballet vocabulary conflicted with the company's neoclassical style. "I am a stickler for the Petipa style," Schergen said. "This was difficult for the Pennsylvania Ballet, because it's a Balanchine company. Their crisp technique was too much. I had to round out the edges a bit so it didn't look so contemporary."[73] In other words, when we analyze down to this level and consider issues such as how authenticity is produced (or not), the importance of physical technique must be at the heart of any analysis of *The Sleeping Beauty* and, in particular of the Aurora role, and any discussion of physical technique can and should include a focus on the dancers. This is how the shift from audience to stage starts to matter.

Dance History from the Stage: Shifting the Gaze

Dancers' understandings of the roles they perform have shaped and continue to shape the trajectory of classical ballet. Explicating this is where this chapter now heads and where the argument now turns. As they inhabit the choreographic material of classical ballets, dancers perform and enact embodied theorizations of dance history (see Figure 5.1). Aurora, then, awakens within the context of her performers' bodies, and each performance reconstitutes the classical onstage as the ballet unfolds. For many reasons, which I outline in Chapter 1 of this book, however, dance history typically has been written from the outside in.

While the lived experience of the ballerina and that of the ballet historian and critic are intertwined, it is only recently that the dancer's perspective has been seen as significant. Certainly the work of dance scholars is important; without it, even dancers would not have the vocabulary they need to describe, interpret, and evaluate choreography and performance deeply and in detail. Certain ballets could be lost to us without the descriptive reviews of critics, and many reviews of premieres capture a certain "essence" of a ballet that continues to guide performers and artistic directors in how the work should come alive in contemporary restagings. As Andrea Harris has stated,

Figure 5.1. An airborne Dede Barfield rehearsing the leading role in *The Sleeping Beauty*, 2002. (Pennsylvania Ballet Records, Special Collections Research Center, Temple University Libraries, Philadelphia, PA.)

writers such as John Martin, Edwin Denby, and Lincoln Kirstein shaped the development and formation of American dance throughout the 1930s, with their opinions influencing what dance audiences, and therefore choreographers, understood as "good" dance.[74]

However, as I also note in Chapter 1, academic writing and academic dance practice (especially since the advent of second-wave feminism), tend to see ballerinas as instruments of male choreographers. In the case of feminist criticism, often borrowing from film theory, ballerinas are also seen as objects of the male gaze on display for audience members and as bodies disciplined by the political and social control of the capitalist patriarchy. However, there is more to the story than this. The voices of female dancers, producers, and choreographers create a discrete intervention into the historian-driven writing in dance studies. The ballerinas I interviewed are articulate and intelligent about their work and their aesthetic field. The author of a recent article in *Dance Research*, in fact, made the claim that ballet training is pleasurable and empowering for participants.[75]

As stated above, *The Sleeping Beauty*'s meaning is derived from the highly technical and plot-driven choreography at its core. Although a good portrayal of Aurora is conveyed to an audience through the physically embodied performance of a dancer, these dancing bodies are always connected to thinking, speaking people. This internal and external process of role creation by dancers, rather than choreographers or restagers, has been overlooked by dance critics, historians, and even choreographers, who do not always see the dancers as equal partners in the creative process. Therefore, dancers offer an important perspective on the meanings embedded in *The Sleeping Beauty* and what the dance can teach us about the world in which we live. In reflecting on their lived experience of dancing Aurora, dancers illuminate the complex and varied ways that they articulate personal understandings and choices through their interpretations of classical choreography.

The three women who performed Aurora for the Pennsylvania Ballet in 2002 are wonderful examples of the women who populate regional ballet companies. Rather than looking to international superstars of ballet, I intentionally stay within the confines of Philadelphia because I believe that it helps keep me true to the premise at the heart of this book. It is not necessarily talent or ability that places one dancer at the center of a dance canon of greatness or genius, although sometimes that may be the case. In many situations, it is simply proximity to a man (or woman) whom scholars and historians have identified as a genius or the progenitor of a tradition that establishes the dancer as significant to the history of ballet. At the same time, many significant dancers' stories have not been told because they lie outside what has been considered the center of the dance world. As much as I advocate for the importance of Philadelphia as an artistic hub for the emergence of American ballet, I also advocate for the importance of dancers, directors, and producers working outside New York who may be less well known than their peers in larger, more visible companies. I believe strongly that history must expand to include these lesser-known women, for they are talented, dedicated artists with significant information to share with scholars and historians willing to listen to voices that are so often overlooked or silenced.

The three dancers I interviewed for this project trained with international faculty, worked with international *repiteurs* and choreographers, and continue to carry out the tradition of Euro-Russian ballet within their dance communities, now teaching and coaching the next generation of ballet dancers. Now active as educators in the field, they pass their knowledge and lived experience on, reawakening Aurora in the bodies of their students, who will reanimate classical ballet as they develop into professional dancers. Because of the Balanchine base of the Pennsylvania Ballet's repertoire, all three Auroras reflect the company's style in their training. Despite their early schooling, all attended the School of American Ballet in New York. Examining the specifics of their early journey in the field of ballet helps provide context for the discussion that follows.

Arantxa Ochoa, now principal teacher for the Pennsylvania Ballet's reestablished school, was born in Valladolid, Spain, and began her movement training as a rhythmic gymnast. At twelve, she moved to Madrid, where she studied at the Centro de Danza Victor Ullate. Ochoa continued her studies at the Académie de Danse Princesse Grace in Monte Carlo. Three years later, she came to the United States and studied at the School of American Ballet. Ochoa spent three years at the Hartford Ballet before joining the Pennsylvania Ballet in 1996 as a member of the corps de ballet. She was promoted to soloist in 1999 and to principal in 2001.

Ochoa has danced many starring roles. In addition to Aurora, she has performed Odette/Odile in the world premiere of Christopher Wheeldon's *Swan Lake*, Juliet in *Romeo and Juliet*, Swanhilde in *Coppélia*, Lise in *La Fille mal gardée*, Katherina in *The Taming of the Shrew*, and the title roles in James Kudelka's *The Firebird* and Marius Petipa's *Giselle*. Her repertoire of George Balanchine ballets includes the leads in *A Midsummer Night's Dream, Agon, Apollo, Ballo della Regina, Bugaku, Concerto Barocco, Divertimento No. 15, Monumentum pro Gesualdo, Movements for Piano and Orchestra, Prodigal Son, Raymonda Variations, Serenade, Theme and Variations, Slaughter on Tenth Avenue, Western Symphony,* and *Who Cares?* She is married to a fellow ballet dancer and has a son, and has recently been promoted to the role of director of the official School of the Pennsylvania Ballet.[76]

Dede Barfield was born in Fort Worth, Texas, and began her training there with Gayle Corkery. She continued at the Etgen-Atkinson Ballet School in Dallas. At fourteen, she began studying during the summers at the School of American Ballet in New York

City, and by sixteen she had moved there to study exclusively. Barfield joined the Pennsylvania Ballet in 1984; she was promoted to soloist in 1987 and to principal in 1990. In addition to Aurora, her repertoire includes a wide variety of classical roles, such as Odette/Odile in *Swan Lake*, Myrtha in *Giselle*, Vera in Robert Weiss's full-length production of *Winder Dreams*, one of the three leading female roles in Fokine's *Les Sylphides*, the title role in Ben Stevenson's *Cinderella*, and Juliet in John Cranko's *Romeo and Juliet*. She has also performed principal roles in Peter Martins's *Fearful Symmetries* and Petipa's *Paquita* and *Don Quixote*. Barfield has danced leading roles in numerous Balanchine ballets, including *The Nutcracker* (as Dewdrop and the Sugar Plum Fairy), *Agon*, *Allegro Brillante*, *Concerto Barocco*, *Divertimento No. 15*, *Donizetti Variations*, *The Four Temperaments*, *Serenade*, *Tchaikovsky's Pas de Deux*, *The Steadfast Tin Soldier*, *Western Symphony*, and *Who Cares?* She is married to a former modern dancer and also has a son. She is now the ballet mistress of Ballet San Antonio and teaches across Texas.[77]

Martha Chamberlain began her dance training at five at the Fellowship House in Media, Pennsylvania, where she was born and raised. She went on to study with Donna Muzio, Paul Klocke, and Cherie Noble at West Chester's Dance Center and the School of American Ballet's summer program from 1985 to 1988. She is a graduate of Friends Select and the School of Pennsylvania Ballet. Chamberlain joined the Pennsylvania Ballet as an apprentice in the fall of 1989 and was promoted to the corps de ballet three months later. She was promoted to soloist in 1997 and to principal after her premiere as Juliet in John Cranko's *Romeo and Juliet* in March 2000.

In addition to Aurora, Chamberlain has danced several leading roles, including Katherina in *The Taming of the Shrew*, Swanhilde in *Coppélia*, Myrtha in *Giselle*, Dewdrop and Sugar Plum Fairy in George Balanchine's *The Nutcracker*, and the Helena and Divertissement pas de deux in *A Midsummer Night's Dream*. She has also danced featured roles in George Balanchine's *Agon*, *Apollo*, *Ballo della Regina*, *The Four Temperaments*, *Rubies from Jewels*, *Serenade*, and *Western Symphony*; Paul Taylor's *Arden Court* and *Company B*; and Christopher d'Amboise's *Franklin Court*. Chamberlain also designs costumes and jewelry and gave birth to her first child in 2013. She is currently a faculty member of the official school of the Pennsylvania Ballet.[78]

All three of these women performed the role of Aurora in 2002. Barfield also performed the role in 1997. In the 1997 ballet, Ochoa and Chamberlain were still climbing through the ranks of the company, performing soloist roles. Despite their different places of birth and early childhood experiences, all of these dancers trained in a similar aesthetic system and came to the Pennsylvania Ballet at a young age. For all three, dancing Aurora was a testament not only to their hard work but also to their preeminence in the company and their ascendance to the rank of principal dancer.

Listening from the Wings: Hearing Dancers Speak

My goal in conducting interviews was to hear the women who danced Aurora reflect on the process of learning and performing the role. Instead of bringing preconceived ideas about questions to ask, I allowed themes to emerge during our conversations. In analyzing the transcripts of the resulting interviews, three distinct yet interconnected areas of content surfaced. The first of these areas is the idea of fear. All three dancers discussed how afraid they were of performing the Aurora role because of the mythology that has developed around it within the world of professional ballet. Aurora is seen as the hardest role in the classical canon and for this reason is seen as the ultimate test of a dancer's talent, endurance, and artistry.

Second and also connected to the idea of the role's difficulty is the way the dancers spoke about the intensity and importance of its technical content. All three dancers (as well as the choreographer and director) spoke about the role as "pure technique." It is composed of a highly technical vocabulary, and its performance produces a visual and aesthetic representation of discipline and form and a crystallization of the progressive, developmental architecture of nineteenth-century classical ballet vocabulary. The more fully a dancer executes the Aurora choreography, the more fully she is subsumed and illuminated by that choreography. Reminiscent of the analysis in Michel Foucault's "Docile Bodies," the performance of Aurora works on dancers' bodies in a "disciplinary coercion [that] establishes in the body the constricting link between an increased aptitude and increased domination."[79] The more proficient the performer, the more obedient and docile his or her body is to the overlying structure of ballet technique as a discipline.

In other words, ballet training is related to Foucault's panopticon. In rigorous training in classes and rehearsals, dancers perpetually scan and monitor themselves, ensuring that their dancing is always "correct." However, unlike Foucault's panopticon, which denies individuals the agency to make choices while under surveillance and the ability to move beyond what has been culturally determined, the dancers I interviewed speak to an ability to "convey spontaneous, unscripted meanings through sedimented forms."[80] In other words, the scrutiny of dancers and audience members does not determine the choices made in the embodiment of the Aurora role. Instead, the dancers' words argue against the constructivist metaphor of bodily inscription described by Foucault and speak to the dynamic power of embodied performance as offering dancers room for choice.

Third and last, all three dancers discussed the Aurora role as transformational in both their careers and their self-awareness. How can this be true when the role demands that the dancer face difficult physical challenges that require intense self-monitoring? For the dancers interviewed for this book, the role was a rite of passage in which, like Aurora herself during the ballet, the ballerinas grew from girls to women or from neophytes to respected authorities both within the Pennsylvania Ballet and in their understanding of themselves as dance artists. After performing Aurora's transformation onstage, these women felt a change within the confines of the ballet company, and sensed a new respect from other dancers and the company leadership. They also experienced a new freedom in their own ability to interpret and command the balletic vocabulary with expressive maturity. Carrie Noland, who demonstrates the emancipatory possibilities of gesture by analyzing theater through the lens of phenomenologists such as Maurice Merleau-Ponty, describes this work of dancers this way: "Our freedom to innovate, our plasticity, should be seen to derive from our rich mnemonic store (our library) of socially acquired 'I can's' as well as the proto-signifying resources of bipedal anatomy."[81] This relates to the regimented work of ballet dancers in that their creativity comes from their own, physicalized kinetic library of classical training. This library of acquired movement vocabulary is not limiting but instead makes up an arsenal of embodied practice from which innovation may emerge. Ochoa, for example, spoke about how dancers pass on both fear and deference for the canon when they tell young ballerinas about the difficulty of dancing Aurora. Regardless of this—or, perhaps, because of it—Ochoa felt that dancing Aurora was the most rewarding role of her career. In an interview in 2003, she said that in rehearsals she was coached to dance the role "pure, simple . . . but the very classical is so hard—the arms, the positions."[82] Later, she said that *The Sleeping Beauty* is hard because "it's so pure, so classical. You can't fake it. You can't cover things. If you don't go through the form correctly, you see it."[83]

However, while discussing how she was coached in her interpretation of the Aurora character, Ochoa said, "That was more or less unsaid." This is an important similarity between Ochoa and the dancers of Petipa's era (as well as the dancers from Littlefield's and Weisberger's eras). Ochoa developed her character through a personal interpretation of the choreography presented to her in rehearsals. Rather than being coached in how to understand the role dramatically, she was trusted as a mature artist to make her character believable. As a principal dancer, she was expected to dance a compelling and believable performance. This personal investment and articulate artistic voice is, in fact, part of the skill set required of principal dancers. Ochoa developed her Aurora role through background research and work in the studio. "I thought I was a sixteen-year-old," she said. "I thought I was a princess. As I read *The Sleeping Beauty*, I tried in my mind to be her. The moment I came out on the stage, it was my birthday. There were all these people watching me. I tried to become her. I mean, I was her, being the princess."[84] In preparation for the role, Ochoa researched the ballet's visual history by watching a videotape she had borrowed from the video archives of the Pennsylvania Ballet, as well as from the Free Library of Philadelphia. These videos held valuable archival sources of the ballet's history. Part of Ochoa's research was to study tapes from the 1950s, including a Russian tape of Maria Kolpakova in Saint Petersburg and a tape of the Rose Adagio performed by Margot Fonteyn in London.[85] The Pennsylvania Ballet, too, has an extensive archive of tapes, which undoubtedly included tape from the 1997 production and of the three women who performed Aurora for those performances. Watching other women dancing the role did not result in mimicry. Rather, it allowed Ochoa to notice how other women have brought their personalities, stylistic and physical differences, and technical strengths to the role. In addition, Ochoa went to the Children's Department at the Free Library of

Philadelphia and studied the illustrations in a beautiful picture book of *The Sleeping Beauty.*

Unlike some dancers who rely primarily on themselves for artistic guidance, Barfield hired an outside coach to assist in her mastery of the Aurora role. In preparation for her debut, she drove to New York City and rented a studio, where she worked with Cynthia Gregory, a former ABT dancer.[86] Although she had the help of experienced dancers, she called dancing Aurora for the first time "frightening." Along with her coach, Barfield also relied on videotapes and went through them section by section.

Despite her nerves and self-doubt, Barfield was critically acclaimed for her performance. Many who saw her dance praised her acting ability. Brian Caffall, for example, wrote, "Dede Barfield is a completely charming Aurora; sweet, innocent, and thoroughly involved."[87] Another reviewer stated, "Barfield dances this long role with precision and flair. . . . Barfield dances with such concentration and focus she earns plaudits from the audience."[88] Yet another opinion was that "Dede Barfield is particularly winsome in her leading role as Princess Aurora. Barfield's performance of the ingénue role is expert, her face mirroring the surprise and wonder of love's adventures, her body exhibiting an eas[e]ful control that rarely slipped beneath first-class execution."[89]

The experience of dancing Aurora twice (in 1997 and 2002) gave Barfield significant insight into herself as an artist. She talked with me about how the changes that had taken place in her personal life filtered into her dancing persona and how they changed the ways in which she interpreted *Beauty.* Commenting on her new understanding of the work after the birth of her son, she stated:

> The second time [I performed Aurora,] everything seemed to have gotten easier in a way, after I had [my son]. It was very hard to come back with nursing. It took me forever to get to a certain stage, but once I got in shape, I had more stamina, more strength. I had a Russian teacher tell me childbirth matures you, gives you power. . . . I felt because I was getting older it would be harder. I was thirty-four the first time. I thought thirty-nine would be harder, but it was actually easier. Artistically I had a different understanding as a mother because I

almost went into the mother role as I was acting. I was thinking of a young girl who gets pricked and dies or goes to sleep.
She's sixteen; it's so heartbreaking.[90]

Barfield continued to discuss her interpretation of the ballet, talking about how she developed her conceptualization of the Aurora
character:

I initially see her as a baby. Whether a kingdom or a small family, everybody loves this baby before it's born. She happens to
be a princess, but she's just a little girl who is loved very much
and adored. Because of her place, she's worried about being
cursed just because of who she is. She is very special, not so
much because she's a princess, but because she's cursed just for
being born to a mom who is queen. She's sweet and innocent,
protected. [There is the] excitement of being sixteen, coming
of age. The debutante ball, whatever you want to think of it, it's
very exciting. She's an innocent being, a child. . . . So when she
comes down in the beginning . . . [w]hen she's told she has to
choose [one of the men] for marriage, she gets very afraid. Her
mother calms her, knowing if she thinks of it as just dancing, it
will be easier. Then she falls in love, with a typical story about
falling in love. A fairy tale. At the very end, the last solo is a
combination of everything—her birth, how she grew up, how
she was cursed, the party where she pricked her finger, how she
fell in love. Then she's a mature woman or ballerina.[91]

As I got to know her through interviews, Martha Chamberlain
was the least cerebral of the dancers who performed Aurora in 2002.
She focused her comments on how the role was passed to her by another dancer in the company. She discussed how dancers teach Aurora's role to the next generation and in doing so translate their own
understandings of the choreography and narrative. "I got a lot of help
from Janek [Schergen, the choreographer]," she said. "I got a lot of little tips from other people. Jodi Gates, who had done it before—I had
been talking to her about it a little bit. She gave me tips about what
she had learned, what they told her, what she had been coached to do
. . . that you were young, then you grew up."[92] Going on to discuss her

own interpretation of Aurora, she said, "She's only sixteen, so you have to emphasize that she's a girl, young and playful. . . . [T]he vision scene is so much more ethereal because you are just a vision. Facially you're not animated. It is very calm. Reaching should be more in the body than in the face. . . . [T]he third act is the basic wedding, happy bride. It is pretty straightforward. It's more about the actual dancing, the variation, than any kind of specific acting."[93]

For Chamberlain, then, as stated earlier, and for the scholar Tim Scholl, the ballet is about technique.[94] Chamberlain's understanding of Aurora focuses on the technical demands of the role. Her feelings about dancing the role successfully revolved around her ability to perform the choreography as accurately and proficiently as possible. "It's important just to make yourself look as much of a ballerina as you can," she said. "It's the quintessential ballerina role. They're always throwing out, 'Your leg's not turned out; your foot is not pointed here,' so you get a lot of that. Everyone was telling me it's the hardest ballet [I would] ever do. Once you hear the music, when you come out, you're . . . sucked in. You know it's not over till it's over. It's a lot."[95]

Chamberlain's comments also testify to the ways in which dancers embody roles. Their interpretation, as well as their ability to exercise agency, is enacted through their learning processes and their approach to kinesthetic performance. In focusing on the body and the sensations produced by moving the body in space, dancers *become* the role they perform. When she says, "You're sucked in," Chamberlain is speaking about the transformational state achieved through the kinesthesia of dance performance much like some other physical and spiritual practices, such as yoga, meditation, martial arts, and parkour. The transformative power of dance is stated so often it has become cliché. Although outside the purview of this study, it bears mentioning that not only ballet but many other structured and regimented repetitive physical practices offer practitioners (as well as audience members) the prospect of a momentary shift or transcendence from the mundane yet mentally cluttered experience of daily living.

Barfield felt that the technical difficulty of the ballet was part of its meaning as well as the pathway for her to experience a fundamental psychic change while she performed the role. The challenging choreographic material made the dance a transformative event as she channeled her energy and focus in a way that allowed her to lose awareness of her physical body, instead becoming engrossed by choreographic vocabulary based on unachievable perfection. The understanding that perfection is never reached—that it is merely an aesthetic, intellectual, and philosophical concept that each performer will forever seek—allowed Barfield to lose herself inside the dancing. Barfield also believes that the ballet gained meaning from the external process of being performed:

> For me, the ballet is a place for the audience to come and get away from the harsh things, get away from reality—[to] see what life can be . . . the beauty of it. Like, I was talking about the birth of a child, . . . whether it's a boy or a girl, marriages. This is what life is. It's about births, weddings, death. It's a magical place. . . . Putting on that costume makes me a magical character, and I must be that. That, to me, is what the whole ballet is. It's a place for little girls and boys to come and see incredible magic.[96]

Barfield's self-reflection was fascinating. "Children can have horrible mothers but think they're the best mothers in the world, because that's what they want," she continued. "I always wanted to be better, better, better. I realized that they don't see me. They're not really seeing me, and they shouldn't see me. They should see what they think is the Sugar Plum Fairy, what they think is Dewdrop, what they think Aurora should be."[97]

I relate to what Barfield had to say and know that she sensed this in our discussions. Our similar experiences as dancers and mothers helped us to connect in ways that may have been different from those of other academics approaching this project. In addition, I believe that small moments of my story are not superfluous inclusions in a discussion about something in which I did not take part. Rather, as a woman shaped by my experiences in the ballet world, and in the academic world of feminist studies, I know that despite their irrelevance to the *New York Times*, my personal stories highlight how a writer's subjective stance contributes to the stories she or he tells and the theories she or he generates to make meaning of cultural phenomena. This furthers the overall aim of this chapter and much of poststructuralist feminism. Speaking about the philosophy of the writer Elizabeth Bowen, Renée Hoogland writes, "Having thus established the inescapable dynamic in which writer, text and reality are mutually caught up, she is able to formulate, in a rather circular manner, precisely why 'impersonality' in writing is impossible: 'The . . . writer is using his own, unique susceptibility to experience, in a sense, the susceptibility is the experience. The susceptibility, equally is the writer, who therefore cannot be absent from what he writes.'"[98]

Therefore, in this chapter I insert a few of my own stories into the discussion. This is done with the intention of opening the chapter up into a discussion rather than an authoritative representation of truth. This discussion between these dancers and me has much to say about ballet as a cultural and political practice. It is only by listening to the details of these stories that a methodological shift can take place in which knowledge is seen as mutually valid from multiple perspectives, allowing readers to realize through what channels insights are drawn.

The transformative power of the ballerina role was what drew me into the field of ballet. Barfield's comments resonate with me, and they draw me back to my own early memories of ballerinas and their evocative power. In 1982, at nine, I danced onstage for the first time with the Maryland Youth Ballet, the performing group of a pre-professional ballet school in Bethesda, Maryland. I performed the role of a beetle in *The Coronation of the Dragonfly Queen*, a ballet by Hortensia Fonseca. Julie Kent, then fourteen but now a longtime principal dancer for ABT, danced the role of the Dragonfly Queen. Backstage, before the performance, she taught me how to apply mascara and blush. I remember sitting in front of the mirror with her while she held the mascara wand in front of my eyes and used a gentle and maternal voice to direct me to "blink, blink, blink." My brown polyester leotard and tights and red papier-mâché shell stood out as awkward and ungraceful compared with her sparkling blue-and-silver tutu, with its gossamer and iridescent wings, but her loveliness and kindness were an inspiration. I felt a connection to her and could imagine nothing better than to grow up to be just like her.

The following fall, Julie Kent traveled to Switzerland to compete in the Prix de Lausanne, one of the most prestigious ballet competitions in the world. For the competition she performed the wedding pas de deux and Aurora's variation from the third act of *Beauty*. She won the gold medal at Lausanne, as well as the attention of Mikhail Baryshnikov, then the director of ABT, who hired her on the spot and cast her in his upcoming movie, *Dancers*. I remember watching her rehearse the pas and variation from *Beauty*, taking in each and every nuance of her delicate and demure performance. She was the beautiful princess of the story, and nothing was more inspiring to me than witnessing another (slightly older) child achieving an amazing level of competence and beauty through hard work and perseverance.

Before leaving suburban Maryland and moving to New York City, Kent (then Julie Cox) performed one more time with the Maryland Youth Ballet. This time, I performed the role of Lilac Fairy Attendant in *Aurora's Wedding*, a condensation of the third act of *Beauty*, performing for the first time in my newly won pointe shoes. Sitting in the partially darkened audience of the University of the District of Columbia, where we performed, I watched Julie rehearse the wedding pas de deux from *Beauty*. She knelt low before her partner and then slowly took his hand, placed her foot en pointe, and raised herself up to a magnificent attitude derrière. Her poise and control radiated from a centralized and stable place of calm. In the variation that follows the duet, there is a long diagonal in which the princess rolls an imaginary orange (a symbol of wealth and prosperity in the Russian court) between her hands as she walks across the stage en pointe, with tiny développés en effacé. I can still see her strong, lifted arches gently pawing the ground while her torso leaned forward with yearning into space and her long, delicate fingers entwined, beckoning the audience toward her and bringing us all into her fascinating dance. After those performances, when Kent left the school and joined ABT, her performance of Aurora stayed with me, having shown me the art form's magic and wonder. As Aurora, Kent was not fully human. She transcended the ugliness of reality and was transformed into an ethereal creature more graceful and more magnificent than anyone I knew.

Cynthia Novack describes a similar experience in "Ballet, Gender and Cultural Power": "As a child watching the prima ballerina on stage, her evocative power for me resided only minimally in the role she played (the Firebird or the Swan Queen)—I never even got the stories straight until I studied dance history as an adult. The ballerina was an admired female (like my sister), a public figure who had achieved technical perfection, a woman of great accomplishment and agency."[99] Novack goes on to describe the ways in which ballet links women's virtuosity and role models with a physical practice in a way that gives the form cultural dominance and power while simultaneously offering up problematic representations of gender for audiences' and participants' consumption. The Pennsylvania Ballet's 2002 Auroras also noted this when they recounted performing *Beauty*.

Chamberlain felt that as Aurora, she escaped the limitations of reality. Her character was removed from rational portrayals grounded in realism:

> She's a fairy tale. There's kind of a cartoonish quality you put on top of it rather than if you were doing *Romeo and Juliet*, where it's a tragic character. [Aurora is] almost silly. As far as portraying a character, you know there's going to be a lot of kids watching, and you want to do a job and make it clear so they understand, but also an elegance. She's a princess, so you have to have the carriage of being elegant overall, be groomed and the right manners. When she does something that's wrong, you make her apologetic, humble. . . . I don't find a huge amount of depth in the character. The depth is more in the history of the ballet itself, and you have to hold up your end because of the ballet's significance. The story has a lot of significance in ballet, and you're paying homage to years past.[100]

For Chamberlain, then, the ballet's meaning and beauty are found not in complex emotional or dramatic expression of Aurora's psyche, but in the clear and proficient performance of her choreography. Harking back to authors such as Walter Benjamin, Chamberlain feels that the ballet's performance is about tradition and lineage as traced through the steps Aurora performs onstage. For this dancer, the choreography trumps any idea of the dramatic and narrative content of the work. The complex layers of meaning that unfold onstage in performance are evident in her ideological framing of the narrative story. "There's always the typical 'every woman is looking for her Prince Charming,'" Chamberlain said, "but I would hate to think that's all it's about."[101] The stereotypical narrative was beside the point for her; the dance was about bringing the past to life and resuscitating Aurora through historically significant choreography.

Barfield, too, was deeply reflective about the Aurora role and the ways in which her interpretation and performance of the role caused a shift in her sense of self and dance. She internalized the character and was serious about making her dancing embody Aurora's essence. Like Ochoa, she had internalized the view that dancing Aurora is a test for a dancer. "I think every ballerina should do Aurora," she said. "It's so funny. I think the younger dancers today feel like ballerinas very early. I don't know if it is because I'm from a different generation or who I am, but I was a principal dancer for years [and] I didn't feel like a ballerina. I felt like I was a principal dancer doing great roles."[102]

Barfield went on to note that the Aurora role matures a dancer and transforms her into a ballerina. This transformation implies belief in her competence as a mature woman and paralleled her lived experience of motherhood and how that shift in identity changed her sense of self. It was not only dancing Aurora but also becoming a mother that made Barfield feel that she was an authentic and unique ballerina, confident in her authority onstage. "The moment I stepped onstage [as Aurora], I was calm," she told me. "I realized I was given a gift from God to dance. I always tried my best, but if I didn't do my best, it would throw me, and I felt like I was cursing God. It took me a long time—actually, it took the birth of [my son]—for me to think I am doing my best, and if I trip during the glory of a live performance, how do I recover from that, and how do I make it so the audience doesn't see it or stay with it? Let it go."[103]

Barfield also described the physical sensations she experienced while dancing Aurora, especially those that convinced her she was indeed a ballerina. In dancing Aurora well, she was finally able to fulfill the ethereal ideals of transcendence and balance that are embedded in ballet aesthetic and kinesthetic training. Doing this, she felt confident about her dancing and her interpretive power as a ballerina:

> It's like flying. . . . Such a floating sensation, yet you are completely aware. There were times when I was nervous before I started. I was hyperaware. But I didn't have a sense of the floor. I didn't have a sense of my body. Then it almost reversed—a floating-free feeling that I was totally connected to

the floor. I totally connected to my partner and was totally aware of what my body was doing. Even though I want to stay free to fly, I was completely grounded. . . . The Rose Adagio is really incredible, an incredible feeling. It wasn't as free. You're concentrating. That last bow when you're onstage is eerie, exciting, if you do it well.[104]

Speaking with these dancers and listening to their words led me to revisit my own experiences as a dancer and coach. Reminded of the words of Linda Alcoff, I tried to examine my own location in relation to the ways I chose to represent the knowledge and contributions of these women to the dance field. As Alcoff writes:

The problem of speaking for others is a social one, the options available to us are socially constructed, and the practices we engage in cannot be understood as simply the results of autonomous individual choice. Yet to replace both "I" and "we" with a passive voice that erases agency results in an erasure of responsibility and accountability for one's speech, an erasure I would strenuously argue against. . . . When we sit down to write, or get up to speak, . . . we experience having the possibility to speak or not to speak. So I [seek] to address . . . that small space of discursive agency we all experience, however multi-layered, fictional, and constrained it in fact is.[105]

As I sat and listened to Barfield and wrote her words on the page, I felt, sensed, and, indeed, knew in my body what she was describing. For I had a similar bodily experience to the one she described when I performed the same variation. I danced Aurora's birthday solo from the first act of *Beauty* in the spring of 1999 during a performance fundraiser for a pre-professional ballet school outside Philadelphia. At the time I had been working as a visiting artist at Mount Holyoke College in South Hadley, Massachusetts, and I learned the variation at the Five College Dance Library at Hampshire College from a videotape of Viviana Durante, a ballerina for the Royal Ballet in London. I was left to my own resources in terms of rehearsal and coaching, as I was working in South Hadley while rehearsing for a concert in Philadelphia. I was able to use studio space at the college to work through the details of the choreography and build familiarity with the role.

When I stepped onstage, I did not think about movement sequencing or proficiency issues. Instead, I focused on mental imagery I had developed to guide my execution of the technically rigorous choreography. Initially, I used the imagery to guide myself into a performative mode. However, as I began dancing, I felt my entire analytical brain let go. It was a meditative experience, in which my brain was thinking about everything and nothing at the same time. I became the dance, and I was able to let myself dissolve completely. The choreography felt easy and natural and flowed from my body so that the series of balances and multiple pirouettes required by Petipa's hyper-technical choreography became effortless.

This absorption of the choreography into my being now manifests at unexpected moments. Sometimes while teaching ballet class creating a new work of choreography, or trying to think of a specific example of an aesthetic or historical concept I am discussing in a dance history class, moments from this variation emerge, seemingly out of nowhere. Creating a new phrase of movement, I may be searching for a moment of lightness, an inflection of youth, or simply a pedagogical tool to help improve pirouettes, and—lo and behold—a snippet of the variation comes to mind. This is one way that the choreography literally transforms a dancer, becoming part of her or his stored memory of bodily knowledge, and also how tradition flows forward.

Chamberlain also had very specific mind-body memories from dancing Aurora. Her most vivid were from the rehearsal studio. She enjoyed the process of preparing for the performance. Like Barfield, she commented on how she transcended her body onstage, letting go of her mental checklist (what some authors have described as the internalization of Foucault's panopticon), or the self-scanning processes that dancers often hear in their minds while dancing:

> I remember rehearsing the Rose Adagio in the studio the most. I liked that part. It was fun. I guess balancing is one thing I can do. Once I get perched, I can stay. It was so technically pure. . . . Janek [Schergen] is really funny. I enjoyed his quirkiness, his weirdness. . . . I enjoyed being coached by him. The funny thing is, performing it, I don't remember that much

about it. I remember being in the dressing room changing, all the changing, and barely having enough time to go over and practice anything onstage.[106]

The difficulty of the choreography is a significant theme that runs through every dancer's experience of *Beauty*. Intimidated, excited, overwhelmed, or pleasantly surprised and self-satisfied, each dancer's comments circulated around the idea of the difficulty of dancing Aurora. Despite—or perhaps because of—the difficulty of performing the role, it was also one of Ochoa's favorites. She told me that dancing Aurora was different from dancing other ballets and that it left her with a greater feeling of accomplishment and joy. "I came out of dancing that, and I was so happy," she said. "It was something I hadn't felt [before]. You always feel different things when you dance. Coming out of *Sleeping Beauty* was very gratifying. Before I did it, a lot of ballerinas would come up and say all these things about *Sleeping Beauty*. You think, 'I'm scared.' You have to rehearse so much. Then maybe because you think, 'I've done it [performed Aurora].' The first time is so hard. When you do it, when you're finished, you think it's wonderful. It really is."[107]

For Ochoa, then, the challenge of the role made the performance experience more satisfying and transformative than that of other classical roles. "When you do a ballet that is not challenging," she said, "you finish performing, and you're unhappy because [you] feel, 'Yes, I performed, but I do not feel like I improved.'" The feelings of pride and joy stayed with Ochoa not only after performing but also while she danced. Talking about her most distinct memories from dancing the ballet, she said, "I remember being onstage and feeling so happy there."[108]

Barfield also commented on the ways in which dancers "talk up" *Beauty*, perpetuating the idea that it is the hardest of the classics to perform. During an interview in her dressing room at the Academy of Music, she said, "We heard so much about *Sleeping Beauty*. It was so frightening. I had done *Swan Lake* before. . . . *Swan Lake* and *Sleeping Beauty* are the biggies in terms of difficulty—difficulty artistically and technically."[109]

As many critics have suggested, the meaning of the *Sleeping Beauty* does lie in the choreography but perhaps differently from how we usually think, once we entertain and interpret the layers of meaning added to this discussion by the ballerinas' reflections. Earlier chapters established that each performance of *The Sleeping Beauty* is a ritual enactment of tradition for the dancers who perform it, as well as critics and audiences, and during performance they come together, experiencing the embodiment and personification of the spirit of classical ballet. Aurora's dancing body translates and communicates ballet's aesthetic traditions for audience members and for young dancers. Coaching, rehearsals, and classes become another step in this meaning-making process. They bring dancers closer to the essence of classicism that they hope to embody as Aurora. The ballet must be danced well if its performance is to be meaningful. Petipa's choreography—or what is perceived to be Petipa's "authentic" choreography—is the root of the ballet, and the aspect most often discussed in the critical discourse around the ballet's performance. It is this special language and syntax of classical ballet, connected to Tchaikovsky's music, composed to fit perfectly with the dance steps, that transports dancers and audience members to a performed enactment or representation of tradition in which classical technique flows without effort from highly disciplined and trained bodies.

I am not the first scholar to discuss classical ballet as a ritual enactment or performance. In *Nutcracker Nation*, Jennifer Fisher speaks about that ballet, also created by Marius Petipa and Peter Tchaikovsky, as a secular ritual. She discusses how dancers and audience members experience *The Nutcracker* as a rite of passage, commenting that "for performers the 'passage' through one role after another marks various status changes in a dancing life."[110] This echoes what many ballet dancers say about the Aurora role as the ultimate test for a ballerina when she "comes of age." Fisher notes that *The Nutcracker* marks the elapsing of time for audience members, too, and becomes a ritual event that helps many people celebrate the winter holidays. She also maintains that many of the people drawn to ballet's Apollonian ideals of perfection, balance, and symmetry feel that the experience of dancing or watching ballet is both spiritual and transformative. She quotes one of the people she interviewed for her book as saying, "It's the pursuit of perfection—you suffer for it, work for it; it's a constant struggle, complete and total selfless dedication. I think it has a religious fervor to it."[111]

I agree with Fisher. As a dancer, teacher, and choreographer, I have experienced moments of transformation while dancing, coaching, creating new work, and leading students through intellectual inquiry because of the intensity of focus and interdisciplinary critical thinking required to perform, create, and make meaning of ballet with rigor and high standards. In my work building the ballet component of a large university's bachelor of fine arts degree in dance, I use variations from *The Sleeping Beauty* as a significant part of teaching and assessing my students. I adapt Aurora's variations, as well as those of other roles, to the students' level, allowing (and requiring) them to experience the performative aspect of the danse d'école, building the architecture of the semester's work on the basic movement motifs and thematic structures of one variation. If, for example, the students will perform Aurora's third act variation for their midterm and final examination, we spend time at the barre and in center enchaînements working on first arabesque and attitude derrière. The students observe themselves and their peers dancing the variation on video, assessing their own work and offering feedback to and receiving it from their peers. In this way, students live moments from the ballet, and the choreography becomes a pedagogical tool, as well as inspiration or creative fodder for their compositional and choreographic studies.

As a scholar who values the perspectives of other dancers, I also understand that classical ballet—and, in particular, *The Sleeping Beauty*—is a channel or conduit for dancers to re-create the classical. In dancing the ballet, the dancers themselves circumscribe the art form and define the genre. This is a ritual of self-determination and is a self-reflective act. As they perform elements from what is generally accepted inside and outside the ballet world as part of the "classical" tradition, dancers (steeped in all genres) imagine and create new standards, which emerge from their own creative voices and ideas, to which they must adhere. As *The Sleeping Beauty* is performed in the incredibly wide-ranging and expanding global and diverse reach of ballet, it has become more about the dancer and her individual interpretation, translation, and expression of a role than about the original choreography. The choreography, which the critics cited in this book desire to see presented "authentically" and intact in its nineteenth-century guise, has become a shell that, without the expression of a dancer, is empty and meaningless. This understanding of ballet as more than the choreography and as including the performance of the choreography itself dramatically shifts the usual focus on the choreographer or the critic sitting in the audience as the arbiter of the ballet's meaning.

The embodiment of living tradition is the reason so many critical reviews focus on the dancer who performs the Aurora role. If we are to be fair in analyzing the ballet, perhaps our definition of a good performance needs to focus more on the physical interpretation of the dancers involved. Is Aurora a good performer (according to the ideologies embedded in the genre in which she performs)? Does she draw us into her dancing, allowing us to experience the joy of classical ballet?

In a review of the 1987 ABT production of *Beauty*, performed in 1998, the critic Jennifer Dunning focused on the dancing of Aurora. Using a critical approach that focused on the power of the ballerina's interpretive skill, she opened her review by stating, "*The Sleeping Beauty*, set to one of Tchaikovsky's most sumptuous scores, is a standard against which performers may be measured. It is also a ballet that is capable of a surprising number of interpretations, as American Ballet Theatre suggested in well-danced performances."[112] She then went on to describe one dancer's Aurora as "unusually shy . . . dancing with a dreaming softness and delicacy"; another dancer's as "shifting between grandeur and melting love"; and a third dancer's as "endearingly coltish, and spunky."[113] This kind of judgment is focused less on authenticity than on the quality, shading, and gradations of performance. By looking at the dancing that happens on the stage, and not at questions such as whether the choreography replicates or authenticates the original Petipa choreography, Dunning's review clues her readers in to the physical experience of both dancing and watching *The Sleeping Beauty*. Dunning's focus prioritizes the interpretive power of dancers, as well as the audience's affective experience. In doing so, it more fully determines the ways in which performance constructs an evocative ritual in which dancers and audiences together re-create the classical.

6.

The Power of Dance Technique
and the Agency of the Ballerina

Dancing Women: How Corporeal Strength, Presence, and Creativity Challenge the Male Gaze

The previous chapters of this book have examined a specific historiography focused on the geographic location of Philadelphia and the chronological location of the twentieth century. The significance of dancers' agency and their embodiment of ballet's mid-century legacy, as materialized in Philadelphia and across the country, is even more important now as the Pennsylvania Ballet again undergoes a tremendous turnover of artistic leadership. However, this chapter now moves into a more theoretical realm of interdisciplinary critical and philosophical inquiry in order to frame, or focus, the detailed history archived in previous chapters. Although the material covered in this chapter is indeed chronologically prior to the work already discussed, I use it here in a conclusory fashion to frame how the work of the various dancing sleeping beauties covered throughout this book in fact differs from that of their counterparts in the realms of the literary and visual arts. Thus, I go back to the inspiration for these dance productions in the 1930s, 1960s, and 1990s to draw out the ways in which the dancing body in ballet has always had different capabilities for agency and empowerment because of the very presence of the live woman included in, and instrumental in, the communication of meaning in dance performance. Therefore, although I briefly discussed the premiere of *The Sleeping Beauty*, I now posit how that 1890 ballet creates opportunities and leaves room for women to establish and express their own presence, and how the ballet, unlike writing and painting from the same time period reflective of similar cultural conservatism, offers women a way in which to speak with power and force through the strength of their physical practice. As stated earlier, ballet is often condemned by feminist critics as a gendered throwback and thus not important to study (and, perhaps, as a conservative and culturally reprehensible art form that should no longer be taught and performed). Some authors have even argued that the genre is no longer relevant to contemporary culture and is, in fact, a dying art form. To counter this, I argue that it is much easier to be feminist and forward-looking when one is creating a new genre. However, classic ballets retain their power. They do not just go away; they are perpetuated because in many cases the technique itself is appealing and because classics are culturally familiar. The feminist question within ballet, and any classical tradition, shifts to this one: Are there spaces for difference and resistance? When two women in ballet's history wanted to establish their companies as legitimate front-runners within a culturally elite paradigm, they went back to the classic tradition to assert their authenticity and acceptability. From a feminist reading, what did they accomplish? Within the ballet tradition, was there space for women such as Catherine Littlefield and Barbara Weisberger? And more broadly, are there ways to understand the strength and training of ballerinas in classical dance not as a gender throwback but as a space of vision and women's artistic creativity?

Reawakening *The Sleeping Beauty* and the Power of the Dancing Body

"The Sleeping Beauty" is a timeless story—sometimes told; sometimes read; sometimes danced, acted, painted, or drawn—about the power of emergent adolescent women's sexuality. It has captured, and continues to capture, the imaginations of people across hundreds of geographical and historical locations. Stories often have been used to carry didactic messages to their listeners, and the sleeping beauty story has done this labor in many contexts. The universal interest in the tale and its telling, as well as the story's longevity, are testaments to the compelling and archetypal truths of the story's theme, narrative, and characters, for the protagonist (whose name changes from story to story) is a symbolic figure on a journey of transformation. She grows from child to woman and must face her own weaknesses as well as external danger and violence along the way. The central character, despite her transformation, often has been painted (literally and figuratively) as passive, objectified, or dangerously heedless.

The genre of dance, however, offers both performers and audience members a unique representation of the sleeping beauty tale in its physical enactment and embodied sense making. Marius Petipa's 1890 choreography, at the root of the productions examined in this book, allows Aurora to resist and challenge the disciplinary function of the literary tale from which the ballet's libretto was drawn through her highly physical and athletic performance onstage.

The productions produced and performed by women in Philadelphia between 1937 and 2002 also offer strikingly complex representations of the Aurora character. They stand in stark contrast to many of the written and painted versions of the tale that were created to enforce a cautionary or punitive message about women needing to stay in their proper place. To demonstrate this claim—an important one that shifts the view from women's passivity to their dancerly agency—I turn to the literary tale from which the 1890 ballet was drawn, as well as to a series of paintings featuring the sleeping beauty story created the same year the ballet premiered (1890). In doing so, I am able to contextualize and contrast the ballets and the Auroras explored throughout this book with these other literary and visual interpretations. This highlights the agency and power of the dancing body onstage and demonstrates how dancers give active voice to their characters in the process of creation and in performance.

Many Tales, One Story

Charles Perrault wrote *La Belle au bois dormant* in 1696.[1] It drew from the themes of tales from Ovid, Epimenides, Giambattista Basile, and *Perceforest*.[2] *La Belle* is the source from which Petipa and his collaborators drew the libretto for the 1890 ballet. Perrault was a writer who was part of a flourishing community of artists in the court of King Louis XIV, who was also known as the Sun King. At sixty-three, after a career writing commentary on politics, science, and the creative arts, Perrault began writing collections of moralistic legends in verse.[3] His most famous book was *The Tales of Mother*

Goose, composed in 1697. "The Sleeping Beauty" was part of that collection and was also published separately the previous year in the French journal *Mercure Galant*. The complete collection of *Histoires ou contes du temps passé* was published in 1697. This collection of fairy tales contained eight prose tales that each end with a rhymed moral, including "The Sleeping Beauty."[4]

Perrault collected these tales orally from working-class women who were often illiterate. Perrault's seventeenth-century values and viewpoints, and his intention to entertain and educate the Sun King's royal court transformed these stories. Although the lives of the court members were very different from those of the peasants among whom the tales originated, the stories exerted powerful impressions on their listeners.[5] Jack Zipes has discussed this transformation of the fairy tale genre, referring to it as "an institutionalized symbolic discourse on the civilizing process."[6] Fairy tales, then, both entertained their listeners and subtly persuaded them to conform to dominant social codes.

Toward the end of the seventeenth century, children—especially of the upper classes—became recognized as a category apart from adults. Along with the notion of *civilité*, or good manners, this new understanding of children as individuals with immortal souls that needed to be shaped and educated fostered the blossoming of didactic storytelling in the form of fairy tales.[7] The formalization of dance training was also part of this push toward civilizing children through an ideological education process. In addition to this burgeoning concept of childhood, the seventeenth-century French court saw the changing of many old behaviors and customs. Feudal manners were now seen as savage, and natural behavior was seen as uncivilized and barbaric. King Louis XIV and the French court idealized the *homme civilité* and behaved with intricate social manners, wore wigs and face powder, and spoke in a baroque style.[8] The tales that emerged from this context appealed to the newly cultured children of the court (as well as their socially conscious parents), and the literary fairy tales of Perrault, as well as of the women of *salon* culture, became useful vehicles for promulgating court culture and its ideology. The stories encouraged the maintenance of the status quo through their civilizing and disciplinary form and content, as well as their pro-monarchy political bent.

Perrault was an astute man and a highly perceptive member of Louis XIV's court. One of his finest works was a piece of prose poetry, *Le Parnasse poussé à bout*, a piece of political propaganda that extols the virtues of the war France won against the Spanish Netherlands in 1668.[9] When he turned to the writing of children's literature, Perrault maintained his political and dogmatic intent. His fairy tales were constructed to disseminate notions that would regulate children's behavior and homogenize their values. He had started by indoctrinating his own children into this educational movement.

Critics have seen Perrault's story of the sleeping beauty as representing many things: the struggle between good and evil, the vanquishing of death by life, the ultimate invigorating power of true love, the perennial passing of the seasons from winter to spring, the constant cycle of social and spiritual renewal, and the coming of age of a young woman.[10] The tale opens quickly with the lines, "Once upon a time, there lived a king and a queen who were bitterly unhappy because they did not have any children. They visited all the clinics, all the specialists, made holy vows, went on pilgrimages and said their prayers regularly but with so little success that when, at long last, the queen finally did conceive and, in due course, gave birth to a daughter, they were both wild with joy."[11]

Seven fairy godmothers are invited to the baby's baptism. After the ceremony, they return to the palace, where they are invited to a banquet in honor of the princess. During the feast, each of the fairies bestows a gift on baby: They ordain that she will have beauty, a sweet disposition, and grace, along with skills in dancing, singing, and playing music. Magnificent place settings are laid out for each of the fairies for their celebratory meal. But as the banquet begins, an old fairy enters the hall, greatly angered that she has not been invited to the feast. Although the king orders a place set for her at the table, he neglects to ensure that the setting is made of gold and jewels. Believing she has been slighted intentionally, the old fairy mutters threats under her breath.

A young fairy who hears the threats hides behind a tapestry in case she needs to counteract "any evil which the old fairy might do."[12] That is when the old fairy curses the princess: She will prick her finger on the spindle of a spinning wheel and die. The young fairy then emerges from her hiding place and reassures the court that the princess will not die; instead, she will fall into a deep sleep for one hundred years, and a king's son will come and meet her when she awakens. After hearing the curses and spells, the king bans the use of spinning wheels by all people in the kingdom.

Sixteen years later, despite the king's edict, the princess meets her fate. Wandering through the castle, she sees an old serving woman spinning alone in a small room at the top of the castle tower. The princess is curious about what the old woman is doing. Then, according to Perrault's text, "partly because she was too hasty, partly because she was a little heedless, but also because the fairy decree had ordained it, no sooner had she seized the spindle than she pricked her hand and fell down in a swoon."[13]

No matter what is tried, no one can revive the princess. Then the king remembers the fairy's prophecy and orders that no one disturb the princess. He sets up an apartment for her, where she is arranged on a bed of gold and silver. The good fairy rushes to the castle, where she puts everyone (except the king and queen) to sleep so the princess will not be alone when she wakes up a hundred years later. Everything in the castle subsides into slumber, including the fires; the cooking food; the guards, porters, and footmen; and even Aurora's pet dog, Puff.[14] An impenetrable forest of trees with brambles and thorns grows up around the castle.

After one hundred years' time, a king's son decides to enter the castle, for he has heard stories about a beautiful princess asleep inside. As he approaches, the trees separate and make a path for him to enter. The prince walks through the castle. He passes sleeping people everywhere and finally sees the princess, who is reclining on her bed with the curtains drawn back. He kneels beside her to see her more clearly when the moment of her disenchantment arrives. She wakes up, sees him, and asks, "Is it you, dear prince? You have been long in coming!"[15] The prince declares his love for the princess and the two are quickly married in the castle's chapel. The next morning, however, the prince returns to the city and leaves his bride at her castle in the forest.

The prince keeps his bride secret for two years, during which time she gives birth to two children, a girl named Dawn and a boy named Day. The prince cannot tell his mother about his bride and children, for he is afraid of his mother's cannibalistic nature. Perrault tells the reader, "It was whispered at court that she had ogreish instincts, and that when little children were near her she had the greatest difficulty in the world to keep herself from pouncing on them."[16] After two years, however, the king dies, and the prince ascends the throne. He makes a public announcement of his marriage and brings the princess, Dawn, and Day to the capital city.

Soon after this, the newly ascended king goes off to war. He leaves his mother in charge as regent, and she promptly sends the princess, Dawn, and Day to her country home, where she plans to eat them. She tells the cook that she first desires to eat her granddaughter, Dawn (translated from the French, Aurore), "with a piquant sauce."[17] The cook is unable to kill the adorable child, however, and instead hides her in the servants' quarters in the basement and serves the ogress a dinner of lamb. The queen then asks to eat Day and the princess, so the two of them go into hiding. Later, as the queen mother wanders through her castle, she hears Day crying in his basement hiding place.

Enraged that she has been tricked, the queen mother orders that a huge vat full of "vipers, toads, snakes and serpents of every kind" be brought to the middle of the courtyard. She plans to toss the princess, Dawn, and Day, along with the cook and his wife, into the vat. Before they are to be thrown in, however, the king arrives home, demanding to know the meaning of the horrible scene. The queen mother, frustrated and angry about the situation she has created, throws herself headlong into the pot and is instantly devoured by the animals inside. Although the king is sorry his mother has died in such a gruesome fashion, he and his family live happily ever after.[18]

The Disciplinary Function of the Story

By celebrating the values and manner of the French court, the world portrayed in *The Sleeping Beauty* "served as an imaginative model as well as a marker of royal behavior and hierarchical values," according to Sally Banes, "enacting the triumph of the realm, and reproducing and reinforcing in a charmed arena values that in reality were constantly questioned and under threat."[19] During his long reign (1643–1715), King Louis XIV acted as a divinely ordained absolute monarch. He had grandiose plans for France—and, in fact, for all of Europe—that included a comprehensive vision of culture and civilization, as well as an expansionist foreign policy.[20] Along with philosophers and literary figures such as René Descartes, Blaise Pascal, Pierre Corneille, Jean Racine, Jean-Baptiste Poquelin (known by his stage name, Molière), Jean de La Fontaine, Jean-Baptiste Drouard de Bousset, and many others, Perrault produced work that supported these political efforts as it entertained and educated the large and powerful group of royal courtiers who composed the monarch's governmental apparatus.

The political purpose and outlook of these stories is clear on close examination of *La Belle au bois dormant.* Referred to as *l'école des rois* (the school of kings) by an eighteenth-century French compiler,[21] these stories were intended to guide individuals in power with lessons about morality, truth, and virtue. In the sleeping beauty story, as well as in many of Perrault's other tales, the government is monarchical—led by a strong autocrat who is dependent on the help of an important adviser or consultant.[22] In Perrault's story, the sleeping beauty character never receives a name other than "the princess." (It is only in later revisions of the tale—the Petipa ballet and the Walt Disney film— that she receives the name Aurora.). She is destined for a life of power; from the moment of her royal birth until her marriage to a future king, her destiny reflects the realities of those courtiers born into the power system in both seventeenth-century France and nineteenth-century Russia. Her right (and the rights of her father and husband) to rule is never questioned. The citizens of the realm easily accept the king's edict, "forbidding all persons, under pain of death, to use a spinning wheel or keep a spindle in the house."[23]

Susan Stewart has pointed out that the "falsely naïve" and folksy narrative voice in Perrault's tales reflects his attempts to transcend the limits of historical circumstance by making the lessons implied in the story seem natural, inevitable, and appropriate.[24] She claims that such tales are "reproduced as antique at moments in need of ideological closure: [the story's] rhetorical form lends itself to didacticism and defined meaning, the sublimation of occasion to rule."[25] This can be seen as related to a Foucauldian understanding of the prison state, as part of a creeping control over bodies and thinking that was part of the Enlightenment and its discursive power that systematically developed institutions that enforced social control in deploying the all-encompassing reach of the panopticon.

Perrault's tale is a depiction of order and beauty that is thickly laced with imperialist ideology. Although it represents a community putatively at peace, it speaks to the feelings of a community in the midst of violence, change, and terror. The Russian artists who created *The Sleeping Beauty* ballet saw baroque France as a place of "civilization"—and as a civilization they wanted to emulate. It was a long-standing tradition in Russia to import French culture and cultural technology. To prove how "enlightened" they were to the rest of the world, Russians adopted European habits, as when Peter the Great issued his beard tax to discourage Russians from traditional grooming practices and to steer them toward practices he saw as more up to date and European.[26]

The French Enlightenment sensibilities that emerged from Versailles placed a high value on depictions of a stable and continuous court. Hierarchy, personal politics, and proper decorum were considered supremely important under the Sun King's reign.[27] This is why dance and the physical gestures of courtly decorum were practiced regularly and with unwavering solemnity at Versailles. For example, nobody turned his or her back to a courtier of higher rank, and dancers always performed *reverence* (a bow or curtsy) to the highest-ranking courtier (or *la présence*) in the room before and after performance. Similarly, the imperial culture of late nineteenth-century Russia imagined Versailles as a model of triumphant and successful aristocracy. When Marius Petipa, Ivan Veselovsky, and Pyotr Tchaikovsky used Perrault's seventeenth-century tale as inspiration for their ballet, they modeled their stage designs on their idealized visions of the court society in which Perrault lived. In doing so, they attempted to capture a utopian society of stability, order, safety, and comfort. In *The Sleeping Beauty*, good wins over evil, aristocracy is preserved, and the audience is assured of life's continuity. The ballet articulates the desires of a culture undergoing changes from which it knows it will never return, a culture that wants to reach back to an idealized and imaginary past. The princess's role in this tale is as a vehicle allowing the prince to come into his own as a powerful ruler. In fact, the princess's ability to be an active participant in the unfolding events of the story is never even examined by Perrault.

The tale has been rendered visually, as well, with bridges built among the traditions of dance, storytelling, and art and between visual iconography and cultural symbols. The very same year Petipa choreographed *The Sleeping Beauty* in Russia, the famous Pre-Raphaelite painter Edward Burne-Jones created a series of paintings entitled *The Legend of Briar Rose*. (The Little Briar-Rose is also the princess's name in the Grimm Brothers' 1812 publication of the story.) The paintings, now well known and widely seen, were first shown in 1890 at Agnew's Gallery in London. Wildly popular with Victorians of the time, the series consists of four images, each one six feet long and three and a half feet high.[28] Today, the paintings are in the music room of the stately British home Buscot Park, where Burne-Jones hung them. They create a continuous frieze around the walls so that visitors feel as if they have actually stepped into the wood and are "surrounded by the spellbound sleepers of [Burne-Jones's] imagination."[29]

Although, like the ballet, they were inspired by Perrault's fairy tale,[30] the paintings display no narrative progression, for their theme is not the development of action over time. Rather, in the paintings Burne-Jones emphasizes the timelessness of the imagery and the pervading languor and passivity of the sleeping briar wood. Each image shows another aspect of the lassitude and immobility of these characters as they are trapped within their hundred-year slumber. Among *The Briar Wood*, *The Council Chamber*, *The Garden Court*, and *The Rose Bower*, each displays another scene inhabited by catatonic figures who have collapsed into deathlike poses beneath a canopy of thick, overgrown briars.[31]

In representing this story, Burne-Jones consciously refused to depict the moment of Aurora's awakening. This marks a large difference between the paintings, Perrault's tale, and choreographed versions of the story in which Aurora awakens. In the Perrault tale (drawn from earlier sources, such as *Perceforest* [1528] and Giambattista Basile's "Sun, Moon, and Talia" [also known as *Il Pentamerone* (1636)]), and in the danced versions of the story, the moment of reanimation and the resumption of history are pivotal—a moment that is not only fundamental to the unfolding of the narrative plot of the story but also the crux of the story's theme. In Petipa's ballet and in Perrault's tale, the audience or reader experiences a story about transformation and maturation, about forgiveness and redemption.

In Burne-Jones's visual representation of the tale, however, viewers are consciously prevented from experiencing this resumption of activity and vitality. The figures remain sleeping and inert.

Burne-Jones himself commented on his refusal to undo the bewitchment of the court. In his *Memorials*, he wrote, "I want to stop with the Princess asleep and tell no more, to leave all the afterwards to the invention and imagination of people, and tell them no more."[32] What does this refusal to represent the forward-moving moment of the story say about these images and their appeal? Among Victorian painters, the theme of the sleeping/dead woman was quite popular. Burne-Jones's famous *The Legend of Briar Rose* series therefore was not an anomaly in terms of its thematic content. Although many artists did not choose to focus on mythological or fairy tale characters, as Burne-Jones did, it was quite fashionable among the Pre-Raphaelites to paint sleeping, ill, and wan women in a state of deathlike catatonia.[33] Frederic Leighton's masterpiece *Flaming June*, for example, depicts a voluptuous woman swathed in transparent orange draperies and asleep on a bench. She cradles her head in her arms and tucks her legs around her as her hair flows freely over her shoulders and down her back. Leighton painted this theme more than once. His paintings *Summer Slumber, Summer Moon, Ariadne, Lachrymae,* and *Cymon and Iphigenia* also depict sleeping women caught totally unaware of the voyeuristic gaze of the viewer.[34] In all of these paintings, sleep and death are intertwined, leading some art historians to argue that for Leighton, sleep imagery was a representation of death.

Leighton and Burne-Jones created their images of sleeping women during a time in which white women of the middle class increasingly were drawn into a "cult of invalidism," this new movement coming on the heels of, and as a backlash to, Britain's early feminist movement, which had promoted quite the opposite of sleeping, passive women.[35] In Europe and North American as the end of the century wore on, a proper woman was envisioned as helpless, weak, and ill. In *Woman in America* (1873), Abba Goold Woolson wrote about American women, "With us, to be ladylike is to be lifeless, inane and dawdling. Since people who are ill must necessarily possess these qualities of manner, from a lack of vital energy and spirits, it follows that they are the ones studiously copied as models of female attractiveness."[36] Therefore, it is not surprising that images of ill and dying women were quite popular with late nineteenth-century artists. Leopoldo Romañach's *The Convalescent*, Carl Larsson's *The Invalid*, Alfred Philippe Roll's *The Sick Woman*, and Giovanni Segantini's *A Rose Leaf* show the extent to which artists promoted and fetishized feminine frailty. Once we understand this glamorization of feminine weakness and illness, it is not a far leap to understand Victorian artists' subsequent glorification of women's catatonia, with a favorite image encapsulating this state of feminine cataplexy illustrated by the many artists who chose the character of Ophelia as subject.[37]

It was not only images of sick women that were popular. In *Idols of Perversity*, the art historian Bram Dijkstra devotes an entire chapter, titled "Dead Ladies and the Fetish of Sleep," to the often gruesome late nineteenth-century depictions of women that were tinged with aspects of necrophilia. These depictions included James Bertrand's *Virginia*, Joseph Noel Paton's *The Dead Lady*, Romaine Brooks's *Dead Woman*, Hermann Moest's *The Fate of Beauty*, Paul-Albert Besnard's *The Dead Woman*, John Collier's *The Death of Albine*, Frances MacDonald's *The Sleeping Princess*, and Madeleine Lemaire's *Sleep*.[38] Dijkstra comments on the frequent slippage between representations of sleep and death, suggesting that by the late nineteenth century, art lovers had come to associate a beautiful woman sleeping with a woman safely dead.[39]

These representational trends strongly reframe Burne-Jones's refusal to depict the moment of Briar Rose's awakening. Also, to return us to our consideration of Aurora and *The Sleeping Beauty*, they put into a very new context the muscular force of strong women's bodies dancing the Aurora character onstage, in 1890 and in subsequent productions of the ballet. Like many artists of his time, Burne-Jones participated in the representation of women as languorous, sleepy, exhausted, and weighted down by the materiality of her own imminent sexuality. For many European middle-class men of the late nineteenth century, there was no safer way to experience and observe a woman's sexuality than while she was passively sleeping or dead. This ambivalence toward women's sexuality is clearly demonstrated in Burne-Jones's *The Legend of Briar Rose* series. The sleeping princess represents a contained presence—one that the artist carefully controls through his refusal to allow her to be resuscitated. And unlike some other contemporary images, *The Legend of Briar Rose* series does contain a representation of a potential agent of change and vitality. The character of the prince, while not depicted as particularly active, still "stands on the threshold of the enchanted realm."[40] For Burne-Jones, the prince's arrival was a threat to the sleeping princess's awakening sexuality. While the prince's presence does imply the threat of Aurora's potential arousal, the power of that arousal is placed firmly within the dominion of the prince. A colleague and friend of Burne-Jones's, the poet Algernon Charles Swinburne, combined rose imagery with ambivalence toward female sexuality in his poem "Fragoletta":

> I dreamed of strange lips yesterday
> And cheeks wherein the ambiguous blood
> Was like a rose's—yea
> A rose's when it lay
> Within the bud. . . .
>
> I dare not kiss it, lest my lip
> Press harder than an indrawn breath,
> And all the sweet life slip
> Forth, and the sweet leaves drip,
> Bloodlike, in death.[41]

Like the speaker in this poem, the prince in Burne-Jones's paintings hesitates. In doing so, he leaves Aurora in a state of perpetual catatonia. In this sense, the theme of Burne-Jones's *Briar Rose* series is death: The immobilization and infantilization of a young girl on her way to female maturity becomes the focus of his visual tale.

The late nineteenth-century trend in visual depictions of women generally showed them to be at once objects of erotic desire and creatures of peculiar self-containment, as beings who were not really interested in—and hence, were not likely to make any demands on—the viewer's participation in their personal erotic gratification. Such images permitted the late nineteenth-century man to have his voyeuristic peek into the world of women and yet leave him with what one might term a soothing sense of "restful detumescence." These images formed the constituent elements of the late nineteenth-century artistic phenomenon of the "collapsing woman."[42]

The 1890 Ballet

The Sleeping Beauty ballet, as produced in 1890, along with the ballet's many subsequent restagings—including the productions that took place in 1937, 1965, and 1997/2002 in Philadelphia—give Aurora or the princess far more agency than do these other, debilitating and disciplinary portrayals of women's passivity, exhaustion, and death. Petipa's ballet cannot be seen as a perfectly emancipatory artistic production for women. It can be argued, however, that given this cultural history of women's immobilization and acculturation, by providing Aurora with an active, lively story and a physical choreography that embodies the characteristics of strength, power, independence, and shaded nuance, Petipa and his collaborators provided space for dancers to resist the more common representations of the sleeping beauty character. Often within feminist re/searchings of history, a space for women's resistance and the opportunity for a bit of agency and liveliness is exactly what we are looking for.

Carrie Noland defines "agency" as "the power to alter those acquired behaviors and beliefs for purposes that may be reactive (resistant) or collaborative (innovative) in kind." For Noland, this agency "depends on the role of *kinesthesia*, without which the subject would not be able to distinguish her own body from other bodies; would have no capacity for independent movement; and thus would be incapable of assuming any agency at all."[43] In other words, it is the work of the body that allows people to resist the overpowering force of acculturation described by writers such as Foucault. A comparison of written, painted, and danced versions of the sleeping beauty story also demonstrates how the physical labor of the body, with its unpredictable possibilities and immediate presence and engagement, can combat many of the coercive powers of historical determinism. Within Perrault's story and Burne-Jones's painting, there is little room for Aurora to resist the force of hegemonic ideology. Petipa's ballet, however, enacted through the physical language of classical ballet technique, offers dancers spaces for agency in their active embodiment and articulation of the roles they perform. Although the ballet perpetuates and enforces many of the notions of civility and restricted femininity inherent in the seventeenth-century tale, Aurora's growth, transformation, and maturation from girl to woman is structured within her highly athletic choreography and is the central focus of Petipa's 1890 version of *The Sleeping Beauty* as established earlier as the model upon which all later productions would emerge. The ballet uses the highly physical and impressively virtuosic syntax of movement to represent a strong woman dancing progressively more difficult and intricate choreography that celebrates her expanding emotional and physical prowess. The embodied nature of this representation gives the Aurora character a powerful presence within the story that changes the meaning of the danced tale.

Description of the 1890 Premiere

The premiere of *The Sleeping Beauty* ballet took place on January 15, 1890, in Saint Petersburg, Russia, at the Maryinsky Theater. Tchaikovsky composed the famous score that indicates the grandiosity and splendor of the ballet. Audiences were stunned and captivated by the magnificence of the production, which as discussed earlier, quickly established itself as the standard by which all later ballets would—in some way—be judged.[44] In the ballet, the princess Aurora is plunged into a deep sleep on her sixteenth birthday because of a curse by an evil witch. While she sleeps, her palace is overgrown with weeds and brambles, and her fate seems to be to remain forever frozen in time. She is saved, however, by the kiss of Prince Désiré. The union of Aurora and Désiré guarantees their kingdom safety and prosperity.[45] The opposing forces of light and dark, good and evil, and order and chaos form a thematic core for the ballet. They also reflect the cultural environment in which Petipa lived and worked.

Collaborators and Context

The ballet *The Sleeping Beauty* was conceived by Ivan Veselovsky, the director of the Imperial Theaters of the Russian Ballet from 1881 to 1889. He wrote the scenario, designed the costumes, commissioned the score from Tchaikovsky, and worked closely with Petipa on the choreography. He wanted to create a court ballet like those produced by King Louis XIV in his opulent Court of Versailles, reflecting the desire of the Russian royal court to emulate the absolutist state of the French Sun King.[46]

The ballet did manage to evoke the Golden Age of both France and the Russian aristocracy. At the start of the nineteenth century, the Russian aristocracy began to see cracks form in the impenetrable power of its grand tsarist façade. Political unrest was spreading throughout the country, and the elite upper classes began to see their potential downfall.[47] Perhaps because of this new sense of insecurity, members of the royal family and others of the royal elite desired theatrical productions that would quell these fears—that is, a theater that projected an image of a strong monarchy resplendent in both prosperity and culture. For these reasons, the court and culture of Louis XIV was the perfect source for Petipa's new ballet. Again I use the words of Sally Banes to highlight the didactic purpose of both Perrault's tale and Petipa's ballet. In celebrating the values and manner of the French court, the milieu—or the fantasy world—depicted onstage in *The Sleeping Beauty*, the ballet's collaborators created an onstage world that "served as an imaginative model as well as a marker of royal behavior and hierarchical values, enacting the triumph of the realm, and reproducing and reinforcing in a charmed arena values that in reality were constantly questioned and under threat."[48]

The ballet's third act fully evokes a world of childhood fantasy created by Petipa's vision. It begins with the pageantry of a processional entrance by many costumed characters, all of whom are from seventeenth-century French fairy tales, who arrive at court to celebrate the wedding of Aurora and Désiré. Tom Thumb and his brothers, Little Red Riding Hood and the Wolf, Puss and Boots and the White Kitten, Princess Florine and her Bluebird, and others march through the palace court and greet the betrothed royal couple. After a series of dances by these fairy tale characters and by more fairies representing prosperity (Silver, Gold, Sapphire, and Diamond), the royal couple dances the apotheosis of the ballet, their wedding pas de deux. This dance is classicism at its apex. Petipa's choreography resolves both Tchaikovsky's score and the themes of the ballet, creating a masterpiece of classical danse d'école; it is a superb expression of Petipa's vision.[49]

The fantastic aspect of the fairy tale ballet is precisely what interested Tchaikovsky in *Beauty*. He wanted to test himself in a fantastical musical drama. His friend Herman Laroche said that "in that magical world there was no room for words[;] it was pure fairy tale expressed by pantomime and dance. . . . Tchaikovsky could not stand realism in ballet."[50] Léon Bakst, an important contributor to the heir of Russian classical ballet, the Ballets Russes, expressed the same perspective when he recalled watching a performance of *Beauty*: "I lived in a magical dream for three hours, intoxicated by fairies and princesses, by splendid palaces dripping in gold, by the enchantment of a fairy tale."[51]

However, *Beauty* not only reflects the desires of Russian aristocrats to escape the political and cultural instability of the prerevolutionary world. The ballet is also the fullest expression of Petipa's artistic and ideological vision and therefore reflects the artistic and theatrical style valued by the imperial system in which he worked. Petipa's masterpiece is connected to his early dance training as well as to the autocratic world in which he produced art. It is the acme of Petipa's career; the ultimate realization of the majestic aesthetic that defined Russian ballet throughout his tenure as choreographer at the Imperial Theaters and, in many ways, continues to define classical ballet at large.

Themes also emerge from the work choreographically and technically, especially, as I have already referenced Fyodor Lopukhov noting, the liberation from darkness and stagnation to freedom and rebirth. The music of Tchaikovsky, like the en dehors principle of Petipa's dance, is built on openness. It is major, open, and melodic. In choreography, music, and narrative, therefore, each section builds to a calm and complete resolution. This openness and liberation is danced by the figure of Aurora. It is precisely a female character that represents the desired new.

Aurora's role is supremely important because, unlike in Romantic ballets and even many of Petipa's other classical works, in *The Sleeping Beauty* there is very little pantomime. Some critics have argued that *Beauty*, in all of its purity of technique and classicism, is about the history of ballet itself.[52] By relying on the choreographic themes of tendu devant (representing baroque dance), attitude derrière (representing Romantic ballet), and first arabesque (representing the danse d'école of Petipa), the ballet displays a panorama of perpetual sleep and rebirth of classical ballet as an art form.[53] Although scholars and audiences today see *Beauty* as a perennial favorite of classical ballet, the critics of the 1890s did not see the ballet as a success. In fact, many critics felt it lacked narrative, choreographic interest, and drive. To many, its calm and resolved themes and choreography felt as if they lacked drama. As one writer commented on the ballet, "It is a sweet and poetic tale, but has little movement and is too simple. The plot is pale and watery for the stage. The ballet has no intrigue, drama or action and leads on to special effects and fairy scenes. The dances are distinguished neither by their originality [n]or their character and they don't provide the ballerina gratifying material."[54] This type of reaction to the ballet was not uncommon. Many other reviewers held similar opinions. Another Russian critic wrote about the famous premiere, "The plot is not very poetic, banal and unworthy of the Petersburg stage; the production is nothing more than a museum of props."[55] But despite these condemnations, the ballet did not go away. It stayed in the memory of many audience members and artists and, in fact, was the inspiration for Diaghilev and his followers, later known as Mir Iskusstva (World of Art), to create thematically unified dance productions.[56]

Aurora's Agency and the Possibility of Resistance to Women's Passivity and Death

Aurora is the central focus of Petipa's ballet. She is the protagonist, and she performs the largest portion of stage action. Over the course of the ballet's four acts, audience members grow familiar with her dancing. In a well-known image, Carlotta Brianza, the very first Aurora, stands alone, balancing en pointe on one leg.[57] Her right leg is straight and long, the arch of her foot en pointe a graceful yet powerful curve. Her left leg is bent slightly at the knee, and her left foot is softly crossed across the front of her right ankle. Her elbows are daintily bent, and her hands gently come together under her chin, fingertips pressing lightly together. She is a vision of delicacy and elegance, calmly floating on balance, caught in a perpetual state of independent flight. In the image, her eyes are focused directly on the camera, and they are wide open and unflinching. Her gaze is calm and elegant; it fits a woman wearing an exquisite black tutu and fantastic golden crown.[58] She is not passive; she is not waiting to be seen. Rather, she is doing the looking, and she stares directly out of the frame of the photograph, a vision of strength and elegance. She does not hide from the camera, and she is aware of her onlookers. She uses her physical strength and charm to create a regal and dignified character for the camera, and in doing so, she memorializes herself as an independent princess—something quite culturally new.

Not only in 1890 did the role of Aurora carry with it the possibility for women's independent and creative expression. Many stagings of the ballet have taken place since then, each a unique vehicle for another woman to embody the character of Aurora. Many reviews of the ballet revolve around the interpretation of the role by the leading ballerina because of the importance of the principal performer's nuance and shading of the canonical role. Because this chapter focuses on comparing written, painted, and danced versions of the story, I recount the details of the 1890 premiere. I did not see that performance, of course. However, I was able to see the 1999 reconstruction of Petipa's original work undertaken by the Maryinsky Ballet, the current instantiation of the Russian Imperial Ballet, during the company's 2002 tour.

Despite the controversy about whether an authentic reconstruction is actually possible, I have decided to reference as a valid comparison the observations and interpretations I made when I saw the 2002 performance of the 1999 reconstruction at the Kennedy Center for the Performing Arts in Washington, DC.[59] The ballerina Irma Nioradze danced the role of Aurora.[60] Nioradze, like many of the Auroras I have seen, danced the first act of the ballet beautifully. From the moment she sprang onstage at her sixteenth birthday party, she was full of energy and vitality. She entered the stage space at top speed, with an allégro ménage that covered the entire stage. Aurora was no catatonic sleeper here. In this scene, the choreography, the dancer's interpretation of the choreography, and the ballet's libretto all show Aurora to be strong, lively, and longing for independence. Four princes from distant lands have arrived at the party with a desire to win Aurora's hand in marriage. Once she has arrived onstage and settled down after her exuberant and youthful burst of joy, the king and queen urge her to choose a fiancé from the elegant, handsome, and smitten princes in attendance. Aurora, however, wants no part of marriage. "I'm still so young," she says. "Let me enjoy my freedom."[61]

Throughout the Rose Adagio, the partnered dance for Aurora and her four suitors that follows, Aurora displays her strength and independence, as well as her agility and grace. The most recognizable moment in the Rose Adagio is the promenade en attitude derrière that Aurora performs with each prince. She gently steps to pointe on her long, straight right leg, lifting her left leg in attitude derrière. When a prince offers his hand to the princess, she delicately offers her right hand, palm up, in return. She gently places her hand on his and lifts her left arm above her head, with the long slender curve of her arm, rounded at the elbow and wrist, creating an elongated frame around her face. The prince then walks around her, continuing to hold her hand, slowly rotating her body in a full circle.

Aurora maintains her position during the promenade en attitude through incredible physical power. Her calm regal character is a result not of passivity but of steely strength and vigor. Aurora then displays even more fortitude by releasing the prince's hand: Without support, Aurora remains suspended on balance while one man steps away from her and another approaches. The moment is thrilling, as the audience watches Aurora—at center stage—defy the forces of gravity and momentum. They see her assert her power, independence, and control. She sends her gaze directly out to the audience, dazzling all with her supreme confidence and joy at her physical feat. She surveys the court around her with an elegant, joyful smile and her confident gaze. She then turns to look at the approaching prince, and when *she* is ready, she takes his hand, and he graciously accepts the honor of her gesture. It is Aurora who grants the princes the privilege of dancing with so special a creature—not the princes who display Aurora as a passive object for the consumption of a lascivious and voyeuristic audience.

This difference between contemporary visual art and the narrative of the fairy tale with the choreography of what is being danced onstage cannot be underestimated. In the Rose Adagio, princes who want to marry Aurora are courting her. Her parents are ready to see her married and are offering her to princes who are seeking a wife. The physical text, however, is about Aurora's strength, beauty, and independence. The princes act as a backdrop for Aurora's beauty and force, and they manage to enhance her beauty and power by occasionally offering a hand to support her or take a rose from her. Their moments of support also intensify the true focus of the choreographic piece: Aurora's balance, stability, and autonomy. The most dramatic and famous movements are found at those moments in which Aurora is unsupported. Her spine is the axis around which the ballet rotates. When one mentions the Rose Adagio, what comes to mind immediately is the moment when Aurora, at center stage, performs her series of promenades en attitude derrière and, while balancing, extends her arms and legs in beautiful, unsupported allongé. She is the center of the court and the center of the stage, a strong and balanced woman. Her technique is concerned with a strong core and a calm, progressive, and open body that negotiates the challenges of the choreography with muscular strength, aplomb, and coordination. What I experienced as an audience member viewing the Kirov's performance, as well as what I experienced as a dancer who has performed and coached the work, is Aurora's centrality, her strength, her self-reliance, and her steely composure.

CONCLUSION/CURTAIN CALL

The Sleeping Beauty works so beautifully as a case study of American classical ballet because of its canonical status and importance in the field and because it provides a metaphorical window through which to view the emergence of the balletic genre in the United States throughout the twentieth century. Through its chapters and reviews of female ballet producers, American premieres, and ballerinas' perspectives, this book has explored four major themes.

1. It has pointed to the historical presence of female producers within the world of ballet and their particular activity in producing the first and second U.S. productions of *The Sleeping Beauty*, shifting the usual sense that men have been the primary leaders of ballet.

2. It has demanded that dance scholars' perspectives accommodate dancers' point of view, because taking dancers' thoughts seriously provides new understandings about how we can think about continuity, authenticity, tradition, and change in a ballet.

3. It argues that taking a diachronic view of dance history dismantles the current linear narrative that regards dance history as flowing from one important site directly to an-

other, rather than envisioning dance history as a concurrent web of activity in which multiple nodes of equally significant action occur simultaneously. Philadelphia is just one of many places where ballet creativity happens, and like many other places in the web, it both takes from and gives to the center.

4. It suggests shifting the current discourse of dance studies within the academy to allow for more acceptance of ballet dancers' embodied knowledge, despite their frequent lack of postsecondary education.

I have expanded on these points, addressing further issues regarding the agency of ballerinas. This shift in discourse will influence dance teaching both outside and within the academy. It would diversify modern dance's current domination of the academic field by embracing the valuable assets embedded in ballet training and other codified and structured traditional dance techniques. This would also create a new critical space that could account for the living breathing-ness of all dancing bodies, a topic of interest to everyone engaged in aspects of feminist and cultural studies and critical theory. It is also a topic about which dance studies has a lot to say, as it is more connected with the actual body than other disciplines. The body is dance studies' contribution, its singular expertise that is not borrowed from other disciplines.

The experience of learning, practicing, and performing transforms the identity of the many female performers of ballet, making them literate in the syntax of classical balletic vocabulary and immersing them within the historical and cultural world of the tradition. This is not purely a process of subordination; it is a process of transformation. Transformation (for both the dancer and the audience) is the end goal of ballet training, and this book makes concrete how dancers have used, and continue to use, creative power, physical strength, and transformative potential in their work in the studio and on the stage.

I use the idea of agency as defined by Laura Ahearn—that is, a "socio-culturally mediated capacity to act."[1] How women exercise this capacity within the confines of the strict discipline of classical ballet is a profound example of how agency is "something individuals exercise within existing cultural confines through a process of internalizing cultural norms and images."[2] Recent research has urged scholars to move beyond a conceptualization of agency as more complex than a dualistic battle between social pressure and free will. In addition, reconceptions of agency move beyond an understanding of its only possibility as through acts of resistance to a hegemonic discourse. In keeping with the work of writers such as Saba Mahmood, who writes about the agency of Islamic women, and Patricia Gagne and others who have written about women who elect to undergo cosmetic surgery,[3] I believe that ballet dancers demonstrate a "modalit[y] of agency whose meaning and effect are not captured within the logic of subversion and resignification" and that "taking up the idea of agency at this level of individual consciousness does not require, and in fact works against, a notion of agency as necessarily resistant."[4] It is in this regard that *The Sleeping Beauty* works as an important example of how women can operate creatively, finding spaces for action and expression within confining disciplinary frameworks. As dancers find ways to understand and express the roles of the classical canon, embodying these roles through physical practice, they have also stretched and evolved the balletic tradition itself.

Writing about the pervasive and persistent presence of feminine beauty in children's fairy tales, Lori Baker Sperry and Liz Grauerholz noted that "the institution of gender relies in part . . . on gender imagery—"the cultural representations of gender and embodiments of gender in symbolic languages and artistic productions that reproduce legitimate gender statuses."[5] This book has demonstrated how *The Sleeping Beauty*, which emerged from the canon of Marius Petipa and Pyotr Ilyich Tchaikovsky's work in Saint Petersburg during the late nineteenth century, stages gendered representations that both perpetuate and challenge traditional constructions of femininity. Although certain dominant values are enforced in the playing out of the fairy tale narrative at the heart of the ballet, *Beauty* is also an opportunity for women to show their creativity and athleticism and to articulate an empowered expression of agency.

Paula Kelso has written, "All of ballet looks the same, with cookie cut-out dancers expressing themselves in the same way to the same music. There is no individual creativity to be explored here, only the creativity of the director is seen. The director's feelings are then described to the dancer, and the dancer's job is to express that feeling to the audience."[6] Claims such as this one do not hold water when we look at the history of *The Sleeping Beauty* in the United States between 1937 and 2002. Women are producing and directing both ballet companies and important restagings of canonical work. In addition, when focusing on the individual interpretations of each dancer in performance and how her particular idiosyncrasies and physical strengths shade the meaning of the work, we find a broad range of expressions. In my work as a dancer, teacher, and coach—and as a researcher speaking with dancers about their lived experiences in performance—I have discovered that dancers are indeed expressing their own ideas in the ways they come to inhabit canonical roles. When I turn to the work I do in the studio and think about the sensitivity and strength necessary to perform Aurora's variations, as well as the confident smiles and contented walk of a dancer who has had successful rehearsals or performances of *Beauty*, I know the role provides opportunities for women to manifest innovation and power. Time after time, dancers have told me about the absolute freedom they feel onstage, as well as the authority and transformation that they experience when performing a classical ballerina role. In inhabiting these iconic roles and bringing them to life with power and emotional maturity, ballerinas are both expressing agency and moving the balletic tradition forward.

Appendix: Plot and Stage Action

The Sleeping Beauty opens with a Prologue at the royal palace, with the christening of Aurora, the daughter of a king and queen. The master of ceremonies checks his guest list to ensure everything is in order for the coming party. The princess's six fairy godmothers attend the christening and perform dances that reflect their gifts for her: beauty and purity, grace and energy, abundance and fertility, song and eloquence, power and passion, and wisdom.[1] Throughout the ceremonies, the fairies and other courtiers pay homage to the new princess until Carabosse, an old and ugly fairy, bursts onto the scene, enraged that she was not invited to the party. She puts a curse on Aurora that she will one day prick her finger on a spindle and die. The Lilac Fairy then steps in and mitigates the curse, announcing that rather than killing Aurora, the prick of her finger will merely put her to sleep for one hundred years.[2]

Act I opens to Aurora's sixteenth birthday party, also at the royal palace. The king and queen arrive at the party, along with four foreign princes who desire to marry Aurora. A large garland waltz takes place; then the Rose Adagio begins—the famous dance in which Aurora dances with her four suitors. Aurora then dances a solo variation that reflects her vitality and joy for life. She then impulsively rushes over to an old woman holding a spindle, seizes the object, and dances with it. She pricks her finger and dances until she falls down, unconscious. The old woman reveals herself as Carabosse, and the Lilac Fairy appears, puts the entire court to sleep, and covers the court in a thicket of roses brambles, lilacs, and trees.[3]

Act II begins one hundred years after Aurora's collapse into sleep. The action starts in the forest with Prince Désiré hunting with his courtiers.

The prince and courtiers perform a series of baroque dances until the Lilac Fairy appears and shows the prince a vision of Aurora. She leads him to Aurora, and the three characters perform a trio in which Prince Désiré longs to reach Aurora, who is but a fleeting vision, blocked from his reach by the Lilac Fairy. Finally, Aurora disappears, and the prince, smitten, vows to marry Aurora. He travels with the Lilac Fairy to the castle where Aurora lies sleeping and awakens her with a kiss. The entire court comes to life, and the thicket of brambles surrounding the court magically disappears.[4]

Act III, the final act of *The Sleeping Beauty*, is a celebration of the wedding of Aurora and Prince Désiré. It is a representation of the Court of Versailles under King Louis XIV and a wonderful vehicle for displaying the technical virtuosity of the danse d'école developed by Marius Petipa during his reign at the Russian Imperial Theaters. Various fairytale creatures from Charles Perrault's many stories appear as wedding guests at the opulent royal court. The guests wish prosperity for the new couple—for example, the fairies of gold, silver, sapphire, and diamonds appear and dance a pas de quatre for Aurora and Désiré. The grande pas de deux for Aurora and Prince Désiré follows; it is a bridal dance in which both dancers display their strength, technical prowess, and grace. The ballet finishes with a large mazurka and apotheosis for the entire court and the royal couple.[5]

As the curtain lowers, the story of Aurora has unfolded, showing the audience the many stages of her life: her birth and growth into womanhood, as well as her marriage and ascendance to the throne. We are left with the idea that the couple will live "happily ever after" and that the balance between good and evil has once again been restored.

NOTES

INTRODUCTION/PROLOGUE

1. Serge Lifar, *A History of Russian Ballet from Its Origins to the Present Day*, trans. Arnold Haskell (New York: Roy, n.d.); Natalia Roslavleva, *Era of the Russian Ballet* (London: Victor Gollancz, 1966); Tim Scholl, *From Petipa to Balanchine: Classical Revival and the Modernization of Ballet* (London: Routledge, 1994); Gennady Smakov, "Marius Petipa and the Creation of 'The Sleeping Beauty,'" in *100 Years of Russian Ballet, 1830–1930*, ed. Nancy Van Norman Baer, 17–22 (New York: Nakhamkin, 1989); Solomon Volkov, *Balanchine's Tchaikovsky*, trans. Antonia W. Bouis (New York: Simon and Schuster, 1985).

2. Simone de Beauvoir, *The Second Sex* (Harmondsworth, UK: Penguin, 1972); Judith Butler, *Gender Trouble: Feminism and the Subversion of Identity* (New York: Routledge, 1993); Gayle Rubin, "The Traffic in Women," in *Toward an Anthropology of Women*, ed. R. Reiter (New York: Monthly Review Press, 1975); Monique Wittig, *The Straight Mind and Other Essays* (Hempstead, UK: Harvester Wheatsheaf, 1992).

3. Linda Nochlin, *Women, Art, and Power and Other Essays* (New York: Harper and Row, 1988), 145–178.

4. Adrienne Rich, "When We Dead Awaken: Writing as Re-Vision," in *On Lies, Secrets and Silence: Selected Prose, 1966–1978* (New York: W. W. Norton, 1995), 35.

5. Linda Alcoff. "The Problem of Speaking for Others," *Cultural Critique* 20 (Winter 1991–1992): 5–32.

6. Ibid.

7. Katerina Kolozova, *Cut of the Real: Subjectivity in Poststructuralist Philosophy* (New York: Columbia University Press, 2014), 67.

CHAPTER 1

1. Elena Daprati, Marco Iosa, and Patrick Haggard, "A Dance to the Music of Time: Aesthetically-Relevant Changes in Body Posture in Performing Art," *PLOS One* 4, no. 3 (March 2009): 2.

2. Andrea Harris, "Gendered Discourses in American Ballet at Mid-century: Ruth Page on the Periphery," *Dance Chronicle* 35, no. 1 (March 2012): 51.

3. Ibid.

4. Alastair Macaulay, "Timeless Alchemy, Even When No One Is Dancing," *New York Times*, November 28, 2010, available at http://www.nytimes.com.

5. See Stephen Kosloff, "Jenifer Ringer: Why the New York Times Thinks This Ballerina Is Too Fat," December 13, 2014, available at http://www.lemondrop.com; John Springer, "I'm Not Fat, Says Ballerina Faulted for 'Too Many Sugarplums,'" December 13, 2010, available at http://today.msnbc.msn.com.

6. See Alastair Macaulay, "Judging the Bodies in Ballet," *New York Times*, December 3, 2010, available at http://www.nytimes.com.

7. Gelsey Kirkland, *Dancing on My Grave* (New York: Doubleday, 1986); Toni Bentley, *Winter Season: A Dancer's Journal* (New York: Random House, 1982); Suzanne Farrell, *Holding On to the Air: An Autobiography* (Mandaluyong City, Philippines: Summit, 1990); Allegra Kent, *Once a Dancer: An Autobiography* (New York: St. Martin's Press, 1997).

8. Clive Barnes, "It Must Be Fun to Be Funded," *New York Times*, April 2, 1972, D14.

9. See Martha Ullman West, "What Is American Dance?" 2008, available at http://www.danceheritage.org/whatisamericandance.pdf.

10. The summer of 2012 I attended the ballet intensive at Jacob's Pillow with a conference. While there, I had the opportunity to speak with the program's director, Anna-Marie Holmes, who stated that she felt young emerging dancers must learn Petipa repertoire to become polished classical dancers.

CHAPTER 2

1. George Balanchine and Francis Mason, *Balanchine's Festival of Ballet* (London: W. H. Allen, 1978), 337.

2. This is certainly a complex statement, but it can be supported both by evidence drawn from dance scholars such as Sally Banes, Mary Clarke, Jennifer Homans, Deborah Jowitt, Tim Scholl, and Roland John Wiley and by the ballet's continued inclusion in the repertoire of not only all of the largest, but also many small, ballet companies in the world today. It has taken on a great deal of cultural capital as the finest and most definitive collaboration between Petipa and Tchaikovsky in structure, form, and style; in the dance world and popular culture, *Beauty* (along with *Swan Lake* and *The Nutcracker*) remains a symbol of classical ballet at its zenith. Part of this is due to the collaborative manner in which Petipa and Tchaikovsky worked, making the choreography and scoring of the ballet fit each other like a glove. Another significant factor is that the formula

Petipa developed for producing evening-length works perfectly fit the format of *Beauty*, and the ballet became a template for the structure and aesthetic of the majority of full-length works that followed—even when those works moved away from the classicism of Petipa, for they still were developed in relation (though oppositional) to the template developed and performed in 1890.

3. Vera Krasovskaya, "Marius Petipa and 'The Sleeping Beauty,'" *Dance Perspectives*, Spring 1972, 6.

4. Tim Scholl, *From Petipa to Balanchine: Classical Revival and the Modernization of Ballet* (New York: Routledge, 1994), 11.

5. Tim Scholl, "Anticipating a New Sleeping Beauty," *Ballet Review* 19, no. 1 (Spring 1991): 44.

6. Arsen Degen, "Then and Now at the Maryinsky Theatre," *Ballet Review* 18, no. 2 (Summer 1990): 41.

7. Krasovskaya, "Marius Petipa and 'The Sleeping Beauty,'" 6.

8. Paul Dukes, *A History of Russia: 1882–1996* (Durham, NC: Duke University Press, 1998), 145.

9. George Vernadsky, *A History of Russia* (New Haven, CT: Yale University Press, 1961), 226.

10. Solomon Volkov, *Saint Petersburg* (New York: Free Press, 1995), 246–248.

11. Lynn Garafola, *Diaghilev's Ballets Russes* (New York: Oxford University Press, 1989), 21–22.

12. What does it mean that this is the ballet chosen to legitimize ballet in Philadelphia, the "cradle of liberty"? Is it a move to establish Philadelphia—and, indeed, the United States—as a stable and ordered environment in which, originally European, the fine arts can flourish?

13. Krasovskaya, "Marius Petipa and 'The Sleeping Beauty,'" 12.

14. Ibid., 12.

15. Katia Canton, *The Fairy Tale Revisited: A Survey of the Evolution of the Tales, from Classical Literary Interpretations to Innovative Contemporary Dance-Theater Productions,* New Connections: Studies in Interdisciplinarity, vol. 9 (New York: Peter Lang, 1994, 46–48.

16. Ibid.

17. Grace Robert, "The Sleeping Beauty," in *The Borzoi Book of Ballets* (New York: Alfred A. Knopf, 1946), 280–301.

18. Alastair Macaulay, "The Big Sleep: The Sleeping Beauty at Its Centenary," *Dancing Times*, May 1990, 805.

19. Ibid., 806.

20. Sally Banes, *Dancing Women: Female Bodies on Stage* (London: Routledge, 1998), 44.

21. Tim Scholl, "Sleeping Beauty: Ballet-Féerie as Gesamtkunstwerk," in *From Petipa to Balanchine: Classical Revival and the Modernisation of Ballet* (London: Routledge, 1994), 30.

22. For more on the baroque dance, see works on French dance in the seventeenth century and eighteenth century—for example, Joellen Meglin, "Sauvages, Sex Roles and Semiotics: Representations of Native Americans in the French Ballet,

1736–1837," *Dance Chronicle* 23, no. 3 (2000): 275–320; Joellen Meglin, "Feminism or Fetishism: La Revolte des Femmes and Women's Liberation in France in the 1830s," in *Rethinking the Sylph: New Perspectives on the Romantic Ballet*, ed. Lynn Garafola (Hanover, NH: University Press of New England, 1997), 69–90; Joellen Meglin, "Le Diable Boiteux: French Society behind a Spanish Façade," *Dance Chronicle* 17, no. 3 (1994): 263–302.

23. Macaulay, "The Big Sleep," 809.

24. Fyodor Lopukhov, "Annals of 'Beauty': Choreography," *Ballet Review* 5, no. 4 (1975–1976): 24.

25. Ibid., 25.

26. Krasovskaya, "Marius Petipa and 'The Sleeping Beauty,'" 50.

27. Solomon Volkov, *Balanchine's Tchaikovsky* (New York: Simon and Shuster, 1985), 169.

28. David Vaughan, "Revivals, 1976," *Ballet Review* 6, no. 1 (1977–1978): 29.

29. Mary Clarke, "A Tale of Three Ballets: *Cinderella, The Sleeping Beauty* and *Sylvia*," *Dancing Times*, December 1993, 254.

30. Tim Scholl, "Anticipating a New 'Sleeping Beauty,'" *Ballet Review* 19, no. 1 (Spring 1991): 45.

31. Quoted in Volkov, *Balanchine's Tchaikovsky*, 171.

32. Macaulay, "The Big Sleep," 808.

33. Grace Robert, "The Sleeping Beauty," in *The Borzoi Book of Ballets* (New York: Alfred A. Knopf, 1946), 281.

34. See https://www.balletmet.org/backstage/ballet-notes/185#anchor43082

35. Wiley has dated the choreographic notation to circa 1903, in connection with a revival of *The Sleeping Beauty* at the Maryinsky Theater. Nicholas Sergeyev (1876–1951), for whom the Harvard collection is named, was an Imperial Ballet dancer who took over notation teaching duties from Alexander Gorsky (1871–1924) in 1900 and was appointed régisseur in charge of notation and rehearsals in 1903. His exodus from Russia with the Stepanov notations and his subsequent career in the West are now legendary. Are the *Sleeping Beauty* notations in Sergeyev's hand? It is likely that most of them are, but the work of other scribes appears in the notations of several of the numbers in the third act: see Doug Fullington, "The Kirov's Reconstructed Sleeping Beauty," 1999, available at http://www.for-ballet-lovers-only.com/Beauty1.html.

36. Alex C. Ewing, *Bravura? Lucia Chase and the American Ballet Theatre* (Gainesville: University Press of Florida, 2009), 27.

37. Ibid., 34.

38. Ibid., 34, 58.

39. "The Sleeping Beauty," *Philadelphia Evening Bulletin*, February 12, 1937, 22.

40. Ibid.

41. Image from the *New York Times*, February 12, 1937, clipping files, New York Public Library.

42. "Sleeping Beauty," *Time Magazine*, February 22, 1937, clipping files, New York Public Library.

43. Ibid.

44. Ewing, *Bravura?* 245.

45. Ibid.

46. Brenda Dixon Gottschild, *Joan Myers Brown and the Audacious Hope of the Black Ballerina* (New York: Palgrave Macmillan, 2012).

47. Clive Barnes, "Ballet Theatre's 'Sleeping Beauty'—A Promise Fulfilled," *New York Times*, June 27, 1976, 56.

48. Gottschild, *Joan Myers Brown*, 41–45.

49. Henry Pleasants, "Miss Littlefield Introduces a Saga of the Negro," *Philadelphia Evening Bulletin*, December 14, 1937.

CHAPTER 3

1. Russell F. Weigley, ed., *Philadelphia: A 300-Year History* (New York: W. W. Norton, 1982), 668.

2. Herbert Kupferberg, *Those Fabulous Philadelphians: The Life and Times of a Great Orchestra* (New York: Scribner's, 1969), 64.

3. "José Limon to Lead Dance," *Temple University News*, October 12, 1938, 1; "Dancer Limon Upholds Big 'Apple'; Illustrates Virility of the Dance," *Temple University News*, October 14, 1938, 4; "Mops, Brooms, Showerbaths to Appear in Dance Recital," *Temple University News*, January 16, 1939, 2; "Painting Depicts a Scene When Tyler Was Temple's Newest School," *Temple Times*, May 25, 1989, 12, all in clipping files, Special Collections Research Center, Urban Archives, Paley Library, Temple University, Philadelphia (hereafter, UA).

4. A list of all of the national and international artists who performed in Philadelphia at the Robin Hood Dell during this time period is available at http://manncenter.org/artists/past/1930-1975.

5. Henry Pleasants, "Men and Things," *Philadelphia Evening Bulletin*, August 24, 1936, UA.

6. See http://manncenter.org/artists/past/1930-1975.

7. "Ballet on Dell Program," *Philadelphia Evening Bulletin*, September 2, 1932, UA.

8. "At the Dell," *Philadelphia Evening Bulletin*, July 28, 1937, clipping files, UA.

9. B. Amidere, "Styles in Strikes, Amalgamated Cuts a New Pattern for Philadelphia," *Survey* 63 (December 1, 1929): 261–264.

10. Frederic M. Miller, Morris J. Vogel, and Allen F. Davis, *Philadelphia Stories* (Philadelphia: Temple University Press, 1988), 45.

11. Sam Bass Warner, *The Private City: Philadelphia in Three Periods of Its Growth* (Philadelphia: University of Pennsylvania Press, 1968), 178.

12. "Housing Problems in Philadelphia," *Monthly Labor Review* 37 (September 1933): 626–631.

13. Miller, Vogel, and Davis, *Philadelphia Stories*, 46.

14. Barbara Ferreri Malinsky, "Catherine Littlefield," in *International Encyclopedia of Dance*, vol. 4, ed. Selma Jeanne Cohen (New York: Oxford University Press, 1998), 210.

15. Ann Barzel, "The Littlefields," *Dance Magazine*, June 1945, 10.

16. Ibid.

17. Nancy B. Schmitz, "A Profile of Catherine Littlefield, a Pioneer of American Ballet" (Ed.D. diss., Temple University, Philadelphia, 1986).

18. Lisa Jo Sagolla, *The Girl Who Fell Down* (Boston: Northeastern University Press, 2003), 18.

19. Florence Cowanova clippings, file of undated and unidentified newspaper clippings pertaining to dance drawn from Philadelphia newspapers, Theatre Collection, Rare Book Department, Free Library of Philadelphia, Philadelphia.

20. Sagolla, *The Girl Who Fell Down*, 21–22.

21. Malinsky, "Catherine Littlefield," 209.

22. Nancy Brooks Schmitz, "The Contributions of the Littlefields to Concert Dance in Philadelphia," in *Proceedings of the Ninth Annual Conference of the Society of Dance History Scholars*, 1986, 133–147.

23. Ibid, 134.

24. Egorova performed Aurora for both the Maryinsky Ballet in 1911 and the Ballets Russes in 1921: see http://www.ballerinagallery.com/egorova.htm; Schmitz, "A Profile of Catherine Littlefield," 34.

25. Doris Hering, "An American Original, Part One: The Rise of The Littlefield Ballet," *Dance Magazine*, August 1993, 42–46, and "An American Original, Part Two: The Littlefield Legacy," *Dance Magazine*, September 1993, 48–51.

26. Jennifer Homans, *Apollo's Angels: A History of Ballet* (New York: Random House, 2010), 455.

27. Alex C. Ewing, *Bravura! Lucia Chase and the American Ballet Theatre* (Gainesville: University Press of Florida, 2009), 34.

28. Schmitz, "A Profile of Catherine Littlefield," 34.

29. Luigi Albertieri, *The Art of Terpsichore* (New York: De Vinne, 1923); Anatole Chujoy and P. W. Manchester, eds., *The Dance Encyclopedia* (New York: Simon and Schuster, 1967), 9.

30. Norman Abbott, "Terpsichore, Thy Last Name Is Littlefield," *Philadelphia Record*, October 11, 1937, UA.

31. Homans, *Apollo's Angels*, 449.

32. Lynn Garafola, "Lincoln Kirstein, Modern Dance, and the Left: The Genesis of an American Ballet," *Dance Research* 23, no. 1 July, 2005, 20.

33. Schmitz, "The Contributions of the Littlefields to Concert Dance in Philadelphia," 135.

34. George Dorris, "Léo Staats at the Roxy, 1926–1928," *Dance Research* 13, no. 1 (Summer 1995): 84–99.

35. Ibid., 84.

36. Schmitz, "The Contributions of the Littlefields to Concert Dance in Philadelphia," 133–147.

37. Ibid., 41.

38. Schmitz, "A Profile of Catherine Littlefield," 40.

39. "Catherine Littlefield Muses about the Muse," *Philadelphia Evening Bulletin*, March 29, 1936, clipping files, UA.

40. "Littlefield Ballet," *Philadelphia Evening Bulletin*, November 11, 1935, clipping files, UA.

41. Hering, "An American Original, Part One," 43

42. Ibid., 44.

43. Ibid.

44. Schmitz, "A Profile of Catherine Littlefield," 59–64.

45. Abbott, "Terpsichore, Thy Last Name Is Littlefield."

46. Barzel, "The Littlefields," 8.

47. "Program Notes," Littlefield ballet program, December 28, 1935, clipping files, Theatre Collection, Rare Books Department, Free Library of Philadelphia.

48. Schmitz, "A Profile of Catherine Littlefield," 66.

49. Ibid., 68.

50. "Philadelphia Ballet Gives Famous Work an American Premiere," *Philadelphia Evening Bulletin*, February 12, 1937, 22, UA; "Philadelphia Ballet to Give First American Performance of Tchaikovsky Work," *New York Times*, February 7, 1937, 16.

51. "Dance in Review," *Dance Magazine*, April 1937, clipping files, New York Public Library (hereafter, NYPL).

52. "Program Notes," *The Sleeping Beauty* program, Littlefield Ballet, 1937, clipping files, Free Library of Philadelphia.

53. Alberta Vitak, "Dance Events Reviewed," n.d., clipping files pertaining to Catherine Littlefield, Library for the Performing Arts, Jerome Robbins Dance Division Research Collection, NYPL.

54. John Martin, "Tchaikovsky Work Is Given as Ballet" *New York Times*, February 14, 1937, N3.

55. Ibid.

56. Cecil Smith, "Chicago Cheers Ballet," *Chicago Tribune*, December 5, 1938, clipping files, Free Library of Philadelphia.

57. Martin, "Tchaikovsky Work Given as Ballet," N3.

58. Dorathi Bock Pierre, "Dance Events Reviewed," *Hollywood Bowl Magazine*, November 1939, clipping files, NYPL.

59. "Philadelphia Ballet Gives 'Sleeping Beauty,'" *Philadelphia Inquirer*, February 13, 1937, clipping files, NYPL.

60. "Philadelphia Ballet Gives Famous Work and American Premier," *Philadelphia Evening Bulletin*, February 12, 1937, 22, UA.

61. "Dance in Review."

62. John Martin, "Sleeping Beauty Given at Stadium," *New York Times*, July 30, 1937, L22.

63. Ibid.

64. "Philadelphia Ballet to Give First American Performance of Tchaikovsky Work," 8X.

65. Martin, "Sleeping Beauty Given at Stadium," L22.

66. Ibid.

67. Martin, "Tchaikovsky Work Given as Ballet," N3.

68. Publicity brochure, clipping files, NYPL.

69. Garafola, "Lincoln Kirstein, Modern Dance and the Left," 25.

70. "Catherine Littlefield Dies, Noted Ballet Dancer Was 46," *Philadelphia Evening Bulletin*, November 19, 1951.

71. "Miss Littlefield Kisses Mayor: Ballet Head Happy over Ovations Received on European Tour," *Philadelphia Evening Bulletin*, June 23, 1937, clipping files, UA. Another way Littlefield achieved this status was by creating American-themed dances choreographed and danced by Americans. In this regard, the other dances the Philadelphia Ballet Company premiered that season are quite significant. After *Beauty*, Littlefield created two short ballets to show throughout the 1937 season. These dances, *Barn Dance* and *Terminal*, were groundbreaking in their embrace of a modern American aesthetic. In Littlefield's push to establish the Philadelphia Ballet as a truly "American" company, therefore, she took on the creation of new ballets with American themes, music, and choreography.

72. "All Philadelphia Dancers List 'Sleeping Beauty,'" *Camden Inquirer*, January 29, 1937, clipping files, NYPL.

73. "A Tale of Two Cities: Philadelphia Supplies the Ballet for Chicago's City Opera," *Philadelphia Evening Bulletin*, November 17, 1938.

74. Henry Smallens, "Music in Review," *Philadelphia Evening Bulletin*, February 20, 1937, clipping files, UA.

75. Edwin H. Schloss, "Philadelphia Ballet to Tour Europe This Summer, First Company to Go in Immortal Duncan's Footsteps," *Philadelphia Evening Bulletin*, February 2, 1937, clipping files, UA.

76. "Quarter Century Old Dream Comes True in Littlefield School of Dancing," *Philadelphia Evening Bulletin*, September 18, 1929.

77. "Meet Men of the Ballet—He-Men at That," *Philadelphia Evening Bulletin*, December 10, 1937.

78. "Catherine Littlefield Muses about the Muse."

79. "A Bouquet for the Ballet," *Philadelphia Evening Bulletin*, November 15, 1937.

80. Usually the story goes something like this: Ballet began in the French courts of the Renaissance. It migrated to England during the Romantic period, then to Russia during the late nineteenth century, and then through the Ballets Russes from Russia to Europe to New York, where it now lives on in the New York City Ballet.

81. Cohen, *International Encyclopedia of Dance*, 4:210.

82. Barzel, "The Littlefields."

CHAPTER 4

1. Russell F. Weigley, ed., *Philadelphia: A 300-Year History* (New York: W. W. Norton, 1982), 668.

2. Ibid., 662–675.

3. Peter O. Muller, Kenneth C. Myer, and Roman A. Cybriwsky, *Philadelphia: A Study of Conflicts and Social Cleavages* (New York: Ballinger, 1976), 11–34.

4. Miriam Ershkowitz and Joseph Zikmund, eds., *Black Politics in Philadelphia* (New York: Basic Books, 1973), 55–100.

5. Weigley, *Philadelphia*, 675.

6. Frederic M. Miller, Morris J. Vogel, and Allen F. Davis, *Philadelphia Stories* (Philadelphia: Temple University Press, 1988), 283.

7. See the Pennsylvania Ballet website at http://www.paballet.org/history

8. Barbara Weisberger, telephone conversation with the author, July 23, 2014.

9. Olga Maynard, "Barbara Weisberger and the Pennsylvania Ballet," *Dance Magazine*, March 1975, 48.

10. Ibid., 50.

11. Shawn Marie Avery, "A Chronological History of the Pennsylvania Ballet" (senior honors thesis, Goucher College, Baltimore, 1993).

12. Leonard Boasberg, "Once Before the Ballet 'Died' and Was Brought Back to Life," *Philadelphia Inquirer*, March 12, 1991.

13. Arthur Bronson, "New Ballet Has Gotham Astir: Don't Look Now—But Aren't Those Stars Philadelphians?" *Philadelphia Record*, February 4, 1940, Philadelphia Dance Collection, Special Collections Research Center, Temple University, Philadelphia (hereafter, PDCAT).

14. Linton Martin, "Ballet Born in America Has Its Own Distinction," *Philadelphia Record*, November 8, 1942.

15. Arthur Bronson, "Americans Have 'Discovered' the Ballet," *Philadelphia Record*, November 1, 1943.

16. A driving force behind American Ballet Theatre during the first four decades of its existence, Lucia Chase (1907–1986) was born to a wealthy family in Waterbury, Connecticut. She studied ballet with Mikhail Mordkin and danced leading roles with his company in the late 1930s. She was a founding member of Ballet Theatre and proved her mettle as a dramatic dancer in works by Antony Tudor, Agnes de Mille, and Michel Fokine. In 1945, with the designer Oliver Smith, she was named co-director of American Ballet Theatre, a position she held until she stepped down in 1980. Responsible for programming as well as casting, she pursued the vision of Ballet Theatre as a showcase for classical and contemporary works, international in scope and national in spirit, with remarkable success. By the last decade of her tenure, the company had become an outstanding classical ensemble, with an acclaimed roster of principals. During her forty-year association with the company, Chase contributed generously from her private fortune to its maintenance and survival. In 1980, she received the Presidential Medal of Freedom: see http://www.danceheritage.org/chase.html.

17. Rita Katz Farrell, "The Philadelphia Story: Pennsylvania Ballet Ascendant," *Ballet News*, vol. 3, no. 4, October 1981, 12.

18. Michael Kimmelman, "Whatever Its Real Age, the Forum Is Going Strong," *Philadelphia Inquirer*, October 26, 1986.

19. Barbara Weisberger interview, October 2014.

20. Avery, "A Chronological History of the Pennsylvania Ballet," 13.

21. Ibid., 10.

22. "Israel Variety Show at Academy Tonight," *Philadelphia Record*, May 23, 1965; "Recitals to Grana," *Philadelphia Record*, December 12, 1966; "Jazz at the Academy," *Philadelphia Record*, March 5, 1967; "Benefit Concert," *Philadelphia Record*, January 8, 1967; "Bossa Nova Makes Local Bow Friday," *Philadelphia Record*, November 18, 1962, all in UA, Academy of Music file.

23. Harry Harris, "Wonderland Ballet Stars Alice . . . of Course," *Philadelphia Evening Bulletin*, March 14, 1950.

24. William Smith, "Young, Old Dance in Ballet Program," *Philadelphia Evening Bulletin*, May 16, 1951.

25. Kay Mott, "Ballet in the Alley," *Philadelphia Inquirer*, September 16, 1956.

26. "Royal Ballet Flies Here to Do 'Cinderella' on TV," *Philadelphia Record*, April 28, 1957.

27. Jack Brady, "African Dancers Enliven Locust Stage," *Philadelphia Record*, November 8, 1960.

28. "American Dance History, from Hoofers to Ballet," *Philadelphia Record*, February 24, 1963, UA.

29. Frank Bookhouser, "Season Treat on Way for Balletomanes," *Philadelphia Record*, September 7, 1964.

30. Ann Ragni, "She's Put Philadelphia on the Map with Her Dedication to Dance," *Philadelphia Inquirer*, August 11, 1971, UA, Stella Moore file.

31. Barbara Weisberger, telephone interview with the author, July 26, 2014.

32. Farrell, "The Philadelphia Story," 15.

33. Maynard, "Barbara Weisberger and the Pennsylvania Ballet," 54.

34. Eileen Foley, "Ballet School Makes Its Point," *Philadelphia Inquirer*, March 19, 1963.

35. Ragni, "She's Put Philadelphia on the Map."

36. Foley, "Ballet School Makes Its Point."

37. Eugene Palatsky, "These Dancers Have Character," *Dance Magazine*, November 1967, 44.

38. Ibid.

39. Allen Hughes, "New Dance Group Makes Its Debut," *New York Times*, October 31, 1964.

40. Peggy Constantine, "The Woman Who Brought Forth a Ballet for Philadelphia," *Chicago Sun Times*, December 17, 1969.

41. Avery, "A Chronological History of the Pennsylvania Ballet."

42. "A Birthplace of Ballet," n.d., clipping files, PDCAT.

43. Marie Van Patten, "Debut of Ballet Group Glows with Promise," *Philadelphia Evening Bulletin*, April 20, 1964, G 27.

44. "Presstime News," *Dance Magazine*, January 1964, clipping files, New York Public Library (hereafter, NYPL).

45. Alex C. Ewing, *Bravura! Lucia Chase and the American Ballet Theatre* (Gainesville: University Press of Florida, 2009), 245.

46. The Ford Foundation would continue to fund the Pennsylvania Ballet for ten years, with a fifth grant of $2.9 million.

47. Daniel Webster, "Ballet Plans Ahead," *Philadelphia Inquirer*, April 24, 1966.

48. Academy of Music, *The Sleeping Beauty* program, November 26–27, 1965, Theatre Collection, Rare Book Department, Free Library of Philadelphia.

49. Barbara Weisberger, telephone interview with the author, September 21, 2001.

50. "Proposed Performance and Rehearsal Schedule from September 13, 1965 to May 30, 1966," Pennsylvania Ballet clipping file, PDCAT.

51. "Beauty Budget B," Pennsylvania Ballet clipping file, PDCAT.

52. Ibid.

53. Samuel Singer, "Pennsylvania Ballet in 'Sleeping Beauty,'" *Philadelphia Inquirer*, UA, Pennsylvania Ballet "Sleeping Beauty" file.

54. Clive Barnes, "A Vital Role for Tradition," *New York Times*, December 12, 1965, 34X.

55. Alexandra Grilikhes, "The Sleeping Beauty Wakes Up in Philadelphia," *Dance Magazine*, January 1966, 20–21.

56. Palatsky, "These Dancers Have Character," 42–45.

57. Samuel Singer, "Dancer Tampers with Tradition in 'Sleeping Beauty,'" *Philadelphia Inquirer*, October 24, 1965, Pennsylvania Ballet clipping files, Jerome Robbins Dance Collection, NYPL.

58. "Beauty Awakens—Streamlined," *Philadelphia Evening Bulletin*, November 21, 1965, UA.

59. Ibid.

60. Susan Goodwin and Becky Bradley, "1960–1969," *American Cultural History*, Lone Star College–Kingwood Library, 1999, February 7, 2011.

61. Ibid.

62. Ibid.

63. Ibid.

64. Otto Dekom, "P[ennsylvania] Ballet Group Does 'Sleeping Beauty' Well," *Morning News*, Wilmington, DE, January 5, 1967.

65. Pennsylvania Ballet, 1968–1969 season souvenir program, Music Collection, Free Library of Philadelphia.

66. Sleeping Beauty clipping file, UA.

67. Weisberger, telephone interview, July 26, 2014.

68. Daniel Webster, "Penn[sylvania] Ballet Offers 'The Sleeping Beauty' for Young People," *Philadelphia Inquirer*, December 30, 1966.

69. Ibid.

70. Ibid.

71. Daniel Webster, "Restaged 'Beauty' Is Holiday Gift from Pennsylvania Ballet," *Philadelphia Inquirer*, December 25, 1966, 13.

72. This is demonstrated by the referencing of the 1890 Petipa version of the ballet in almost every one of the thousands of newspaper and magazine clippings that I have collected, as well as in the interviews I conducted with choreographers, artistic directors, and dancers involved in these productions. The performance is never discussed without an allusion to or mention of the 1890 version, and in some cases Littlefield's version of 1937 is also referenced.

73. Macaulay "The Big Sleep: The Sleeping Beauty at Its Centenary," *Dancing Times*, May 1990, 806.

74. Ibid.

75. Fyodor Lopukhov, "Annals of 'The Sleeping Beauty': I. The Choreography," *Ballet Review* 5, no. 4 (1975–1976): 33.

76. Boris Asafiev, "Annals of 'The Sleeping Beauty': II. The Music," *Ballet Review* 5, no. 4 (1975–1976): 43.

77. Littlefield left the grand pas de deux from the third act intact. Most productions of *Beauty* retain what is believed to be Petipa's choreography for the role of Aurora. This is considered the heart of the ballet, and—although individual ballerinas add to or subtract from the role with their interpretive skills—many audience members, critics, and dancers have specific expectations about the presentation and performance of this choreography.

78. P. W. Manchester, "The Pennsylvania Ballet in 'The Sleeping Beauty,'" *Dance News*, January 1966, 10–11. Manchester was a pioneer in the world of dance criticism, an editor, a historian, and a gifted writer whose wide-ranging career spanned more than half a century. A native of London, she was an adjunct professor at the College-Conservatory of Music, University of Cincinnati, from 1969 to1993. "She was a brilliant teacher with a very deep knowledge of the field of ballet. . . . She had the ability to make it come alive. She knew all the lives of the dancers. You go to London, Moscow, St. Petersburg or Paris and mention her name and everybody knows her": Oleg Sabline, professor of dance, University of Cincinnati, quoted in Janelle Gelfand, "P. W. Manchester, 91, Led in Dance Criticism," *Cincinnati Enquirer*, May 19, 1998. Manchester's career started during World War II, when she was dance critic for *Theatre World* in England. In 1942, she wrote the nonfiction best-seller *Vic-Wells: A Ballet Progress*, the story of the first ten years of the Sadler's Wells Ballet (now the Royal Ballet). From 1944 to 1946, she was secretary to Marie Rambert, director of Ballet Rambert, England's oldest dance company. "She was one of the first of the major English dance critics during World War II. She was very important in establishing the reputation of what is now the Royal Ballet": Clive Barnes, quoted in ibid. Manchester was invited to the United States in the early 1950s by Anatole Chujoy, the founder and editor of *Dance News*, to become assistant editor and principal critic of that publication. Manchester's *Dance Encyclopedia* (1967), which she co-wrote with Chujoy, is regarded as the bible of the dance world.

79. Anna Kisselgoff, "'Sleeping Beauty'—The Crown Jewel of Ballet," *New York Times*, June 13, 1976, 77.

80. Ibid.

81. Clive Barnes, "Revamped 'Sleeping Beauty' Proves Livelier," *New York Times*, May 7, 1977; Clive Barnes, "'Beauty' by Helpmann," *New York Times*, December 20, 1976.

82. Clive Barnes helped bring dance to a broad audience with an exuberant, highly personal style as a critic in Britain and later for the *New York Times* and *New York Post*. He made his mark by waging a sustained assault on British dance criticism as it was practiced just after World War II. Writing for several publications simultaneously—chiefly *The Spectator* and the *Times of London*, which hired him as its first full-time dance critic in 1961—Barnes exposed his readers to foreign dance companies and choreographers, including George Balanchine and Martha Graham, whom most British critics had dismissed. His thirteen years as dance critic at the *Times*, from 1965 to 1977, coincided with a rapid expansion of the dance world and an explosion of new talent. He witnessed and described "dance's finest hours in all its brief history," as he later observed in *Dance Magazine*, a period in which Jerome Robbins and Balanchine

were at their peak, Merce Cunningham and Paul Taylor moved from strength to strength, and new choreographers such as Eliot Feld and Twyla Tharp were beginning to make a stir. In 1978, Barnes accepted a position with the *Post* and remained there for the next thirty years: see William Grimes, "Clive Barnes, Who Raised Stakes in Dance and Theater Criticism, Dies at 81," *New York Times*, November 19, 2008.

83. Clive Barnes, "Wrongheadedness," *New York Times*, November 29, 1965, UA.

84. Ibid.

85. Barbara Weisberger, interview with the author, Philadelphia, October 3, 2001.

86. Ibid.

87. Donal J. Henahan, "Young Dancers Heading Up," *Chicago Daily News*, November 23, 1966.

88. Hubert Saal, "The Young Philadelphians," *Newsweek*, Philadelphia Dance Collection, undated clipping files, UA.

89. Clive Barnes, "Welcome to the Pennsylvanians," *New York Times*, January 28, 1968.

90. Manchester, "Pennsylvania Ballet," 10.

91. Ibid.

92. Grilikhes, "The Sleeping Beauty Wakes Up in Philadelphia," 20–21.

93. Henahan, "Young Dancers Heading Up."

94. Barnes, "Wrongheadedness."

95. Manchester, "Pennsylvania Ballet," 10.

96. Melissa Hayden began her career with American Ballet Theater from 1945 to 1947 and returned there in 1953 and 1954. Essentially, however, she was a charter member of the New York City Ballet (NYCB), joining the troupe shortly after it was founded by George Balanchine and Lincoln Kirstein in 1948. She retired in September 1973. Unlike other Balanchine ballerinas who were about to leave the company, Hayden was honored with a new ballet that Balanchine created for her. Although that work, "Cortège Hongrois," was considered a *pièce d'occasion*, it remains in the NYCB's repertoire, bringing back memories of Balanchine as a flower boy giving Hayden a bouquet onstage. In a tribute to Hayden, Kirstein wrote, "Melissa has been the nearest thing to a 'star' in our starless company. We have never encouraged stardom on programs, posters or publicity; managers can't make stars. The public does": quoted in Anna Kisselgoff, "Melissa Hayden, a Vibrant Star of New York City Ballet, Dies at 83," *New York Times*, August 10, 2006.

97. Nancy Love, "Superman in a Tutu," Barbara Weisberger clipping file, PDCAT.

98. Anna Kisselgoff, "Ballet Director: No to Guest Stars," *New York Times*, April 5, 1971.

99. Cited in Ame Wilson, "Literary Theory and Dramaturgy: Interpreting the Dust," *Theatre Studies* 45 (2001): 5.

100. Lincoln Kirstein to Barbara Weisberger, personal correspondence, December 4, 1965, in Weisberger's possession.

101. Mark Franko, "Repeatability, Reconstruction and Beyond," *Theatre Journal* 41, no. 1 (March 1989): 56–74.

102. For a detailed account of that work, see Chapters 2 and 6 in this volume.

103. Tim Scholl, *From Petipa to Balanchine: Classical Revival and the Modernization of Ballet* (New York: Routledge, 1994), 11.

104. Ralph Harper, *The Sleeping Beauty and Other Essays* (New York: Cowley, 1966), 13.

105. Barbara Saltzman, "Founder vs. Board: Weisberger and Penna. Ballet," *Philadelphia Inquirer*, Letters to the Editor, March 8, 1982.

CHAPTER 5

1. See http://www.cnn.com/SPECIALS/2002/yir.

2. William Tinning, "From Riches to Ruin: The Enron Story," *The Herald* (Glasgow), May 26, 2006, 13.

3. Michael Petrou, "Media Frenzy Trails Cardinals to Rome," *National Post* (Canada), April 23, 2002, A14.

4. Carolyn Adams, "The Philadelphia Experience," *Annals of the American Academy of Political and Social Science*, no. 551 (May 1997): 228.

5. Carolyn Adams, David Bartelt, David Elesh, and Ira Goldstein et al., *Philadelphia: Neighborhoods, Division, and Conflict in a Postindustrial City* (Philadelphia: Temple University Press, 1991).

6. Joellen Meglin and Lynn Matluck Brooks, "Where Are All the Women Choreographers in Ballet?" *Dance Chronicle* 35, no. 1 (2012): 4.

7. Barbara Weisberger, interview with the author, Philadelphia, October 3, 2001.

8. Jean Battey Lewis, "Two Cheers for Ford Grant," *Washington Post*, May 16, 1971; "Pennsylvania Ballet to Get Ford Grant," *Los Angeles Times*, May 21, 1971.

9. Elizabeth Kendall, "Dancing: A Ford Foundation Report" (monograph), December, 1983.

10. Rodham was originally trained by Barbara Weisberger in Wilkes-Barre, Pennsylvania. He went on to train as a scholarship student at Balanchine's School of American Ballet and then joined the New York City Ballet. He rejoined Weisberger as a dancer and choreographer in 1965 and was appointed ballet-master in 1966, devoting his full attention to coaching, rehearsing, and choreographing for the company: Craig Palmer, "Robert Rodham Bio," n.d., and Daniel Webster, "Pennsylvania Ballet Focuses Attention on Rodham, New Master," *Philadelphia Inquirer*, April 29, 1936, both in Pennsylvania Ballet Archives, PDCAT.

11. Meglin and Brooks, "Where Are All the Women Choreographers in Ballet?" 2.

12. Harkarvy, a former director of the Royal Winnipeg Ballet and the founder and director of the Netherlands Dance Theater, came to the Pennsylvania Ballet from the Harkness Ballet, where he had shared the artistic director position with Robert Rodham.

13. Clive Barnes, "It Must Be Fun to Be Funded," *New York Times*, April 2, 1972, D14.

14. *Dance Magazine*, March 1975.

15. Alex C. Ewing, *Bravura! Lucia Chase and the American Ballet Theatre* (Gainesville: University Press of Florida, 2009). Ewing writes about this moment. "For Lucia, after nearly four decades of performing, touring, underwriting practically every deficit working day and night for Ballet Theatre, never complaining but always encouraging and exhorting . . . to have all heads turning to greet the new figure about to walk in and take over center stage was almost too much to bear": ibid., 302. He then quotes a psychologist speaking about the effect this had on Chase's dancers. "With Chase retiring, the dancers feel even more exploited because they identify with her being abused": ibid., 304.

16. Anna Kisselgoff, "Ballet: Pennsylvanians Dance a New Harkarvy," *New York Times*, March 2, 1979.

17. Jennifer Dunning, "Founder-Director of Pennsylvania Ballet Resigns," *New York Times*, March 3, 1982, C23.

18. Ibid.

19. George Balanchine to Charles Rannells, president, Pennsylvania Ballet Company, letter, April 21, 1982, in the possession of Barbara Weisberger.

20. David Brenner, chairman, Board of Trustees, to the dance editor of the *New York Times*, letter, February 19, 1982, in the possession of Barbara Weisberger.

21. Barbara Weisberger, conversation with the author, July 26, 2014.

22. Valerie Scher, "Pennsylvania Ballet Opens Alert, Confident and Lean," *Philadelphia Inquirer*, February 4, 1983, F22.

23. Nancy Goldner, "Pennsylvania Ballet Performs 'Sylphide,'" *Philadelphia Inquirer*, March 8, 1985, C1.

24. Ibid.

25. Nancy Goldner, "Tale of Two Cities with One Ballet, Milwaukee and Pennsylvania Ballet's 'Swan Lake' Opens Here Wednesday," *Philadelphia Inquirer*, June 5, 1988, E1.

26. Nancy Goldner, "Weiss Quits as Artistic Director of P[ennsylvania] Ballet," *Philadelphia Inquirer*, January 17, 1990.

27. Nancy Goldner, "Ballet Board Members Resign over Weiss's Departure," *Philadelphia Inquirer*, February 1, 1990, C5.

28. Nancy Goldner, "Director Supports Ballet's Traditions," *Philadelphia Inquirer*, May 24, 1990.

29. Lucinda Fleeson, "Pas de Deux with Disaster," *Philadelphia Inquirer*, March 17, 1991, L1.

30. Ibid.

31. Lucinda Fleeson, "Of Dance and Debt," *Philadelphia Inquirer*, March 12, 1991, E1.

32. "The Pennsylvania Ballet Raises $2.5 Million" *New York Times*, July 16, 1991, C18.

33. "Pennsylvania Ballet Names a New Boss," *San Francisco Chronicle*, March 28, 1991, E2.

34. "P[ennsylvania] Ballet Drops 10 Dancers in Shakeup," *Philadelphia Inquirer*, June 17, 1992.

35. Nancy Goldner, "Kaiser Is Appointed [Pennsylvania] Ballet Artistic Director for One Year," *Philadelphia Inquirer*, June 10, 1994.

36. "Roy Kaiser Appointed by Pennsylvania Ballet," *New York Times*, June 11, 1994, 17.

37. David Mead, "Pennsylvania Ballet: Everything You Ever Wanted to Know," *Ballet Magazine*, September 2002.

38. Nancy Goldner, "A New Posture in Leadership at the Ballet," *Philadelphia Inquirer*, June 26, 1994.

39. Nancy Goldner, "P[ennsylvania] Ballet: Trying to Look on the Bright Side," *Philadelphia Inquirer*, July 24, 1994.

40. Robert Baxter, "P[ennsylvania] Ballet Awakens 'Sleeping Beauty,'" *Cherry Hill [NJ] Courier Post*, May 23, 1997.

41. Anne Levin, "'Sleeping Beauty' Closes Pennsylvania Ballet Season," *Trenton Daily Times*, May 28, 1997.

42. Barbara Malinsky, "Arduous 'Sleeping Beauty' Closes P[ennsylvania] Ballet Season," *Chestnut Hill Local*, June 5, 1997.

43. Joyce Mullins, "P[ennsylvania] Ballet's First Staging of 'Sleeping Beauty' Opulent, Exciting," *Philadelphia Pride Weekly*, May 27, 1997.

44. Janek Schergen studied ballet at the American Ballet Center and the Harkness House for Ballet Arts in New York. In 1971, he joined the Royal Winnipeg Ballet and the following year became a member of the Pennsylvania Ballet. Later, he taught and staged works at the School of the Pennsylvania Ballet. In 1981, he joined the Washington Ballet in a full-time position as ballet-master and teacher and toured with the company through the Asia, Europe, and South America, as well as the United States. In 1988, he was invited to be ballet-master and company teacher for the Royal Swedish Ballet in Stockholm, rehearsing full-length classics. In 1991, he completed his studies in written dance notation in London, receiving his certification in Benesh Movement Notation. He later became a ballet-master for Pittsburgh Ballet Theatre, where he rehearsed the full-length classics and other important additions to the repertoire. He has staged his own production of *The Sleeping Beauty* for Ballet Met (1994), the Milwaukee Ballet (1995), Pittsburgh Ballet Theatre (1996, 2000, and 2005), Pennsylvania Ballet (1997, 2002), and the Norwegian National Ballet (2006). In January 1994, he was appointed artistic director of the Nashville Ballet, as well as director of the company's school: see http://www.arts2013.sg/janek-schergen.html.

45. Levin, "'Sleeping Beauty' Closes Pennsylvania Ballet Season."

46. Ibid.

47. Malinsky, "Arduous 'Sleeping Beauty'"; emphasis added.

48. Brian Caffall, "P[ennsylvania] Ballet's 'Sleeping' Unfolds Beautifully," *Philadelphia Gay News*, May 30, 1997.

49. John Berger coined the phrase "ways of seeing" in the four-part television series and accompanying book *Ways of Seeing*, British Broadcasting Corporation, London, and Penguin Books, 1972.

50. See the Internet Movie Database, available at http://www.imdb.com/year/1997.

51. Lewis Whittington, "Unsleeping Beauty," *Philadelphia Forum*, May 29, 1997.

52. Schergen, quoted in Levin, "'Sleeping Beauty' Closes Pennsylvania Ballet Season."

53. Sharon Skeel, "Awakening 'Sleeping Beauty,'" *Philadelphia Inquirer*, May 21, 1997, D5.

54. Janek Schergen, telephone interview with the author, June 15, 2001.

55. Ibid. Authenticity is a highly contested idea that has been exposed as an unstable concept by many theorists in dance studies, cultural studies, musicology, sociology, and anthropology. The idea of an "original" or "essential" culture or cultural production is flawed, as cultures are not static, but always in a process of change, migration, expansion, and transformation as elements from outside and inside a community are borrowed, incorporated, referenced, or even satirized (Ben Agger, *Cultural Studies as Critical Theory* [London: Falmer, 1992], chap. 2; Pierre Bourdieu, *The Rules of Art: Genesis and Structure of the Literary Field* [Stanford, CA: Stanford University Press, 1992]; Jane Desmond, "Embodying Difference: Issues in Dance and Cultural Studies," in *Meaning in Motion*, ed. Jane Desmond [Durham, NC: Duke University Press, 1997]; Sherril Dodds, *Dancing on the Canon: Embodiments of Value in Popular Dance* [Basingstoke, UK: Palgrave, 2011]; Gay Morris, "Dance Studies/Cultural Studies," *Dance Research Journal* 41, no. 1 [2009]: 82–100; Edward Said, *Culture and Imperialism* [New York: Vintage Books Reprint, 1994]; John Storey, ed., *What Is Cultural Studies? A Reader* [London: Arnold, 1996]; and John Tomlinson, *Globalization and Culture* [Cambridge, UK: Polity Press in association with Blackwell Publishing, 1999]).

56. Ibid.

57. Schergen, quoted in Malinsky, "Arduous 'Sleeping Beauty.'"

58. Schergen interview.

59. Malinsky, "Arduous 'Sleeping Beauty.'"

60. Levin, "'Sleeping Beauty' Closes Pennsylvania Ballet Season."

61. Schergen, quoted in Anne Levin, "Pennsylvania Ballet Gets 'Beauty' Advice," *Trenton Daily Times*, May 23, 1997.

62. See http://www.paballet.org/history.

63. Malinsky, "Arduous 'Sleeping Beauty.'"

64. Schergen interview.

65. Berger, *Ways of Seeing*.

66. Mullins, "P[ennsylvania] Ballet's First Staging of 'Sleeping Beauty'"; emphasis added.

67. Berger, *Ways of Seeing*, 23.

68. Walter Benjamin, "The Work of Art in the Age of Mechanical Reproduction," in *Illuminations* (London: Fontana, 1973), 222–223.

69. Levin, "Pennsylvania Ballet Gets 'Beauty' Advice."

70. Schergen interview.

71. Ibid.

72. Ibid.

73. Schergen interview.

74. Andrea Harris, "Gendered Discourses in American Ballet at Midcentury: Ruth Page on the Periphery," *Dance Chronicle* 35, no. 1 (2012): 30–53.

75. Alexandra Kolb and Sophia Kalogeropoulou, "In Defence of Ballet: Women, Agency and the Philosophy of Pleasure," *Dance Research* 30, no. 2 (Winter 2012): 107–125.

76. See http://arantxaochoa.com/#/aboutus.

77. See http://www.balletsouthtexastest.org/wp-content/uploads/2012/09/Dede_barfield_bio_full.pdf.

78. See http://forms.paballet.org/dancers/principals/Chamberlain.html.

79. Michel Foucault, *Discipline and Punish: The Birth of the Prison* (New York: Pantheon, 1977), 183.

80. Carrie Noland, *Agency and Embodiment* (Cambridge, MA: Harvard University Press, 2009).

81. Ibid., 92.

82. Arantxa Ochoa, interview with the author, Philadelphia July 14, 2003.

83. Ibid.

84. Ibid.

85. Ibid.

86. Gregory was also well known for her interpretation of Aurora, a role she performed in 1977 and 1978. The critic Anna Kisselgoff wrote, "Miss Gregory's nuanced performance brought in an appropriate lyricism, while the wedding pas de deux was marked by a glitter and clarity of movement that made her whole performance one big wave into crescendo. Rarely has she danced better": Anna Kisselgoff, "'The Sleeping Beauty' with Cynthia Gregory," *New York Times*, May 28, 1978, 47.

87. Caffall, "P[ennsylvania] Ballet's 'Sleeping' Unfolds Beautifully."

88. Baxter, "P[ennsylvania] Ballet Awakens 'Sleeping Beauty.'"

89. Lesley Valdes, "P[ennsylvania] Ballet's 'Sleeping Beauty' Is Exceptionally Beautiful," *Philadelphia Inquirer*, May 23, 1997.

90. Dede Barfield, interview with the author, Philadelphia, June 8, 2003.

91. Ibid.

92. Martha Chamberlain, interview with the author, Philadelphia, June 25, 2003.

93. Ibid.

94. Tim Scholl, *The Sleeping Beauty: A Legend in Progress* (New Haven, CT: Yale University Press, 2004).

95. Chamberlain interview.

96. Barfield interview.

97. Ibid.

98. Elizabeth Bowen, "Preface to *Stories by Elizabeth Bowen*," in *Afterthought* (London: Longmans, Green, 1962), quoted in Renée C. Hoogland, "Feminist Theorizing as 'Transposed Autobiography,'" *Journal of Lesbian Studies* 11, nos. 1–2 (2007): 138.

99. Cynthia Novack, "Ballet, Gender, and Cultural Power," in *Dance, Gender and Culture*, ed. Helen Thomas (London: Macmillan, 1993), 37.

100. Chamberlain interview.

101. Ibid.

102. Barfield interview.

103. Ibid.

104. Ibid.

105. Linda Alcoff, "The Problem of Speaking for Others," in *Cultural Critique*, no. 20 (Winter 1991–1992): 5–32, available at http://www.alcoff.com/content/speaothers.html.

106. Chamberlain interview.

107. Ibid.

108. Ibid.

109. Barfield interview.

110. Jennifer Fisher, *Nutcracker Nation: How an Old World Ballet Became a Christmas Tradition in the New World* (New Haven, CT: Yale University Press, 2003), 172.

111. Ibid., 176.

112. Jennifer Dunning, "Spectrum of Interpretations in Three 'Sleeping Beauties,'" *New York Times*, June 5, 1998, E4.

113. Ibid.

CHAPTER 6

1. Perrault's *La Belle au bois dormant* was first published in February 1696 in the journal *Mercure Galant*. In January 1697, *La Belle au bois dormant* was published (along with seven other tales) in *Histoires, au contes du temps passé, avec des moralités*, under the name of Perrault's son, Pierre Perrault Darmancour. The caption on the front of the first edition read "Contes de ma mère l'Oye," which has been translated into English as *The Tales of Mother Goose*: Humphrey Carpenter and Mari Prichard, *The Oxford Companion to Children's Literature* (Oxford: Oxford University Press, 1984), 402.

2. Nancy L. Canepa, *Out of the Woods: The Origins of the Literary Fairy Tale in Italy and France* (Detroit: Wayne State University, 1997); Maria M. Tatar, *The Annotated Classic Fairy Tales* (New York: W. W. Norton, 2002); P. L. Travers, *About the Sleeping Beauty* (New York: McGraw-Hill, 1975); Marie-Louise von Franz, *The Interpretation of Fairy Tales*, repr. ed. (Boston: Shambala, 1996 [1970]); Jack Zipes, ed., *The Great Fairy Tale Tradition: From Straparola and Basile to the Brothers Grimm* (New York: W. W. Norton, 2001).

3. Bettina A. Knapp, *French Fairy Tales: A Jungian Approach* (Albany: State University of New York Press, 2003), 65.

4. Katia Canon, *The Fairy Tale Revisited: A Survey of the Evolution of the Tales, from Classical Literary Interpretations to Contemporary Dance-Theater Productions*, New Connections in Interdisciplinarity, vol. 9, ed. Shirley Paoli (New York: Peter Lang, 1994), 25.

5. Martin Hallett and Barbara Karasek, eds., *Folk and Fairy Tales* (Peterborough, ON: Broadview, 1996), 14.

6. Jack Zipes, *Fairy Tales and the Art of Subversion: The Classical Genre for Children and the Process of Civilization* (New York: Wildman, 1995), 7.

7. Jack Zipes, *Beauties, Beasts and Enchantments—Classic French Fairy Tales* (New York: Meridian, 1991), 2–3.

8. Philippe Airès, *Centuries of Childhood: A Social History of Family Life* (New York: Vintage, 1965).

9. Canon, *The Fairy Tale Revisited*, 24.

10. Sally Banes, *Dancing Women: Female Bodies on Stage* (London: Routledge, 1998), 45.

11. Charles Perrault, "The Sleeping Beauty in the Wood," in Hallett and Karasek, *Folk and Fairy Tales*, 40.

12. Charles Perrault, "The Sleeping Beauty in the Wood," in *Perrault's Fairy Tales*, trans. A. E. Johnson (New York: Dover, 1969), 4.

13. Ibid., 5.

14. Perrault, "The Sleeping Beauty in the Wood," in Johnson, *Perrault's Fairy Tales*.

15. Ibid., 13.

16. Ibid., 16.

17. Ibid., 17.

18. Ibid., 20.

19. Banes, *Dancing Women*, 44.

20. Ibid.

21. Dorothie R. Thelander, "Mother Goose and Her Goslings: The France of Louis XIV as Seen through the Fairy Tale," *Journal of Modern History* 54, no. 3 (September 1982): 472.

22. Ibid., 473–475.

23. Perrault, "The Sleeping Beauty in the Wood," in *Perrault's Fairy Tales*, 5.

24. Susan Stewart, "Notes on Distressed Genres," *Journal of American Folklore* 104, no. 411 (Winter 1991): 23.

25. Ibid., 18.

26. Marc Raeff, *Origins of the Russian Intelligentsia* (New York: Harcourt, Brace, 1966), 14–20.

27. This was also true of good dancing. King Louis XIV established the Académie Royale de Danse in 1661 and was himself an established performer of dance. The beginnings of classical ballet were born in his court and with his support.

28. John Spurling, "Awake to the World," *The Spectator*, November 21, 1999, 66–67.

29. See http://www.artmagick.com/articles/article.aspx?id=11778

30. Larry D. Lutchmansingh, "Fantasy and Arrested Desire in Edward Burne-Jones's Series," in *Pre-Raphaelites Reviewed*, ed. Marcia Pointon (Manchester: Manchester University Press, 1989), 125.

31. See http://thetextileblog.blogspot.com/2013/12/edward-burne-jones-and-legend-of-briar.html

32. Edward Burne-Jones, *Memorials*, vol. 1 (New York: Macmillan, 1906), 195.

33. Allan Staley, "The Condition of Music," *Art News Annual* 33 (1967): 80–87.

34. Kenneth Bendiner, *An Introduction to Victorian Painting* (New Haven, CT: Yale University Press, 1985), 123–126.

35. Gillian Brown, "The Empire of Agoraphobia," *Representations*, no. 20 (Autumn 1987): 134–157; Rosemarie Garland Thomson, "Benevolent Maternalism and Physically Disabled Figures," *American Literature* 68, no. 3 (September 1996): 555–586.

36. Woolson, quoted in Bram Dijkstra, *Idols of Perversity* (New York: Oxford University Press, 1986), 27.

37. See, e.g., Arthur Hughes, *Ophelia* (1852); Sir John Everett Millais, *Ophelia* (1851); Ernest Herbert, *Ophelia* (1890s); Adolphe Dagnan-Bouveret, *Ophelia* (1910); Madeleine Lemaire, *Ophelia* (1880s); George Richard Falkenberg, *Ophelia* (1898).

38. Dijkstra, *Idols of Perversity*, 51–63.

39. Ibid., 63.

40. Kirsten Powell, "Edward Burne-Jones and *The Legend of Briar Rose*," *Journal of Pre-Raphaelite Studies* 6, no. 2 (May 1986): 16.

41. Available at http://swinburnearchive.indiana.edu/swinburne/view#docId =swinburne/acs0000001-01-i014.xml;query=;brand=swinburne.

42. Dijkstra, *Idols of Perversity*, 69–70.

43. Carrie Noland, *Agency and Embodiment* (Cambridge, MA: Harvard University Press, 2009), 9.

44. George Balanchine and Francis Mason, *Balanchine's Festival of Ballet* (London: W. H. Allen, 1978), 337.

45. Marius Petipa, *Russian Ballet Master: The Memoirs of Marius Petipa*, ed. Lillian Moore, trans. Helen Whittaker (New York: Macmillan, 1958), 12–20.

46. Banes, *Dancing Women*, 42.

47. Nicolas Berdyaev, *The Origin of Russian Communism* (Ann Arbor: University of Michigan Press, 1969); Hans Koh, ed., *The Mind of Modern Russia* (New York: Harper and Row, 1955).

48. Banes, *Dancing Women*, 44.

49. Baird Hastings, *Choreographer and Composer* (Boston: Twayne, 1983), 99–101.

50. Solomon Volkov, *Balanchine's Tchaikovsky*, trans. Antonia Bovis (New York: Simon and Schuster, 1985), 153.

51. Tim Scholl, *From Petipa to Balanchine: Classical Revival and the Modernization of Ballet* (New York: Routledge, 1994), 19.

52. Alastair Macaulay, "The Big Sleep: The Sleeping Beauty at Its Centenary," *Dancing Times*, May 1990, 805–808.

53. Ibid., 806.

54. "Bukva" I. F. Vasilevsky, "The New Ballet Sleeping Beauty," *Russkie Vedemosti*, January 14, 1890, cited and translated in Tim Scholl, *"Sleeping Beauty": A Legend in Progress* (New Haven, CT: Yale University Press, 2004), 186.

55. Quoted in ibid., 201.

56. This is a whole other train of study that is pursued in Scholl's *From Petipa to Balanchine* and many other works that focus on Diaghilev and the World of Art.

57. See Banes, *Dancing Women*, 50.

58. Ibid.

59. The Kirov's 1999 version of *Beauty*, undertaken after consulting the extensive collections of manuscripts, notations, scores, and sketches of the ballet housed in the Harvard Theater collection and in the Kirov's own archives, is as close as a modern audience can come to experiencing the authentic aesthetic sensibilities of the late nineteenth-century ballet. Because of the Kirov's devotion to the nineteenth-century style and form of the ballet, the reconstruction serves as useful evidence of some of the ways Petipa represented the sleeping beauty story in 1890.

60. Harlow Robinson, "A la Russe," *Stagebill*, John F. Kennedy Center for the Performing Arts, Washington, DC, 19A.

61. Ibid., 20A.

CONCLUSION/CURTAIN CALL

1. Laura Ahearn, "Language and Agency," *Annual Review of Anthropology* 30 (2001): 112.

2. Katherine Frank, "Agency," *Anthropological Theory* 6, no. 3 (2006): 284.

3. Saba Mahmood, *Politics of Piety: The Islamic Revival and the Feminist Subject* (Princeton, NJ: Princeton University Press, 2005); Patricia Gagne and Deanna McGaughey, "Designing Women: Cultural Hegemony and the Exercise of Power among Women Who Have Undergone Elective Mammoplasty," *Gender and Society* 16, no. 6 (December 2002): 814–838.

4. Maureen Mahoney and Barbara Yngvesson, "The Construction of Subjectivity and the Paradox of Resistance: Reintegrating Feminist Anthropology and Psychology," *Signs* 18, no. 1 (1992): 70.

5. Lori Baker Sperry and Liz Grauerholz, "The Pervasiveness and Persistence of the Feminine Beauty Ideal in Children's Fairy Tales," *Gender and Society* 17, no. 5 (October 2003): 711–726.

6. Paula T. Kelso, "Behind the Curtain: The Body, Control and Ballet," *Edwardsville Journal of Sociology* 3, no. 2 (2003): 8.

APPENDIX

1. Sally Banes, *Dancing Women: Female Bodies on Stage* (London: Routledge, 1998), 50.

2. Ibid., 50–54.

3. Ibid., 54–56.

4. Ibid., 56.

5. Ibid., 56–59.

INDEX

Page numbers in italics refer to illustrations.

Agency, 154–155, 164–166; Aurora role and, 154–155, 158–161
Ahearn, Laura, 164–165
Albertieri, Luigi, 53
Alcoff, Linda, 3–4, 135
Alexander, Dorothy, 74
Alexander III, 31, 32
Alton, Robert, 56
"America Dances," 76
American Ballet Theatre, 20, 40, 53; during the 1940s, 72–73; *The Sleeping Beauty* (1976) of, 40, 89, 140
Asafiev, Boris, 87
Aurora role, 6, 17; agency and, 154–155, 158–161; Arantxa Ochoa in, 126–127, 137; baroque-influenced choreography of, 33; Carlotta Brianza in, 36, 158–159; dancer's performance fear and, 124; Dede Barfield in, *120*, 127–128, 129–131, 134–135, 137; expressive dimensions of, 117–118; first act variation of, 17–18; Irma Nioradze in, 159–160; Julie Kent in, 132; Laura Katz Rizzo in, 131, 135–136; Lucia Chase in, 37, 53; Martha Chamberlain in, 128–129, 133–134, 136–137; Melissa Hayden in, 42–43, 93; metaphoric interpretation of, 44, 86–87, 96; pirouettes of, 33–34; Rose Adagio of, 10, 17, 86, 159–161; second act variation of, 18–19; solo variations of, 17–19, 25–26, 87; in teaching and coaching, 139; technical content of, 117–118, 124–125, 138; third act variation of, 19; transformative nature of, 28–29, 125–126
Authenticity: concept of, 6–7, 35; context and, 94–95; recreation and, 95–96; reinvention and, 95; reproduction and, 115–116; reviewers' preference for, 60–61, 62, 94; of *The Sleeping Beauty* (1937), 59–60; of *The Sleeping Beauty* (1965), 80–82, 90–91; of *The Sleeping Beauty* (1997/2002), 112–113

Bakst, Léon, 36, 156–157
Balanchine, George, 3, 14, 22, 57, 66, 67; Barbara Weisberger's relationship with, 39–40, 68, 74, *75*, 102–103, 105; on *The Sleeping Beauty*, 34, 35
Balanchine's Tchaikovsky (Balanchine), 34

Ballerina(s): identity as, 28–29, 134–135; interviews of, 41–42, 101–102, 124–140, 163 (*see also* Barfield, Dede; Chamberlain, Martha; Ochoa, Arantxa); physicality of, 43–44, 141–142, 154–155
Ballet Guild, 76
Ballets Africains, Les, 76
Ballet Society, Inc., 79
Ballets Russes, 36
Banes, Sally, 33, 147–148
Barfield, Dede, *120*; on artistic maturation, 127–128, 129–130, 134–135; on Aurora role coaching, 127; on Aurora role conceptualization, 128; on Aurora role difficulty, 137; on Aurora role interpretation, 134; critical reviews of, 127; life history of, 122–123
Barn Dance, 61
Barnes, Clive, 21, 104; on *The Sleeping Beauty* (1965), 80–81, 89–90, 92, 93
Baryshnikov, Mikhail, 132
Battement tendu jeté, 10
Battement tendus, 10
Belle au bois dormant, La (Perrault). See *La Belle au bois dormant* (Perrault)
Benjamin, Walter, 116
Berger, James, 116
Biohistory, 40
Bok, Edward W., 73
Bolender, Todd, 76
Boston Ballet, 40
Bowen, Elizabeth, 131
Breaking Pointe, 16
Bremer, Lucille, 50
Brenner, Claude, 93
Brenner, David, 106
Brianza, Carlotta, 36, 158–159
Bronson, Arthur, 73
Brooks, Lynn Matluck, 101
Brown, Joan Myers, 40
Bunheads, 16
Burne-Jones, Edward, 150–151, 152–153

Caffall, Brian, 127
Cannon, Thomas, 76
Carabosse, 84, 113–114
Caroline Littlefield Ballet, 55
Carpenter, Romulus, 48

Cecchetti, Enrico, 3
Chamberlain, Martha: on Aurora role interpretation, 133–134; on Aurora role preparation, 136–137; on Aurora role technique, 128–129, 133; life history of, 123
Chase, Lucia, 2, 13, 14, 40; in American Ballet Theatre establishment, 73, 104–105; as Aurora, 37, 53; *The Sleeping Beauty* (1976) of, 89
Chavez, Carlos, 56
Chicago Civic Opera, 67
Childhood, 144
Cinderella, 76
Civil Rights movement, 70
Clarke, Mary, 34
Classical ballet, 9–11, 17–19; agency and, 154–155, 164–166; basic movements of, 10; contemporizing of, 35; dancer-to-dancer communication of, 26–27, 53–54; embodiment of, 139–140; feminist reading of, 3–5, 142; hierarchy in, 31; identity and, 11, 28–29; in popular media, 16; semiotics of, 11; transformative nature of, 138–139, 164. See also Dance history; *Sleeping Beauty, The*
Comelin, Jean-Paul, 103
Conrad, Karen, 50
Coralli, Jean, 3, 14
Coronation of the Dragonfly Queen, The, 131
Corruption, institutional, 99–100
Costumes: for *The Sleeping Beauty* (1937), 38, 60; for *The Sleeping Beauty* (1965), *83*, 84; for *The Sleeping Beauty* (1997/2002), 111
Coudy, Douglas, 50
Cowanova, Florence, 50
Curtis, Margaret, 71
Cut of the Real: Subjectivity in Poststructuralist Philosophy (Kolozova), 6

D'Amboise, Christopher, 107, 108–109
Dance history: Catherine Littlefield in, 66–68; decentralization in, 19–22; feminist analysis in, 3–5, 14–15, 142; from outside, 14, 23, 119–120; from within, 14–19, 25–26, 27, 115, 119–140 (*see also*

Barfield, Dede; Chamberlain, Martha; Ochoa, Arantxa); linear narrative in, 3, 12, 14, 20, 163–164; place in, 19–22; subjectivity of, 43; web narrative in, 12–13, 163–164
Dance studies, academic approaches to, 23–26, 101–102, 115, 163–164
Danton, Henry, 97
Daprati, Elena, 10
Deering, Jane, 50
Degen, Arsen, 30
De Mille, Agnes, 13
Denby, Edwin, 12, 62
Denham, Serge, 51
De Valois, Dame Ninette, 2, 13, 36
Diaghilev, Serge, 36, 51
Dijkstra, Bram, 152
Dollar, William, 50
Dorris, George, 54–55
Duncan, Irma, 46, 62
Duncan, Isadora, 23–24
Dunning, Jennifer, 140
Durante, Viviana, 135

Edwardian drama, 114–115
Egorova, Lubov, 51, 63
Enlightenment, 118
Ewing, Alex, 39

Facelli, Kante, 76
Fairy Doll, 50
Fairy tales, 143–144. See also *La Belle au bois dormant* (Perrault)
Feldman, Emma, 73
Felton, James, 82–84
Film, ballet in, 16
Fisher, Jennifer, 138–139
Flaming June (Leighton), 151
Fokine, Michel, 3, 14, 46, 66, 67, 103
Fokine Ballet, 62
Fonseca, Hortensia, 131
Fonteyn, Margot, 76, 94, 126
Ford Foundation, 12, 39–40, 67, 78–79, 103
Forsythe, William, 3, 12
"Fragoletta" (Swinburne), 153
Franca, Celia, 2
Franko, Mark, 95

Gagne, Patricia, 165
Garafola, Lynn, 31, 54, 63
Gates, Jodi, 128
Gender imagery, 165
Gentner, Norma, 50
Golden, Miriam, 50
Gottschild, Brenda Dixon, 40
Graham, Martha, 22, 24, 62
Grand battement jeté, 10
Grauerholz, Liz, 165
Gregory, Cynthia, 127
Gribler, Jeffrey, 107
Grilikhes, Alexandra, 92–93
Gunn, Janet, 64

Haggard, Patrick, 10
Harkarvy, Benjamin, 103–104, 106
Harmati, Sandor, 46
Harper, Ralph, 97–98
Harris, Andrea, 12, 119–120
Hayden, Melissa, 42–43, 93
H'Doubler, Margaret, 23
Henahan, Donal, 93
Herman, Billy, 50
Hierarchy in Marius Petipa's choreography, 31
Histoires ou contes du temps passé (Perrault), 144
Holmes, Anna-Marie, 25
Homans, Jennifer, 53–54
Hoogland, René, 131
Humphrey, Doris, 24, 46, 62
Hurok, Sol, 73

Identity, 11, 28–29, 134–135
Idols of Perversity (Dijkstra), 152
Invalidism, 151–152
Iosa, Marco, 10
Ivanov, Lev, 3

Jacob's Pillow Summer Ballet Intensive, 25
Jelinic, Franco, 78

Kaiser, Roy, 7, 13, 41, 109–111
Katz Rizzo, Laura, 36, 42–43, 131, 132, 135–136
Keil, Mildred, 104

Kelso, Paulo, 165–166
Kendall, Elizabeth, 103
Kenny, Evelyn, 78
Kenny, James, 78
Kent, Julie, 131–132
Kirov Ballet, 41, 95, 159–160
Kirstein, Lincoln, 12, 57, 74, 94–95
Kisselgoff, Anna, 94
Kolozova, Katerina, 6
Kolpakova, Maria, 126
Krasovkaya, Vera, 30

La Belle au bois dormant (Perrault),
    32–33, 44, 143–147; disciplinary func-
    tion of, 147–149; imperialist ideology
    in, 149; literature inspired by, 151–152;
    monarchical system in, 148–149; paint-
    ings inspired by, 150–151; summary of,
    145–147
LaFontsee, Dane, 106
Lakoff, George, 11
Laroche, Herman, 156–157
La Sylphide, 107
Leadership: female, 12 (*see also* Littlefield,
    Catherine; Weisberger, Barbara); male,
    104–109
Legat, Nicholas, 32
Legend of Briar Rose, The (Burne-Jones),
    150–151, 152–153
Lehman, Marian, 71
Leidy, Phillip Ludwell, 57
Leighton, Frederic, 151
Le Parnasse poussé à bout (Perrault), 145
Les Ballets Africains, 76
Let the Righteous Be Glad, 43
Levin, Anne, 111–112, 114
Liliac Fairy, *83*, 84
Limon, José, 45, 62
Littlefield, Caroline, 48–49
Littlefield, Catherine, 2, 5–6, 22, 37, *49*,
    52; choreography by, 56–57, 59, 63;
    historical significance of, 66–68; hybrid-
    ized ballet style of, 63–64; international
    influences on, 51–54; leadership role
    of, 13–14, 65–66; life history of, 48–51;
    popular dance influences on, 54–55;
    racism of, 43; at Robin Hood Dell, 57;
    at Roxy Theatre, 56–57; teaching style

of, 55–56. See also *Sleeping Beauty, The*
    (1937)
Littlefield, Dorothie, *52*
Littlefield Ballet, 67
Littlefield School, 50–51, 55–56
Lopukhov, Fyodor, 33–34, 87
Lopuszanski, Michael, 78
Loring, Eugene, 22
Louis XIV, 14, 17, 31, 32, 33, 44, 144,
    147–148

Macaulay, Alastair, 15–16, 33, 35, 86
Mahmood, Saba, 165
Male dancer, 17
Malinsky, Barbara, 114
Manchester, P. W., 88, 91–92
Martin, John, 12, 60, 62, 63
Martin, Linton, 73
Martins, Peter, 106, 107
Maryinsky Theater, 29
Maryland Youth Ballet, 131, 132
Massine, Léonide, 67
Maynard, Olga, 72
McCracken, Joan, 50
Medieval music, 114–115
Meglin, Joellen, 101
Military aesthetic in Marius Petipa's cho-
    reography, 30–31, 32
Milwaukee Ballet, 107
Modern dance: emergence of, 61–62; in
    Philadelphia, 45–46
Moore, Stella, 77
Mordkin, Mikhail, 14, 37; Catherine Little-
    field's study with, 51–52, 53
Motherhood, 127–128, 130
Mullins, Joyce, 116
Musical revues, 54–55

New York, 20–21
New York City Ballet, 15–16, 71, 79
Nicholas I, 31
Nijinska, Bronislava, 2, 13, 36
Nijinsky, Vaslav, 66
Nioradze, Irma, 159–160
Nochlin, Linda, 2
Noland, Carrie, 125
Novack, Cynthia, 132–133
Nureyev, Rudolf, 94

Nutcracker, The, 15–16, 107–108
Nutcracker Nation (Fisher), 138–139

Ochoa, Arantxa: on Aurora role difficulty,
125–126, 137; on Aurora role research,
126–127; life history of, 122
Oklahoma City Ballet, 20

Page, Ruth, 2, 12, 13
Paintings of sleeping/dead woman,
150–153
Paris Opera Ballet, 51
Parnasse poussé à bout, Le (Perrault), 145
Pavis, Patrice, 94
Pavlova, Anna, 13, 36, 51
Pennsylvania Ballet Company, 39–40;
1970–1990 administrative crises
of, 104–109; Barbara Weisberger's
leadership of, 102–103, 104, 105; Barbara Weisberger's resignation from,
105–106; Benjamin Harkarvy's leadership of, 103–104, 106; classical canon
in, 114; corporate male leadership
of, 104–109; d'Amboise's leadership
of, 108–109; dancers' resignations
from, 104–105; emergence of, 70–71,
76–79; first season of, 79; funding for,
39–40, 78–79, 103, 108, 109; George
Balanchine's ballets for, 102–103,
105; Milwaukee Ballet venture with,
107; naming of, 77; Robert Weiss's
leadership of, 106–107; Roy Kaiser's
leadership of, 109–111; "Save the Ballet" campaign of, 108; temporary closure of, 109. See also *Sleeping Beauty,
The* (1965); *Sleeping Beauty, The*
(1997/2002)
Perrault, Charles, 32–33, 44, 143–147
Perrot, Jules, 3, 14
Petipa, Marius, 3, 7, 14, 66; choreography
of, 1, 25, 28, 29–32, 63
Pew Charitable Trusts, 108
Philadelphia, 5, 21–22; concert performances in, 74–76; dance teachers in,
50–51; Depression-era, 45–48; industrial decline of, 100; modern dance in,
45–46; 1960s-decade, 69–71, 76–77. See
also *Sleeping Beauty, The* (1937); *Sleep-*

ing Beauty, The (1965); *Sleeping Beauty,
The* (1997/2002)
Philadelphia All Star–Forum, 73–74
Philadelphia Ballet Company, 37; estab-
lishment of, 57–58; European tour of,
64, 67; national recognition of, 66, 67;
performance style of, 64. See also Little-
field, Catherine; Pennsylvania Ballet
Company; *Sleeping Beauty, The* (1937)
Philadelphia Civic Grand Opera Com-
pany, 76
Philadelphia Civic Opera, 51, 55
Philadelphia Grand Opera Company, 56
Philadelphia Lyric Opera, 77
Philadelphia Opera Company, 48, 50, 51
Philadelphia Orchestra, 45, 46, 56, 57
Phillips, Ethel, 50
Pierre, Dorathi Bock, 60–61
Place, 19–22. See also Philadelphia
Poll, Heinz, 82–84, 85–86
Potteiger, Jack, 50
Preobrajenska, Olga, 51

Racism, 43
Rambert, Dame Marie, 2
Ratmansky, Alexei, 3
Reconstruction of dance, 59–60, 94–95
Regional Dance Association, 74
Reproduction of dance, 115–116
Rich, Adrienne, 3
Ringer, Jenifer, 15–16
Ritual, classical ballet as, 138–139
Rivera, Diego, 56
Robin Hood Dell, 38, 46, *47*, 57
Rodham, Robert, 103, 104
Roosevelt, Franklin E., 67
Rose Adagio, 10, 17, 86, 159–161
Roxy Theatre, 54, 56–57
Royal Ballet, 76

Sadler's Wells Ballet, 97
Saltykov-Shchedrin, M. E., 96
Sandonato, Barbara, 77–78, 105
San Francisco Ballet, 40
"Save the Ballet" campaign, 108
Schergen, Janek, 111–114, 117, 119
Scholl, Tim, 30, 33, 35
School of American Ballet, 39, 57, 71

School of the Pennsylvania Ballet, 77–78
Sergeyev, Nicholas Grigorievich, 36, 38–39
Serrano, Lupe, 104
Sexuality, Victorian representations of, 151–153
Shawn, Ted, 62
Skeaping, Mary, 41
Skelton, Thomas, 82, 84
Sleeping Beauty, The, 1, 29–32; archaic elements of, 33; baroque elements of, 33, 149; choreographic options for, 88–89; conservative values of, 32–33, 96–97, 98, 112, 149; critical views of, 30–31, 33, 34–35, 88–89; European stagings of, 38–39, 40–41; grand scale of, 30, 34–35; main characters of, 17 (*see also* Aurora role); metaphoric interpretation of, 44, 86–87, 96, 157; nostalgic elements of, 97–98; summary of, 167–168; thematic content of, 32–33. See also *La Belle au bois dormant* (Perrault)
Sleeping Beauty, The (1890), 29–35, 141–142, 149, 154–155; Aurora role in, 158–159; choreography of, 17–19, 28, 29–32, 33–34, 35, 156, 159–160; critical reviews of, 157–158; monarchical system of, 32–33, 155–156; music for, 156–157; premiere of, 29, 155; third act of, 156
Sleeping Beauty, The (1936), 37
Sleeping Beauty, The (1937), 6, 13, 37–38, 40, 58–64; all-American company for, 63–64; choreography of, 59, 61, 63; costumes for, 38, 60; critical reviews of, 60–63, 65; Depression-era resonance of, 63; economic circumstances and, 47–48; financing for, 60; at Robin Hood Dell, 38, 46; sets for, 38, 60
Sleeping Beauty, The (1965), 6, 13, 40, 79–98; Aurora role of, 93; authenticity of, 80–81, 82–84, 90–91; Balanchine's influence on, 85; budget for, 80; choreography of, 82–85, 85–86, 86–88, 88–89, 92; costumes for, *83*, 84; critical reviews of, 81, 82–84, 85, 88–94, 97; mime elements of, 90; modernization of, 80–81
Sleeping Beauty, The (1976), 40, 89, 140

Sleeping Beauty, The (1997/2002), 7, 13, 41, 100–102, 110–119; Arantxa Ochoa's Aurora role in, 122; Aurora role of, 117, 121–140; authenticity of, 112–113; Carabosse role of, 113–114; casting for, 117; choreography for, 111–113, 119; costumes for, 111; critical reviews of, 111–112, 114, 127; Dede Barfield's Aurora role in, 122–123; Martha Chamberlain's Aurora role in, 123
Sleeping Beauty, The (1999), 41, 95
Sleeping Beauty, The (2002), Kirov Ballet production of, 159–160
Sleeping/dead woman theme, 150–153
Sleeping Princess, The, 36
Sokolow, Anna, 62
Sperry, Lori Baker, 165
Staats, Léo, 51
Stevenson, Ben, 40
Stewart, Susan, 148
Stokowski, Leopold, 45, 56
Subjectivity of history, 43
Swinburne, Algernon Charles, 153
Sylphide, La, 107

Tales of Mother Goose, The (Perrault), 143–144
Tarasoff, Ivan, 53
Tchaikovsky, Pyotr Ilyich, 1, 7, 29, 87, 156–157
Technique: in Aurora role, 117–118, 124–125, 128–129, 133, 138; development of, 9–11, 117–118
Television, ballet on, 16, 76
Terrorism, 99
Terry, Walter, 76
Thomason, Helgi, 40
Tudor, Antony, 76, 103
Turko, Patricia, 78

Van Praagh, Dame Peggy, 2
Vaughan, David, 34
Veitch, Patrick, 107
Veselovsky, Ivan, 32, 155

Wanamaker's Department Store, 75–76
Ways of Seeing (Berger), 116
Webster, Daniel, 85, 86

Weidman, Charles, 45
Weidman, George, 46
Weisberger, Barbara, 2, 5–6, 39–40;
   on authenticity, 90–91; George Balanchine's relationship with, 74, 75, 77,
   102–103, 105; leadership role of, 13–14;
   life history of, 71–72; as Pennsylvania
   Ballet administrative artistic director, 104. See also Sleeping Beauty, The
   (1965)
Weisberger, Ernest, 72
Weiss, Robert, 106, 107

West, Martha Ullman, 22
Wheeldon, Christopher, 12
White, Al, 50
Whittington, Lewis, 112
Whorf, Benjamin Lee, 11
Williams, Raymond, 21
Wilson, C. Colkut, III, 78
Woman in America (Woolson), 151
Woolson, Abba Goold, 151

Ziegfeld Follies, 54
Zipes, Jack, 144

Laura Katz Rizzo is the Program Director of the Bachelor of Fine Arts Program in Dance and an Assistant Professor of Dance at Temple University. She is also a frequent guest speaker, choreographer, and pedagogue at universities and ballet companies throughout the United States and abroad.